The King and the Commentator:
Rashi's Holistic Readings of
Solomon's Song, Proverbs, and Ecclesiastes

Lisa Fredman

The King and the Commentator

Rashi's Holistic Readings of Solomon's Song, Proverbs, and Ecclesiastes

Matan
Maggid Books

The King and the Commentator: Rashi's Holistic Readings of Solomon's Song, Proverbs, and Ecclesiastes

First Edition, 2026

Maggid Books
An imprint of Koren Publishers Jerusalem Ltd.

POB 8531, New Milford, CT 06776-8531, USA
& POB 4044, Jerusalem 9104001, Israel
www.korenpub.com

Cover Design: Studio Dosa

The publication of this book was made possible through the generous support of *The Jewish Book Trust.*

ISBN 978-1-59264-706-4, *hardcover*

A CIP catalogue record for this title is available from the British Library

Printed and bound in the United States

Ann and Jeremy Pava, Trustees Micah Philanthropies

*in deep appreciation of their generous support
for Matan and the Kitvuni Fellowship*

*and their tireless efforts to strengthen women's
Torah scholarship worldwide .*

To the incredible individuals & community who have lifted me during this challenging time.

Your unwavering support has been my strength.

Thank you for your kindness, encouragement, and for being there when I needed it most.

Each of you has had a significant impact on my journey, reminding me that I am not alone.

With deep gratitude,
Sheila Klein

In loving memory of my parents,

Israel and Yetra Goldberg

Janice Bitansky and family

In the 1980s, Rabbanit Malke Bina began teaching a groundbreaking Talmud *shiur* for women, held around the dining room table of Lili Weil *z"l*. Inspired by this pioneering learning, Rabbanit Bina and her students envisioned an advanced Beit Midrash for women. This became a reality in 1988 with the establishment of Matan: The Sadie Rennert Women's Institute for Torah Studies. From its inception, Matan has been dedicated to cultivating high-level scholars, educators, and leaders, revolutionizing opportunities for women to engage deeply with Torah study.

Today, Matan has eleven branches, serving tens of thousands of students in Israel and worldwide. It offers intensive Beit Midrash programs in Bible, Talmud, Halakha and Jewish thought, continually raising the bar for women's Torah study. Additionally, there is a broad choice of weekly classes and series, Yemei Iyun in Israel and beyond, a summer learn-and-tour program, pre-holiday programming, an international mother-daughter bat mitzva program, and weekly *parasha* podcasts in Hebrew and English. Matan remains at the forefront of Torah study, inspiring and empowering the next generation through transformative Torah learning.

Kitvuni – Fellowship Program for Writing Torah Literature

In 2022 the Kitvuni Fellowship was launched, led by Dr. Yael Ziegler, a distinguished Matan graduate and senior lecturer. The initiative nurtures exceptional *talmidot ḥakhamim*, supporting them in writing and publishing books of Torah scholarship across diverse fields. Kitvuni provides a structured framework, mentorship, and professional support for every cohort, ensuring that each scholar's work reaches its highest potential. In collaboration with Koren Publishers, the program is producing books that will enrich the Jewish bookshelf for generations to come.

The second Matan Kitvuni publication in English is *The King and the Commentator: Rashi's Holistic Readings of Solomon's Song, Proverbs and Ecclesiastes* by Dr. Lisa Fredman. It explores how Rashi crafts exegetical frameworks that knit together Solomon's writings and infuse them with deep spiritual and religious resonance that speaks powerfully to the modern reader. Upcoming Kitvuni publications will feature works on Bible, Talmud, Halakha, *Ḥasidut*, and Kabbala, further enhancing contemporary Torah scholarship.

Contents

Acknowledgments

This book is the culmination of my intense study of Rashi's Bible commentary, a scholarly path that commenced with my master's thesis, deepened through my doctoral dissertation, and was further refined through subsequent articles and the compilation of this volume.

This extensive project could not have come to fruition without the generous support of the Kitvuni Matan Fellowship program. For over thirty-five years, Matan, under the visionary leadership of Rabbanit Malke Bina, has pioneered serious Judaic learning for women, successfully enabling thousands of students to deepen their Torah knowledge and rigorously engage with Jewish texts. Recognizing the need for the next plateau of growth, Matan recently introduced the Kitvuni Fellowship to specifically support the authorship of Torah exegesis by women. This innovative program, lovingly conceived and directed by Dr. Yael Ziegler, not only affords financial support but also provides a nurturing and intellectually rigorous environment conducive to serious writing. And it is Matan's CEO, Chaya Bina-Katz, who tirelessly translates this innovative vision into reality. Thank you to Rabbanit Malke, Dr. Yael, and Chaya for your personal support and for your immense contribution to the advancement of Jewish learning for women.

Beyond the institutional structure, I am deeply grateful to my fellow writing cohort – Rabbanit Karen Miller Jackson, Gila Rosen, Dr. Achinoam Jacobs, and Rabbanit Dr. Brachi Elizur – who provided an intellectual sounding board and fostered ongoing encouragement.

My deepest gratitude to Professor Marty Lockshin for mentoring me in this project. Marty, your insightful comments and recommendations, drawn from your profound expertise in medieval biblical exegesis, were instrumental in elevating the quality of this composition. I am especially grateful for your kind and encouraging manner; you are truly a *mensch*. Naturally, all remaining errors and shortcomings are my sole responsibility.

I extend my profound thanks to Professor Jordan S. Penkower, *z"l*, who unlocked the world of Rashi manuscripts to me and guided my Rashi scholarship for almost two decades. His recent death leaves a lasting void in my life.

Thank you to Matthew Miller and Rabbi Reuven Ziegler at Koren Publishers, and to the superb editorial and design staff – Rabbi David Silverstein, Ita Olesker, Debbie Ismailoff, Nechama Unterman, Tani Bayer, and Tomi Mager – who worked with me side by side, despite the fact that we never met in person! I simply could never have done it without you.

How does an English-speaking, New Jersey girl write a book on Rashi scholarship? It is largely rooted in the home in which I was raised. Thank you to my loving parents, Dr. Abraham and Pamela Berman, for cultivating a nurturing and intellectually stimulating environment, and for equipping me with a first-rate education.

To my dear children: Rachel and Steven, Leora and Chaim, Hillel and Ariella, Yishai and Zoe, and Avigail and Yonaton, and my dear grandchildren: Gavriella, Meital, Alan, Liam, Yagel, Helene, Lia and Aria, for all your love and support and for getting used to the fact that I would rather choose the library over the movies!

And, finally, to my beloved husband, Michael, my partner in every sense of the word. Together, we have dedicated our lives to Jewish education, traveling the globe to teach our fellow Jews. Thank you for the unwavering support you have shown me in every challenge I've undertaken. For your steadfast love and friendship, I am forever grateful. May we continue our journey together, inspiring others for many more years!

Introduction

Rabbi Shlomo Yitzhaki (1040–1105), commonly referred to as Rashi, is surely the most illustrious of Jewish commentators. He was the first to write comprehensive commentaries on both the Talmud and the Hebrew Bible (Tanakh), and his commentaries are still the gateway to the study of these fundamental texts. This work examines Rashi's commentaries on the three books attributed to his namesake, King Solomon – the Song of Songs, Proverbs, and Ecclesiastes. In character and method, Rashi's approach to these books differs from his approach to other books of Tanakh.

INTERPRETIVE APPROACH

First, a word about Rashi's approach generally. Rashi's commentaries are two-layered. There is the *peshat*, or "simple" meaning. This has also been called the "contextual" meaning: A word is interpreted in a way that is consistent with the other words in the sentence and with the overall narrative. Kamin explains that *peshat* is an interpretation aligned "with the text's vocabulary, syntax, context, literary form, and structure in their mutual relationships."[1]

Along with *peshat,* there is the level of *derash,* the "homiletical" meaning. Within the realm of *derash,* all components – letters, words, verses, and sections – can be interpreted as independent units capable of forming countless combinations.[2]

Rashi's innovativeness actually lay in the systematic use of the *peshat* method. His development of this method, anchored in linguistic analysis, grammar, and syntax, represented an exegetical breakthrough within the Ashkenazic region. Although Spanish scholars preceding Rashi had engaged in meticulous examination of the biblical text's language and grammar as early as the geonic period, such an interpretative methodology did not permeate the Ashkenazic milieu until the eleventh century. It is pertinent to note that the majority of these Spanish biblical exegeses were composed in Arabic, a language unfamiliar to Rashi.

The *derash* method of exegesis was prevalent in the writings of the Sages, such as the Midrash and the Talmud. Although Rashi draws heavily from this corpus of rabbinic literature, his explications are not merely a potpourri of earlier thought but rather the result of a careful selection process. As articulated in the opening programmatic statement in his Torah commentary:

> I have come for the simple meaning of Scripture and for Aggada which settles (*meyashevet*) the words of Scripture ... each word in its proper place. (Commentary on Gen. 3:8)

Rashi selects Aggada – rabbinic sources that "settle," i.e., conform to, the language and sequence of Scripture. He then reformulates them to create a seamless transition between explanation and verse, thus achieving a fluid integration between the two.

1. S. Kamin, "Rashi's Exegetical Categorization with Respect to the Distinction Between *Peshat* and *Derash*," *Immanuel* 11 (1980): 16.
2. Kamin, "Rashi's Exegetical Categorization," 16–17, citing I.J. Heinemann, *Darkhei HaAggada* [in Hebrew] (Magnes, 1970), 96.

Modern scholarship has identified an additional methodolc innovation: the application of certain homilies to the context of enth-century northern France, where a small Jewish minority coexi with a dominant Christian society. This strategy aimed to strengt internal Jewish values while countering external Christian influer and threats. Rashi's anti-Christian polemic becomes more explici his commentaries on the Later Prophets and Hagiographa.

WHY *PESHAT*?

What can explain Rashi's systematic introduction of the *peshat* herm neutic? Scholars grapple with this question and raise a number of po sible factors.

Grossman posits the impact of the rich Spanish Jewish exegetica tradition, with its strong emphasis on philology and lexicology. Rashi accessed this tradition through the Hebrew writings of Spanish lin guists such as Menahem ben Saruq and Dunash ben Labrat.[3] Touitou notes the influence of the "twelfth-century renaissance," which actually began in the previous century. This intellectual rebirth in Christian Europe emphasized the power of human reason and intellect, challenging tradition and promoting a more literal reading of the Bible.[4] This "new" reading also proved effective in refuting Christian allegorical and typological interpretations, becoming a crucial element in Rashi's anti-Christian exegetical toolbox. More recently, M.Z. Cohen points to the parallels between Latin learning – specifically the hermeneutical model developed in the late-eleventh-century Cathedral school of Rheims – and Rashi's methodological approach.[5]

---

3. A. Grossman, "The School of Literal Jewish Exegesis in Northern France," in *Hebrew Bible/Old Testament: The History of Its Interpretation*, vol. 1: *From the Beginnings to the Middle Ages*, part 2: *The Middle Ages*, ed. Magne Sæbø (2000), 327–28.
4. E. Touitou, "Rashi's Commentary on Genesis 1–6 in the Context of the Judeo-Christian Controversy," *Hebrew Union College Annual* 61 (1990): 159–63.
5. M.Z. Cohen, *Rashi, Biblical Interpretation, and Latin Learning in Medieval Europe* (Cambridge University Press, 2021), 17–25; M.Z. Cohen, "Rashi's Revolutionary Commentary Deviates from Midrash, Why?" TheTorah.com: www.thetorah.com/article/rashis-revolutionary-commentary-deviates-from-midrash-why.

DUAL COMMENTARY

Regardless of the stimulus, Rashi juxtaposes the two senses of Scripture – *peshat* and *derash* – hundreds of times in his Bible commentary. He often distinguishes between them through the use of clear methodological labels, such as "that is *peshat*" (*zehu peshuto*), "that is *derash*" (*zehu midrasho*), or more general phrases like "another explanation" (*davar aḥer*). It is very rare indeed for him to privilege one explanation over the other.[6] Underlying the dual hermeneutic is the belief that the text is divine, thus allowing for explication on multiple methodological levels. Although this "dual commentary" approach becomes Rashi's distinctive exegetical trademark, sometimes he does content himself with a single comment, primarily of the *derash* nature.

FORMAT

We now turn our attention to the question of form, examining the manner in which Rashi presents his exegesis to the reader.

Rashi's commentary adopts a verse-by-verse structure, prioritizing the elucidation of each individual passage. His commentary on the verse may contain one interpretive point, or it may be composed of multiple interpretive units, with each unit initiated by the guiding words of the text (*dibbur hamatḥil*) requiring clarification. This format enables a systematic and comprehensive exploration of the text, allowing every component of the text to receive due attention. It is crucial to note, however, that while Rashi offers exacting verse-level analysis, he never explicitly constructs a cohesive narrative connecting these discrete interpretive units across large expanses of text.

The independent nature of each interpretive unit did not escape the eyes of Christian scholars, as noted by Touitou:

> Christian authors were aware of this particular characteristic of Jewish exegesis, and they regarded it as a weak point that could be exploited; they therefore instructed the Christian polemicists

6. For example, see his commentary on Proverbs 29:25, where he expresses preference for the first answer.

> not to lead the controversy towards narrow exegetical points, but rather to steer the discussion to the broad domains of theological thought, a field in which the Jews seemed to be inferior.[7]

The "broad domains" are not explicitly addressed by Rashi nor by many other medieval Jewish exegetes living in Christian Europe.[8]

TEXT ARRANGEMENT

Rashi does, however, demonstrate a sensitivity toward textual arrangement. Occasionally, he queries the juxtaposition of biblical sections with inquiries such as "Why is this section juxtaposed?" (*lama nismekha parasha*),[9] often providing a midrashic explanation for the thematic shift. Upon the text's return to its original trajectory, Rashi employs terms like "Scripture returns to the original topic" (*ḥozer la'inyan harishon*) to reorient the reader.[10] In other instances, his observations pertain to chronological inconsistencies, marked by statements such as "There is no chronological order" (*ein mukdam umeuḥar*).[11] Nonetheless, Rashi does not engage in a comprehensive analysis of extended textual units to elucidate their thematic interconnections. A holistic examination of

---

7. E. Touitou, "Rashi and His School: The Exegesis on the Halakhic Part of the Pentateuch in the Context of the Judeo-Christian Controversy," in *Medieval Studies: In Honour of Avrom Saltman, Bar-Ilan Studies in History* IV (Bar-Ilan University Press, 1995), 241.
8. In contrast to Jewish exegetes living in southern France and Spain, see Avraham Grossman, *Rashi,* trans. J. Linsider (The Littman Library of Jewish Civilization, 2012), 81–82. An exception in the Ashkenazic zone was Rabbi Eliezer of Beaugency (twelfth century), whose exegesis is marked by the commitment to explicate the broader context; see Yitzhak Berger, "The Contextual Exegesis of Rabbi Eliezer of Beaugency and the Climax of the Northern French *Peshat* Tradition," *Jewish Studies Quarterly,* vol. 15 (2008): 115–29. For a comprehensive analysis of Rabbi Eliezer's exegesis, see *Rabbi Eliezer of Beaugency Commentaries on Amos and Jonah,* introduction, translation and commentary by Robert A. Harris (Western Michigan University, 2018): web.archive.org/web/20201106103509id_/https://scholarworks.wmich.edu/cgi/viewcontent.cgi?article=1000&context=mip_teamscs.
9. E.g., Rashi's commentary on Genesis 38:1.
10. E.g., Rashi's commentary on Genesis 39:1.
11. E.g., Rashi's commentary on Genesis 6:3.

how individual components contribute to the overarching message is conspicuously absent from his commentary.

CONTRADICTIONS

The lack of cohesion is compounded by internal contradictions. It is not uncommon for Rashi to cite a midrash on one verse that contradicts a midrash brought on a different verse. This phenomenon, termed *aggadot ḥalukot* (contradictory homilies) is prevalent in his commentary.[12] While Touitou suggested these discrepancies were later interpolations, manuscript analysis refutes this claim.[13] Many contradictions appear in the most reliable manuscripts of Rashi's commentary. Alternatively, it may be proposed that Rashi, while culling from different midrashic compendiums, was not concerned with creating one overall harmonious commentary. Rather, more important were the pertinent ideas that could be gleaned from each individual verse. This phenomenon of inconsistency is a feature not exclusive to Rashi but characteristic of the broader midrashic corpus from which his commentary derives. As noted by Kugel, midrashic exegesis is fundamentally verse-centric. The midrashist addresses himself not to the chapter or the book as a whole, but rather to the single verse "isolated in suspended animation."[14] The sole desire to resolve the difficulty surrounding a single word or phrase created a situation wherein solutions to individual phrases contradicted one another. Consistency was not an overriding consideration either for midrashic literature or for Rashi himself.

SOLOMON'S WRITINGS

The upcoming pages will demonstrate a stark contrast between Rashi's commentary on the majority of biblical texts and his commentary on

12. This term already appears in the supercommentary of Rabbi Eliyahu Mizrahi on Genesis 1:1. For a thorough analysis of this topic, see Y. Maori, "*Aggadot Ḥalukot*: Rashi's Commentary on Scripture," in *Shnaton: An Annual for Biblical and Ancient Near East Studies* XIX, ed. S. Japhet [in Hebrew] (Magnes, 2009), 138–54.
13. Maori, "*Aggadot Ḥalukot*," 190–95.
14. J. Kugel, "Two Introductions to Midrash," *Prooftexts*, vol. 3 (1983), 146, n. 2.

the Solomonic corpus. While maintaining his characteristic verse-by-verse format, Rashi's commentaries on Song of Songs, Proverbs, and Ecclesiastes deviate from his typical approach by constructing overarching thematic frameworks. These frameworks or schemas enable Rashi to synthesize the disparate textual elements into a unified whole, thus exhibiting a holistic interpretive approach.

TEXT OF RASHI'S COMMENTARIES

The present study relies on authoritative editions of Rashi's commentaries: the *HaKeter* edition for Song of Songs and Ecclesiastes,[15] and the World Union of Jewish Studies edition on Proverbs.[16] These editions are grounded in manuscript analysis, providing the most reliable textual foundation. The prevalence of interpolations within Rashi's commentary is well documented. While some additions can be attributed to Rashi's own revisions, others originate from his close disciples, such as Rabbi Shemaiah, Rabbi Josef Kara, and Rashbam. Furthermore, later scholars introduced marginal notes that were subsequently incorporated into the main text by copyists.[17] Thus, to ensure textual integrity and to uncover Rashi's original anti-Christian polemic – which was subsequently altered or eliminated by medieval censorship – reliance on these authoritative editions is imperative. Passages from these editions are translated into English in order to present this research.[18] We were assisted in this endeavor by the translations at alhatorah.org.

15. *Mikraot Gedolot HaKeter: The Five Scrolls*, ed. M. Cohen [in Hebrew] (Bar-Ilan University Press, 2012). The *HaKeter* edition is accessible online and can be viewed via the following link: www.mgketer.org/mikra/1/1/1/mg/0.
16. *Rashi's Commentary on the Book of Proverbs*, ed. L. Fredman [in Hebrew] (World Union of Jewish Studies, 2019).
17. For more detailed information, see Grossman, "The School of Literal Jewish Exegesis in Northern France," 333–34.
18. These translations have been occasionally modified to facilitate smoother reading or to more accurately reflect Rashi's original language, as it existed before being altered by medieval censors.

Specific Rashi passages throughout this work are indicated by the use of the letter *R* followed by the chapter and verse, enclosed in parentheses, such as (R 1:11).

METHODOLOGY

By documenting Rashi's sources for his midrashic tier, identifying his deviations from source material, and noting his original interpretive contributions, this study will illuminate his exegetical methodology. This analysis focuses upon Rashi's midrashic layer, as it is precisely this tier that offers the latitude for adaptation to his exegetical requirements.

This adaptation includes the creation of frameworks through which Rashi unifies Solomon's writings. While the framework Rashi applies to the Song of Songs is time-sensitive – arranging the verses in chronological sequence – the frameworks applied to both Proverbs and Ecclesiastes are theme-centric, establishing overarching motifs. The specific frameworks chosen are a direct consequence of the inherent nature of the compositions themselves; thus Rashi's selection of frameworks demonstrates his sensitivity to the distinct character of the biblical texts.

Ultimately, this analysis reveals the holistic nature of Rashi's approach to Solomon's writings.

Rashi's Commentary on Song of Songs

Chapter One

Introduction

Shir HaShirim, Song of Songs (henceforth the Song), is a series of poems describing the romance between the Shulamite and her unnamed lover.[1] The reader is swept away by vivid descriptions of lush fruits, fragrant flora, and pulsating wildlife in the land of Zion, in tandem with rich accounts of the protagonists' beauty – her hair is likened to a flock of goats and her teeth glisten like a freshly washed flock of ewes (6:5–6);[2] his eyes are like doves, evenly set and bathed in milk, and his lips similar to lilies, dripping with flowing myrrh (5:12–13).

Why are such tantalizing descriptions included in the biblical canon? After all, didn't Solomon, the wisest of all men, warn that "grace is deceptive and beauty is illusory" (Prov. 31:30)?[3] More surprising, however, is the provocative language invoked to describe the woman's intimate body parts:

1. According to Rashi, the word Shulamite (7:1) does not describe the woman but rather the nation of Israel, who is complete in her faith; see Rashi ad loc.
2. For additional detailed descriptions of the female, see 4:1–7, 7:2–8.
3. English translations of the biblical text are taken from the *New Jewish Publication Society of America Tanakh* (Jewish Publication Society, 2003). These translations have been occasionally modified to better reflect Rashi's understanding of the text.

> Your rounded thighs are like jewels, the work of a master's hand. Your navel is like a round goblet – let mixed wine not be lacking! – your belly like a heap of wheat, hedged about with lilies. Your breasts are like two fawns, twins of a gazelle. (7:2–4)

And most shocking are expressions of physical contact, such as embracing (2:6, 3:6, 8:3), lodging between her breasts (1:13), grasping them (7:9), and even allusions to consummating their love (1:16, 3:4, 7:13).

These problematic passages are compounded by the absence of any spiritual dimension in this composition – devoid of prayer, sacrifice, and even the name of God. Therefore, it is not surprising that concern regarding its abuse emerges in the words of the second-century Sage R. Akiva:

> One who raises his voice in the Song of Songs in the banquet house and makes it into a kind of song, has no portion in the World to Come. (Tosefta, Sanhedrin 12:10)

His warning seeks to obviate the trivialization of the Song through its recitation at secular gatherings or drinking halls; but why not? What could warrant the inclusion of this secular, provocative poetry in the Holy Scripture?

Turning again to R. Akiva to offer a solution, elsewhere he states: "For all the Hagiographa are holy, but the Song of Songs is Holy of Holies" (Mishna Yadayim 3:5),[4] thereby redeeming this composition by emphasizing its holy status. But how can a composition devoid of spirituality be considered "Holy of Holies"? What can possibly propel it from the secular to the spiritual realm? Apparently, R. Akiva's intent is relatively simple – the employment of allegory.[5]

Thus, Song of Songs is sacred because of its applied meaning. But what exactly is the nature of this meaning? Whom or what do the lovers represent?

---

4. *Mishnah, Seder Tohorot,* trans. and notes P. Kehati, vol. 5 (1996), 29.
5. "Allegory is a literary work in which the various details in the text have a transferred meaning" ("Book of Song of Songs," *The Anchor Bible Dictionary,* ed. D.N. Freedman, vol. 6 [Doubleday Books, 1992], 154).

TWO FUNDAMENTAL APPROACHES

Perusal of rabbinic literature uncovers two fundamental approaches. The first views the love story as the yearning of the human soul to cleave to God; as illustrated in the following source:

> R. Akiva entered in peace and left in peace; of him Scripture declares: "Draw me after you, let us run!" (Song. 1:4; Tosefta, Ḥagiga 2:2)[6]

Tractate Ḥagiga describes four great Sages who entered the *Pardes* (the "garden" or "orchard" of esoteric teachings) in order to draw near to God, yet only Akiva exits intact. The proof text employed to describe Akiva's successful spiritual quest is drawn from the Song and is one that describes the maiden's intense desire to be embraced by her beloved (1:4), thus hinting to a mystical understanding of our composition.[7]

The other, more dominant approach identifies the female protagonist (the bride) with the Congregation of Israel and her partner (the groom) with the Divine Presence, thus transforming the composition into a description of the historical relationship between God and His nation, a spiritual, national love story. Viewing the relationship of Israel with the Divine as that of a bride and groom is well documented in Scripture; after all, the prophet Hosea poignantly declares:

6. An alternative mystical approach found in the book entitled *Shiur Koma*, literally, "The Measurement of the Body," explicates the description of the male's physique (5:10–16) as descriptive of the divine body. See David Stern, "Ancient Jewish Interpretation of the Song of Songs in a Comparative Context," in *Jewish Biblical Interpretation and Cultural Exchange*, ed. N. Dohrmann and D. Stern (University of Pennsylvania Press, 2008), 95–96.
7. Similarly, the prohibition against teaching the secrets of the Divine Chariot is connected to a verse in Song of Songs: "We have learned concerning it, 'Honey and milk are under your tongue' (Song. 4:11). The things that are sweeter than honey and milk should be under your tongue" (Ḥagiga 13a). For additional examples, see Ephraim E. Urbach, "The Homiletical Interpretation of the Sages and the Expositions of Origen on Canticles and the Jewish-Christian Disputation," in *Scripta Hierosolymitana* (Magnes, 1971), 249–51.

> And I will espouse you forever: I will espouse you with righteousness and justice, and with goodness and mercy...then you shall be devoted to the Lord. (Hos. 2:21–22)

And, similarly, Jeremiah reminisces, "I accounted to your favor the devotion of your youth, your love as a bride – how you followed Me in the wilderness, in a land not sown" (Jer. 2:2). Yet the flip side also holds true: Breach of the sacred marriage covenant through the act of idolatry is deemed infidelity, "whoring/*zanu* with other gods" (Judges 2:17).

The allegorization of our text, at first blush, is not surprising, for, after all, we are familiar with this exegetical technique from other sections of the Tanakh.[8] Yet, in truth, its application here is somewhat revolutionary, because our text contains no textual hint indicating that our story represents another. Let us elaborate on this point through comparison.

The book of Samuel recounts David's sin with Bathsheba and the prophet's subsequent reprimand, couched in the form of a parable in which a rich man appropriates the sole ewe of a poor man (II Sam. 12:1–4). Immediately upon hearing of this injustice, David decrees that the rogue should be sentenced to death and charged fourfold for the damages he caused, whereupon Nathan the prophet accuses the king of similar behavior: "That man is you!" Nathan's indictment serves as the textual bridge linking the parable – the story of the magnate and the ewe – with its implied meaning – the king and Bathsheba. The Song, by contrast, contains no such explicit textual signpost pointing to a meaning beyond itself.

Additional Challenges

The Song poses additional questions of form: What is the poem's narrative structure? How many voices can be discerned within this composition? To whom are they speaking, and in what context? How can the swift transitions from singular to plural and from third-person to second-person address be explained?

---

8. Such as the book of Proverbs, Jotham's Parable (Judges 9:6–21), Parable of the Vineyard (Is. 5:1–7).

Let us now turn our attention to Rashi's commentary, asking: How does our premier exegete meet the multiple challenges presented above? What exegetical key does he provide to unlock this very challenging text?

RASHI'S PROLOGUE

Rashi's commentary on the Song commences with a formal prologue, which is an unusual phenomenon within his exegetical oeuvre;[9] although introductions to biblical commentaries were standard in other historical periods and provenances, such was not the case in eleventh-century northern France.[10] The mere penning of introductory words, therefore, hints to the complexity of the composition at hand and the author's desire to clarify central points with regard to its explication. Let us take a closer look.

Prologue: Part One

> "One thing God has spoken, two things have I heard" (Ps. 62:12) – One verse can be interpreted in many ways, but in the end a biblical verse does not leave the realm of its plain sense (*mashmao*).[11] And even though the prophets uttered their words figuratively (*dugma*), one must reconcile the allegory on its basis and its sequence, just as the verses are arranged one after the other. I have seen many aggadic midrashim on this book. Some arrange this entire book in one homily; in others, we find isolated verses scattered in many aggadic works, not reconcilable with the language of Scripture or the sequence of the verses. I decided to be attentive to the literal meaning of the verses, to

9. Similarly, see his introduction to the book of Zechariah.
10. See Eric Lawee, "Introducing Scripture: The 'Accessus Ad Auctores' in Medieval Hebrew Exegetical Literature from the 13th to 15th Centuries," in Jane Dammen McAuliffe et al., eds., *With Reverence for the Word: Medieval Scriptural Exegesis in Judaism, Christianity, and Islam* (Oxford University Press, 2003), 159–79.
11. Regarding the relationship between *mashmao* and *peshuto*, see Benjamin J. Gelles, *Peshat and Derash in the Exegesis of Rashi* (Brill, 1981), 119–20. In our composition, they seem interchangeable.

> reconcile their interpretations according to their sequence, and as for the midrashic interpretations of our Rabbis, I shall set each one in its place.

Rashi opens with a quotation from Psalms that serves as the justification for his exegetical approach:[12] Because Scripture is divine, God's word can be explicated on multiple methodological levels; yet notwithstanding the plurality of meanings embedded in the Holy Writ, one cannot ignore the contextual meaning (*mashmao*). He then notes that even in cases such as ours, wherein the biblical text is to be understood as figurative language (*dugma,* a unique term which will be discussed below), the commentator is still required to be attentive to the language and sequence of the verses, because they form the foundation for the text's applied meaning. Recognition of the text's literal, contextual meaning constitutes Rashi's first exegetical innovation in this commentary; because prior to him, rabbinic literature largely ignored this interpretive tier.

He then criticizes the extant homiletical material on the Song for violating the aforementioned criteria of language and sequence, thus arguing that the literal meaning (*mashmao*) and applied meaning (*dugma*) share some common ground rules.[13] This recognition of correspondence between the two tiers, as noted by Kamin, constitutes an additional exegetical breakthrough.[14] Rashi concludes his methodological manifesto with a pledge to present a dual commentary, one that addresses the literal meaning[15] and also gives a midrashic explication in which each homily sits in its appropriate place.

---

12. Rashi is following Sanhedrin 34a.
13. But, of course, not all. Most importantly, midrashic explications generally incorporate extra-biblical data which is untenable in the realm of *peshuto*.
14. Sarah Kamin, *Rashi's Exegetical Categorization: In Respect to the Distinction Between Peshat and Derash* [in Hebrew] (Magnes, 2007), 82.
15. This tier, however, is less systematic and complete than the allegorical one. For a comparison between the two levels of interpretation, see Sara Japhet, "Rashi's Commentary on the Song of Songs: The Revolution of the *Peshat* and Its Aftermath," in *Mein Haus wird ein Bethaus für alle Völker gennant werden (Jes 56,7): Judentum seit der Zeit des Zweiten Tempels in Geschichte, Literatur und Kult; Festschrift für Thomas Willi,*

Then, homing in on the specifics of the composition, Rashi proceeds to tease out both the narrative's framework and central storyline.

Prologue: Part Two

> I say that Solomon saw with divine inspiration that in the future, Israel will undergo exile after exile, destruction after destruction, and they will then mourn for their former glory in this present exile, remembering the initial love by which they were separated from all other peoples, and they will say, "I will go and return to my first husband, for then I fared better than now" (Hos. 2:9), and they will remember His kindnesses and their betrayal, and the rewards promised to them at the end of days. And he [Solomon] established this book with divine inspiration, in the language of a woman secluded in living widowhood (II Sam. 20:3) who longs for her husband, "who clings to her beloved" (Song. 8:5), remembering how she loved him in her youth. And even her Beloved is pained by her pain, and remembers the kindness of her youth, the comeliness of her beauty, and the quality of her deeds, in which He was bound up with her in intense love, and He tells her that He does not willfully bring her grief, nor has she been sent away permanently, for she is still His wife, and He her husband.

Rashi tells us that Solomon, through divine inspiration, foresaw the future trajectory of Jewish history and penned this composition as an allegory, where the female and male lovers represent the Congregation of Israel and God, respectively. There would be a series of exiles, even to "this present exile," i.e., the Diaspora that commenced with the destruction of the Second Temple and extended through Rashi's lifetime. Throughout this history the Jewish people would lament their former glory and closeness with the Divine. Rashi emphasizes that despite the

---

ed. J. Männchen, T. Reiprich (Neukirchener Verlag, 2007), 199–219; and Barry D. Walfish, "Song of Songs: The Emergence of *Peshat* Interpretation," thetorah.com: Song of Songs: The Emergence of Peshat Interpretation – TheTorah.com.

Jewish people's current exiled state, analogous to that of a living widow distanced from her beloved, her husband's love is still intact and their separation is transitory.

Rashi's narrative framework raises several questions. Why did he choose to detach this composition from its original historical setting – Solomon's lifetime – and reframe it within the context of his own era, thousands of years later? Beyond making the text relevant to his contemporary audience, what additional exegetical benefit did he seek? Moreover, why would a composition containing the passionate portrayal of youthful love be transformed into a narrative depicting a period of diminished ardor and passion – living widowhood and separation?

In order to find answers to these questions and others, let us now delve into Rashi's allegorical commentary.

DUGMA

As noted earlier, in his commentary on the Song, Rashi refers to the allegory – more than twenty times – by the term *dugma*.[16] In his glosses to other biblical books, he uses more general terms, such as *midrasho*, to mark this interpretive tier. What is the exact meaning of the term *dugma*, and why coin new nomenclature?

Dugma is actually a Greek loanword meaning illustration;[17] absent from the Tanakh, it first appears in rabbinic literature:

> As in the case where Rabban Gamliel was sitting and he interpreted homiletically: In the future, a woman will give birth every day, as it says: "Those with child and those in labor" (Jer. 31:7). A certain student scoffed at him and said: "There is nothing new under the sun" (Eccl. 1:9). [Rabban Gamliel] said to him: Come and I will show you an example (*dugmatan*) in this world. He took him outside and showed him a chicken. (Shabbat 30b)

16. Introduction, 1:2, 3, 4, 5, 8, 14, 15, 2:3, 4:1, 2, 3, 4, 15, 16, 5:2, 7, 16, 6:5, 7:3, 5.
17. M. Jastrow, *A Dictionary of the Targumim, the Talmud Babli and Yerushalmi, and the Midrashic Literature* (1903), vol. 1, s.v. דוגמא, p. 282.

Rabban Gamliel is teaching that just like a chicken lays eggs every day, so too will women give birth daily in time to come. The term *dugma* highlights the similarity between the two; the chicken's reproductive frequency serves as an illustration of that future capacity in women. Similar, posits Sarah Kamin, was Rashi's thought process when introducing the term *dugma* in his commentary on the Song; the passionate, carnal love story is illustrative of and serves as a model for the spiritual relationship between God and the Congregation of Israel.[18]

Yet Kamin believes that Rashi's specific choice of language, *dugma*, was influenced by an additional consideration – its occurrence at the beginning of the Midrash on the Song of Songs:

> "And more so because Kohelet was wise, he also taught the people knowledge; yea, he pondered and sought and set in order many proverbs" (Eccl. 12:9). He pondered the words of the Torah and investigated the [meaning of] the words of the Torah. He made handles to the Torah. You will find that until Solomon came there was no *dugma*. (Song of Songs Rabba 1:8)[19]

Thus, Rashi adopts a term which appears in the corpus of rabbinic literature and masterfully molds it to signify the allegory, the applied meaning of this composition. But why specifically in his gloss to the Song, when in his commentaries on other books, which also require decoding, he employs other terms such as *mishalo* or *midrasho*? At this point Kamin turns to external factors to supply the answer.

FOREIGN INFLUENCE

The Christian Church had a longstanding tradition of interpreting the Old Testament in a figurative sense, as a prefiguration of important

18. Sarah Kamin, "'Dugma' in Rashi's Commentary on Song of Songs," in *Jews and Christians Interpret the Bible* [in Hebrew] (Magnes, 2008), 71.
19. *Midrash Rabbah, Song of Songs*, trans. M. Simon (Soncino, 1983), 10. The Midrash credits Solomon with implementing a new interpretive skill (*dugma*), which simplified the learning of Torah.

Christian personalities and events. Notably, their historical exposition of the Song was strikingly similar to the Jewish reading, with a significant twist – the female beloved, the bride, was identifiable with the Christian Church, and her lover, with Christ.[20] Christian exegetes employed specific language to signal this mode of reading, such as "exemplar," *figura, forma,* etc.; and Rashi's use of *dugma,* according to Kamin, closely parallels these Latin terms, especially "exemplar."[21] To Rashi, the love story delineated in the Song serves as an exemplar for the relationship between God and His people, wherein almost every detail in the text is painstakingly matched with an important event in Jewish history. Thus Rashi's employment of the term *dugma* was deliberate – a conscious effort to introduce a Hebrew equivalent to the Latin terminology in order to strengthen the legitimacy of the Jewish reading.[22]

Yet not all scholars posit foreign influence. I.M. Ta-Shma asserts that the meaning of *dugma,* as espoused by Rashi, can already be detected in a commentary on an Ashkenazic liturgical poem preceding Rashi's lifetime; therefore, Rashi's use of the term is neither his own innovation nor a reaction to external factors.[23]

Scholars dismissing the idea of outside considerations are forced to turn inward to explain Rashi's exegetical choice, and some highlight the fact that Rashi's *dugma* has a close correspondence with the story in the text. On this basis, Gelles differentiates between Rashi's glosses to Proverbs and Song of Songs:

> Whereas *mashal* in his commentary on Proverbs centres around the Torah, the subject of the individual metaphorical sense in

20. One of the earlier exponents of this type of Christological reading was Origen, a third-century Christian exegete; see Urbach, "The Homiletical Interpretation," 252–75.
21. Kamin, "Dugma," 75–77. Although Rashi did not know Latin (in contrast to his grandson, who did – see Rashbam's commentary on Exod. 20:12), the Christological mode of reading Scripture was known to him.
22. Kamin, "Dugma," 70–88.
23. Israel M. Ta-Shma, *Studies in Medieval Rabbinic Literature,* vol. 1: Germany [in Hebrew] (Bialik Institute, 2004), 85–86. Kamin responds to his critique; see Kamin, *Rashi,* 83, n. 77.

> Canticles [the Song], depends much more on an exact comparison in detail between the story as it reads and a fitting applied meaning.[24]

Thus, *dugma* is more specific than the general term *mashal* and signifies an allegorical explanation composed of particulars that closely correspond to the details written in the text, making it especially suitable for Rashi's commentary on the Song, in which he toils to highlight the correspondence between the two tiers.

24. Gelles, *Peshat and Derash in the Exegesis of Rashi*, 82.

Chapter Two

Dugma

THE HISTORICAL PERIODS

Rashi's *dugma* covers a wide chronological range – from the Exodus from Egypt through the Edomite (i.e., Roman) exile. The timeline can be divided into sections and subsections as follows:

Superscription: Nature of the Composition (R 1:1)

Section One: From Exodus to Tabernacle (R 1:2–4:16)
- a. The Desert Sojourn (1:3–3:3)
- b. In the Promised Land (3:4–4:16)

Section Two: From Solomon's Temple to Second Temple (R 5:1–6:12)
- a. Solomon's Temple (5:1–6:1)
- b. Second Temple (6:1–6:12)

Section Three: From Exile to Redemption (R 7:1– 8:14)

Markers indicating change of theme or period are embedded in the commentary.

In order to accentuate Rashi's exegetical achievement, the analysis below focuses primarily upon the historical thread painstakingly stitched together by Rashi. We shall largely ignore the flashbacks and emotional outbursts which break the time sequence.[1]

Superscription (R 1:1)

The Song opens with the heading: "The Song of Songs which is Solomon's."

The phrase "Song of Songs" is understood as a superlative, denoting the most superb of all songs. Thus, if other canonical books are deemed holy, this Song is elevated to the status of "holy of holies."[2]

And what is the meaning of the heading's concluding phrase: "which is Solomon's"? Based on the Talmud, Rashi's reading substitutes for the name "Solomon" (Shlomo, written שלמה) the term "his peace" (*shlomo,* written שלומו), thus dedicating the Song to the Almighty, to "Him to whom peace belongs."[3] In his introduction Rashi had affirmed Solomon's authorship of this composition.[4] If here he seems to forget Solomon's authorship, this is perhaps because here the name Solomon is not followed by the patronymic "ben David" (son of David), which appears in the superscriptions of Ecclesiastes and Proverbs.[5]

Section One: From Exodus to Tabernacle (R 1:2–4:16)

Part A: The Desert Sojourn

Rashi's historical narrative begins by recounting the Exodus from Egypt, the Revelation at Sinai, and the construction of the Tabernacle. Throughout the Song, Rashi will find allusions to these formative events in the

1. Such as the recurring sections which praise the lovers' bodies: Female lover: 4:1–7, 6:4–7, 7:2–8; Male lover: 5:10–16. These sections will be analyzed in the following chapter, entitled "Additional Manifestations of Symmetry and Wholeness."
2. Rashi is quoting the words of R. Akiva, as noted above (p. 4); see Mishna Yadayim 3:5.
3. Rashi's source is Shavuot 35b.
4. Rashi's introduction to the Song: "And he [Solomon] composed *(yissad)* this book with the Holy Spirit..." The root Y-S-D in medieval Ashkenazic Hebrew is used to describe composing literature; see Cohen, *Rashi, Biblical Interpretation,* 67, n45.
5. See *The Five Megilloth: Esther the Song of Songs Ruth: A New English Translation,* trans. and notes A.J. Rosenberg (Judaica Press, 1992), 3–4.

nation's history.[6] He finds references not only to the high points but also to shameful events, such as the sin of the Golden Calf:

> *My nard gave forth its fragrance* (R 1:12) – This expression is a euphemism for "gave forth its stench." When the Divine Presence was still at Sinai, I sinned with the calf.[7]

Notably, Rashi reads the verse immediately following (1:13, "My beloved to me is a bag of myrrh") as the command to build the Tabernacle, thus teaching that the Tabernacle brought atonement for this grave transgression.[8] The sequence of sin (Golden Calf) followed by forgiveness (Tabernacle) exemplifies the cyclical nature of the relationship between God and the Congregation of Israel. This pattern will repeat itself in Rashi's explication of subsequent units. Although the nation sinned with the calf, Rashi highlights the loyalty of the tribe of Levi, who refrained from sinning, similar to a dove which is loyal to its mate (R 1:15).

In his commentary on chapter 2, Rashi emphasizes God's loving-kindness during the wilderness era, when He nourished the nation with manna and quail (R 2:6). Rashi also finds references to Israel's reciprocal responsibilities, such as offering the Paschal lamb and dedicating the firstborn (R 2:16). This unit draws to a close with the mention of Israel's sins, which result in the distancing of the Divine Presence from her midst (R 2:17), with her reflection on the desert period:

> *On my bed at night* (R 3:1) – In my distress, when I lived in the darkness for the entire thirty-eight years that they were under reproach.[9]

---

6. Exodus: R 1:9–11; 2:10–14; *Matan Torah*: R 1:2, 4; 2:3, 13; 3:11; 8:5; Tabernacle: R 1:13, 16–17; 2:4; 3:6–11; 4:10; 5:1; 8:2.
7. See Shabbat 88b.
8. So too, Rashi viewed the merit of accepting the Torah as offsetting this future sin (R 1:5). Thus, the sin is sandwiched by two modes of atonement: *Matan Torah* preceding the sin, and the construction of the Tabernacle following the transgression.
9. There is no known source for this interpretation. It is unclear why the Congregation of Israel speaks of herself in the third person: "They were under reproach/ שהיו נזופים."

Part B: In the Promised Land

In this unit, the nation shifts into the Promised Land under the fledging leadership of Joshua. After his military campaign succeeds, with divine assistance, the nation establishes a semi-permanent abode for the Tabernacle in Shiloh as an act of thanksgiving:[10]

> *Scarcely had I passed them* (R 3:4) – Soon after their [Moses's and Aaron's] parting from me,[11] at the end of the forty years. *When I found* – That He was with me in the days of Joshua to vanquish the thirty-one kings. *I held Him fast, I would not let Him go* – I did not loosen my grasp on Him until I brought Him to the Tabernacle at Shiloh because of all that He had done for me.[12]

Next, Israel reminisces about the divine protection in the desert and the splendor of the Tabernacle. God compares her to a dove, who is loyal to her mate and willing to surrender to him, as she accepts upon herself the yoke of heaven. He then praises various limbs of her body, which symbolize exemplary behavior traits in the nation's history (R 4:1–5). But then the priestly family in Shiloh forfeits God's protection by embezzling from the holy sacrifices (I Sam. 2:12–17).[13] In consequence, God abandons this spiritual center and designates another:

> *When the day blows gently… I will betake me* (R 4:6) – Meaning: When you will sin[14] against Me by profaning My holy offerings and by despising My meal offerings in the days of Hofni and Pinhas, I will leave you and I will abandon this Tabernacle, and I will choose for Myself the eternal Temple on Mount Moriah.[15]

10. See Joshua 18:1.
11. As Rashi states in his gloss to the previous verse: "The watchmen found me (3:3) – Moses and Aaron."
12. There is no known source for this gloss.
13. Similarly, see Rashi's gloss on 4:1.
14. It is unclear why Rashi refers to the days of Hofni and Pinhas in the future tense.
15. Genesis Rabba 55:7 connects this verse to Mount Moriah.

Only in this new abode will Israel's sacrifices once more be pleasing to Him.

Analysis: This section divides into two, based on the changes in leadership and setting – from Moses and Aaron to Joshua, from the wilderness to the Promised Land. By using identical expressions, Rashi establishes parallels between the two periods:

	Desert	**In the Promised Land**
Biblical verse	When the day blows gently and the shadows flee away, set out, my beloved, swift as a gazelle or a young stag, for the hills of spices. (2:17)	When the day blows gently and the shadows flee away, I will betake me to the mount of myrrh, to the hill of frankincense. (4:6)
Rashi's gloss	And the shadows flee – We *sinned* with the calf; we sinned with the spies...[16] I caused him to *leave me* on mountains which were far away from me....	When the day blows gently... I will betake me – Meaning: when you will *sin* before Me by profaning My holy offerings and by despising My meal offerings in the days of Hofni and Pinhas,[17] I will *leave you* and I will abandon this Tabernacle....

Both periods are stained by serious sins which result in the distancing of the Divine Presence, and Rashi uses identical language to describe these crises.[18] These periods of estrangement, however, are only temporary, with atonement returning the relationship to its former state on both occasions.

16. There is no known source. Note that Rashi delineates two sins: the calf and the spies, ostensibly to accord with the plural form utilized by the biblical text: "the shadows/הצללים."
17. Note Rashi's repetitive language: "by profaning My holy offerings and by despising My offerings in the days of Hofni and Pinhas"; perhaps to match the plural form utilized by the biblical text. See previous note.
18. The roots S-L-K, to remove, suspend; and H-T-A, to sin.

Notwithstanding this subdivision, a constant throughout this first section is the Tabernacle. Knowing no borders, the Tabernacle bridges both the time in the desert and the time in the Promised Land.

Section Two: From Solomon's Temple to the Second Temple (R 5:1–6:12)

Part A: Solomon's Temple

This section opens with the inauguration of Solomon's Temple, which included ceremonial eating and drinking similar to the consecration festivities of the Tabernacle (R 5:1). Unfortunately, the nation's state of peace and tranquility, like the slumber of the female lover, leads her astray. Yet God knocks on her door – He rests His Divine Presence upon the prophets to return her to the proper path (R 5:2). Several of the Judean kings during the First Commonwealth (Ahaz, Manasseh, Amon) persist stubbornly in their idolatrous ways. Others (Hezekiah and Josiah) heed the prophets' voices and lead the nation in repentance (R 5:7). Nevertheless, God does not rescind His decision; and the Temple is destroyed not only by foreign legions but also with the aid of His own celestial messengers:

> *The watchmen met me* (R 5:7) – Nebuchadnezzar and his armies. *Who patrol the town* – To wreak the vengeance of God. *They stripped me of my mantle* – The Temple. *The guards of the walls* – Even the ministering angels, who were guarding her walls, as it states: "Upon your walls, O Jerusalem [I have set watchmen], etc." (Is. 62:6), they set it [the Temple] on fire, as it states, "From above He sent fire down into my bones, etc." (Lam. 1:13).[19]

Part B: Second Temple

This unit introduces the Second Temple period, with Rashi's explicit mention of Cyrus – the Persian king inspired by God – who permits the Babylonian exiles to return and rebuild the Temple in Jerusalem (R 6:1).[20]

---

19. Regarding the ministering angels igniting the fire, see *Eikha Zuta* 1:7, although this source makes no mention of our verse.
20. Note that the transition between the First and Second Temple periods occurs within

The returnees reject the offer of the local heathens to participate in this holy building project, stating unequivocally that the heathens have no portion in Jerusalem, because God, her beloved, belongs exclusively to her. God promises to protect her from the machinations of these locals in order to complete the construction but notifies her that His excessive love, as demonstrated in the First Temple through the presence of the Ark and other furnishings, will be absent in the Second Temple (R 6:5).[21] He then praises and compares her to a flock of goats – just as a goat can be used entirely for sacred purposes, so too, the Congregation of Israel is completely holy (R 6:6).[22]

Turning attention to the realm of politics, the nations take note of Judah's gradual ascendancy in this arena:

> *Like the dawn* (R 6:10) – Which illuminates little by little; so were Israel during the Second Temple. In the beginning, Zerubbabel was the governor of Judah, but not a king, and they were subjugated to Persia and to Greece, but afterward, the house of the Hasmoneans defeated them and they became kings.[23]

But this zenith of power, attained by the Hasmonean kings, is forfeited due to causeless hatred and internecine rivalry. This results in political servitude to Rome and subsequent subjugation by foreign powers.

> *I did not know* (R 6:12) – The Congregation of Israel laments, "I did not know how to avoid sin, and thus remain in my glory and my greatness. I erred over causeless hatred and controversy, which peaked during the reign of the Hasmonean kings, Hyrcanus and Aristobulus, until one of them brought in the Roman king and received the kingship from his hand and became his vassal. Since

---

the same verse. This contrasts with the *Targum*, which posits that the transition to the time of Cyrus takes place in the subsequent verse (v. 2).

21. Yoma 21b lists the missing appurtenances but makes no mention of our verse.
22. Rashi's commentary is similar to *Shir HaShirim Zuta* 6:6.
23. I found no source connecting this verse to the Persian and Greek periods.

> then, "my soul set me" to be like "a chariot" –with the nobility of other nations riding upon me.[24]

Analysis: Rashi's gloss subtly distinguishes between the two Temples. Whereas the First Temple is dedicated with celebratory sacrifices and libations (R 5:1), a much more modest ceremony marks the inauguration of the Second Temple.[25] The Second Temple also lacks certain central fixtures, which diminishes the edifice's holiness. Different reasons are also posited for the destruction of each edifice.

Kamin raises an additional distinction: The actual fate of the Second Temple is never recorded.[26] Let us revisit Rashi's language:

> *I did not know* (R 6:12) – Since then, "my soul set me" to be "like a chariot" – with the nobility of other nations riding upon me.

This gloss employs vague language – "Since then"– and opaque imagery to depict the vulnerable state of the *nation* in the aftermath of the destruction of the Second Temple. By contrast, the description of the fate of the First Temple more explicitly centers on the *edifice*:

> *I met the watchmen* (R 5:7) – Nebuchadnezzar and his armies. *Who patrol the town* – To wreak the vengeance of God. *Stripped me of my mantle* – The Temple.

The Babylonian army, viewed as God's rod, avenges Israel's transgressions through the destruction of the actual edifice.

Rashi's significant omission of the demolition of the Second Temple, Kamin believes, is an outgrowth of the Jewish-Christian debate. Christianity preached that the edifice's destruction and the cessation of sacrificial worship were divine punishment for the slaying of Jesus and

24. Rashi's intent being that the days of Hyrcanus and Aristobulus mark the end of Jewish sovereignty. I found no source connecting this verse to the Greek and Roman periods.
25. See Ezra 6:16–18.
26. Kamin, *Rashi's Exegetical Categorization*, 253.

rejection of his teachings. The linkage between these events was based on a vision in the book of Daniel:[27]

> And after those sixty-two weeks, *the anointed one will disappear and vanish.* The army of a leader who is to come *will destroy the city and the sanctuary*... he will put a stop to the sacrifice and the meal offering. (Dan. 9: 26–27)

By omitting mention of the edifice's destruction and the motif of divine retribution, Rashi seeks to undermine this fundamental Christological claim.[28]

Notwithstanding the aforementioned distinctions, the Temple (both First and Second) symbolizes the spiritual heart of the nation, the meeting point between man and the Divine, similar to the previous role played by the Tabernacle. And indeed, Rashi's commentary, based on rabbinic sources, blends the two:

> *Our couch is in a bower* (R 1:16) –... The *Tabernacle* is called a couch, as it states, "There is Solomon's couch," and similarly, the *Temple* is called a couch.[29]

> *Eat, lovers* (R 5:1) – In the *Tent of Meeting,* Aaron and his sons, and in the eternal *Temple,* all the priests. *Drink deep, lovers* – These are the Israelites who ate the flesh of the peace offerings that they sacrificed at the inauguration of the *Temple.*[30]

---

27. For a better understanding of the Christian interpretation of these verses and the Jewish response, see Robert Chazan, "Rashi's Commentary on the Book of Daniel," in *Rashi et la Culture Juive en France du Nord au Moyen Âge*, ed. G. Dahan, G. Nahon, and E. Nicolos (Peeters, 1997), 119–21; Robert Chazan, "Daniel 9:24–27: Exegesis and Polemics," in *Contra Iudaeos: Ancient and Medieval Polemics Between Christians and Jews*, ed. O. Limor and G. Stroumsa (Mohr Siebeck, 1996), 143–59.
28. Kamin, *Rashi's Exegetical Categorization*, 253–54.
29. See *Tanḥuma*, Buber, *Naso* 16.
30. See Numbers Rabba 13:2.

> *To the house of my mother* (R 8:2) – The Temple. That You should instruct me – As You were accustomed to do in the Tent of Meeting.

As noted by Gottlieb, the Tent and the Temple become a merismus (a figure of speech where two contrasting parts stand for the whole, as in "young and old" for "everybody"):

> The pair Tent and Temple become a binominal, the A to Z of merismus. Tent represents a small and temporary abode, scene of early revelation, while Temple symbolizes the final and everlasting place of Divinity. Tent represents the past, Temple stands for the future.... Contrasting and complementary, the two concepts implied the totality of religious experience.[31]

Section Three: From Exile to Redemption (R 7:1– 8:14)
We meet the Congregation of Israel scattered throughout the Diaspora, as Rashi clearly states:

> *Your breasts are like clusters* (R 7:8) – Up to this point, the nations praised [Israel]. From here on, the words of the Divine Presence address Israel's exiles, dispersed among the nations.

In the chapter's opening verse (R 7:1), the nations attempt to persuade Israel, the Shulamite, who has complete faith in her God, to abandon Him ("Turn back, turn back, O Shulamite. Turn back, turn back"). She refuses, asking what greatness they could offer that would equal that which she possesses ("Why will you gaze at the Shulamite?").

The nations praise her physical features, which symbolize her outstanding national merits when she was in her prime, and they applaud Daniel and his companions for educating others how to properly fear God (R 7:8).

31. Isaac Gottlieb, "The Jewish Allegory of Love: Change and Constancy," *Journal of Jewish Thought and Philosophy*, vol. 2 (Brill, 1992): 10–11.

God charges Israel to remain steadfast in her faith and instructs her leaders to prepare first-rate responses, analogous to fine wine, in order to counter the verbal enticement of the nations (R 7:9–10). The identity of these nations is revealed in a gloss a few verses later, when the Shulamite says:

> *Let us lodge in the villages* (R 7:12) – Among the disbelievers.[32] Come and I will show You the descendants of Esau, upon whom You have bestowed prosperity, but who do not believe in You.[33]

Esau is a code name in Rashi's Bible commentary for the Roman Empire and its Christian successors;[34] thus, "the descendants of Esau," mentioned here by the Congregation of Israel, are the Christians in whose midst they reside. These neighbors often employ both persuasive speech and physical coercion to entice Israel to adopt their belief system (R 8:7, "Nor rivers drown it"), and her refusal sometimes results in martyrdom (R 8:6, "For love is fierce as death").

Despite these external pressures and the material disparity between them, Israel remains loyal to her God through her presence in the synagogues and their diligent learning in the study halls:

> *Let us go early to the vineyards* (R 7:13) – These are the synagogues and the study halls. *Let us see if the vine has flowered* – These are those who are versed in Scripture. *If the blossoms have opened* – And he compares those versed in the Mishna to them

32. Based on the similarity between the Hebrew words for villages (*kefarim)* and disbelievers (*kofrim).*
33. Rashi clearly states that his source is Tractate Eiruvin (21b). Whereas the Talmud speaks in general terms of disbelievers/*kofrim,* Rashi specifies the children of Esau; see the following footnote.
34. See Gerson D. Cohen, "Esau as Symbol in Early Medieval Thought," in *Jewish Medieval and Renaissance Studies,* ed. A. Altman (Harvard University Press, 1967), 19–48; Lisa Fredman, "In Praise of Esau: Between Rashi's Commentaries to the Torah and Nakh," *Tradition* 55:4 (2023): 41–54.

> [i.e., tender grapes]. *If the pomegranates are in bloom* – He compares those versed in the Talmud to them [ripe pomegranates].[35]

These consecrated spaces nurture Israel like breasts (R 8:10). Interestingly enough, similar institutions already existed during the former exile in Babylonia and thus predate the Edomite exile:

> *To browse in the gardens* (R 6:2) – And further, He has gone to graze His sheep in the gardens where they were scattered; those who did not come up from the exile, He rests His Divine Presence upon them in the synagogues and in the study halls.[36]

Thus, during the Second Temple period, the Divine Presence divides between those who return to Jerusalem to rebuild the Temple and those who remain in exile and frequent synagogues and study halls.[37] God's continued presence with exiled Israel represents a significant theological assertion. Exile does not represent a rupture between Israel and her God; to the contrary, it exhibits God's unwavering presence among His people.[38]

In the Song's closing verses, the Congregation of Israel commits to remaining steadfast in her belief. God promises that the nations who financially exploited her through the levying of exorbitant taxes will pay recompense for their actions (R 8:11–12, "A thousand pieces of silver; you may have the thousand, O Solomon, and the guards of the fruit two hundred"), and He calls upon the angels to hearken to her voice. The composition ends with Israel beseeching God to hasten the redemption.

Analysis: The Edomite exile, which by Rashi's time had lasted nearly a millennium, is characterized by a dual reality: intense external pressures

---

35. Rashi's source is Eiruvin 21b.
36. There is some similarity between Rashi's comment and Song of Songs Rabba 6:2.
37. It is noteworthy that earlier in his commentary Rashi mentions God's presence among the exiles irrespective of a specific meeting place: "With me from Lebanon will you come (R 4:8) – And when you return from the exile, I will return with you…from the time of your departure from here until the time of your return, I am with you *wherever* you will go and come."
38. See Jonathan Kaplan, *My Perfect One: Typology and Early Rabbinic Interpretation of Song of Songs* (Oxford University Press, 2015), 168–76.

on the Jewish minority and robust expressions of devotion to the Divine. Recognizing the potent influence of Christian persuasion, God repeatedly encourages Israel to remain steadfast and resist foreign allurements. Israel's enduring loyalty sets the stage for the Song's concluding verses, which Rashi interprets as heralding the era of redemption: "I have my very own vineyard; you may have the thousand, O Solomon, and the guards of the fruit two hundred! ... Hurry, my beloved, swift as a gazelle or a young stag, to the hills of spices!" (8:12–14). These verses present a stark contrast between Israel's current and former circumstances.

During the period of Solomon's Temple, God repeatedly sent prophets to warn Israel of the upcoming catastrophe, but the oracles were mostly ignored (R 5:2–3, "Hark, my beloved knocks; I had taken off my robe"). But now the exiled Congregation of Israel pledges:

> *When I meet you in the street then I could kiss you* (8:1) – I would find Your prophets speaking in Your name, and I would embrace and kiss them (R 8:1).[39]

While earlier periods were stained by acts of disloyalty due to the influence and seduction of foreign beliefs and entities,[40] Israel now promises to be like a wall of brass which the nations cannot infiltrate, neither through intermarriage nor intermingling (R 8:9–10; "If she be a wall, we will build upon it a silver battlement; if she be a door, we will panel it in cedar" [8:9], "I am a wall" [8:10]).

This transformation in Israel's character precipitates a corresponding shift on high. God's ministering angels were instrumental in the destruction of the First Temple (R 5:7, "The guards of the walls"), and thus, in a sense, were Israel's adversaries. Now they are transformed into companions, or *ḥaverim*. Upon hearing Israel's sanctifying prayers, these celestial beings emulate their earthly counterparts:[41]

39. I found no source connecting this verse to prophecy.
40. Mixed multitude: R 1:6; idolatry: R 2:17; 5:3.
41. This is in contrast to our own assertion, in our *Kedusha* prayer, that we will sanctify God's name following the lead of the angels. Thank you to Professor Marty Lockshin for this insightful comment.

> *Companions listen to your voice* (R 8:13) – The ministering angels, your companions, children of God like you, hearken and come to listen to your voice. *Let me hear* – And afterward, they will sanctify."[42]

Likewise, there will be a change in the situation of the nations who exploited Israel. No longer will they enrich themselves through the impoverishment of Israel; rather, on the day of judgment they will repay the "principal" along with a "penalty," thus correcting this injustice:

> They [the nations] say: *You may have the thousand, O Solomon* (R 8:12) – "The thousand silver pieces that we collected from them [from Israel] will all be returned to You." *And to the guard of fruit two hundred* – "And we will add much more of our own, and we will give it to them."[43]

What effectuated the change in Israel's behavior? From where did she garner the strength to withstand?

> *I am a wall* (R 8:10) – Strong in the love of my Beloved. *And my breasts are like towers* – These are the synagogues and the study halls, which nurture Israel with words of Torah.[44]

> *You who sit in the gardens* (R 8:13) – The Holy One, blessed be He, says to the Congregation of Israel, "You, who are scattered in exile, grazing in the gardens of strangers and sitting in synagogues and study halls."

42. Song of Songs Rabba 8:15 identifies the companions as the ministering angels.
43. The repayment of a principal (here, one thousand silver pieces) plus a penalty (one-fifth of the payment, i.e., two hundred more) for benefiting unjustly from holy property (meaning, exploitation of holy Israel) is based on the Talmud (Bava Metzia 54a), but the application of this law to our verse is original to Rashi.
44. Rashi's source is Pesaḥim 87a.

Dedication to prayer, Torah study, and adherence to the commandments[45] spiritually fortify the Jewish people.

Note that the tail end of Rashi's commentary does not clearly delineate the transition point between exile and final redemption.[46] Consciously blurring the lines, Rashi even refrains from mentioning the word "Messiah" or hinting at an eschatological timeline. Instead, he focuses on the here and now, stressing the importance of his reader's contemporary actions in ushering in the nation's final epoch – in tandem, of course, with the Almighty:

> *Hurry, my beloved* (R 8:14) – From this exile, and redeem us from their midst. *Swift as a gazelle* – To hasten the redemption, and to cause Your Divine Presence to rest on the hills of spices – This is Mount Moriah and the Temple, may it be rebuilt speedily in our days.

MAINTAINING CHRONOLOGICAL ORDER

Rashi's construction of a historical narrative within the Song of Songs hinges on strict adherence to chronological order. This commitment is evident in various ways.

Explicit Statement

First, we find an explicit statement disqualifying rabbinic material that violates time sequence. In chapter 2, the female lover's plea to her companions, "I adjure you, O maidens of Jerusalem, by gazelles or by hinds of the field" (v. 7),[47] is equated by the Talmud with God's injunction

---

45. See R 1:8, 3:11, 4:3, 9, 11, 5:2, 6:11, 7:6, 14.

46. Kamin and Saltman read the Song's concluding five verses as describing the final redemption; yet elsewhere Kamin employs more indefinite language ("near the end of the Song"), which I believe is more accurate. Because it is unclear where the dividing line actually lies, I have refrained from subdividing the final section into two. See S. Kamin and A. Saltman, *Secundum Salomonem: A Thirteenth-Century Latin Commentary on the Song of Solomon* (Bar-Ilan University Press, 1989), 28; Kamin, *Rashi's Exegetical Categorization*, 255.

47. Repeated in nearly identical formulation twice more in 3:5 and 8:4. These three

to exiled Israel against hastening the redemption.[48] Rashi rejects this equation:

> *Or rouse* (R 2:7) – There are many homiletical midrashim, but they do not accord with the *seder hadevarim*, for I see that Solomon prophesied and spoke about the Exodus from Egypt and about the giving of the Torah, and the Tabernacle, and the entry into the land, and the Temple, and the Babylonian exile, and the Second Temple and its destruction.

Thus, homilies referring to the subsequent exile are violations of *seder hadevarim* (the sequence of verses or topics), indicating a problem of chronology.[49] Given the talmudic interpretation's grounding in the era of the Roman exile era, and the focus and Rashi's preceding commentary on the wilderness period, the talmudic homily cannot be fitted into Rashi's chronology. Rashi rejects these homilies and promptly presents his delineation of the Song's correct time sequence.

Rashi's choice of the term *seder hadevarim* rather than *seder hazemanin* (time sequences) suggests a potential additional issue beyond chronology: the identification of the speaker. The talmudic homily attributes the adjuration to God addressing the Jewish people, whereas Rashi assigns the speech to the Congregation of Israel addressing the "daughters of Jerusalem."

Rashi's concern with sequential order leads to his assigning different meanings to identical expressions when they occur in passages dealing with different historical periods.

Comparison of Identical Words or Phrases

The image of "your two breasts" occurs twice in the Song. The first appearance is in chapter 4 (v. 5), wherein Rashi identifies the breasts

---

verses, where the female beloved implores her companions, correspond to the three oaths God places upon Israel.

48. See Ketubot 111a.

49. So believes Kamin, *Rashi's Exegetical Categorization*, 78, n. 66.

with Moses and Aaron, or alternatively the twin tablets.[50] In his later gloss (R 7:4) they refer to the twin tablets, or, alternatively, the king and the high priest.[51] The difference is evidently due to chronological considerations: Chapter 4 deals with the Tabernacle period, the period of Moses and Aaron, while chapter 7 deals with the later exilic era, when Moses and Aaron are no longer present.[52]

Similarly "the watchmen" in chapter 3 (v. 3) are identified with Moses and Aaron, whereas in chapter 5 (v. 7) they serve as an allusion to Nebuchadnezzar and his armies.[53]

Rashi's meticulous attention to chronological order is also evident in his treatment of the myrrh spice. In the Song's opening chapter, the female lover characterizes her beloved as a fragrant "bag of myrrh" (1:13). As myrrh is a key ingredient of both the daily incense offering on the Tabernacle's golden altar and the anointing oil prepared in the wilderness (Ex. 30:23), Rashi associates this imagery with the desert period.[54] However, he links a subsequent reference to "the mount of myrrh" (4:6) to the Temple on Mount Moriah, a connection based on the play on words between *mor* (myrrh) and "Moriah."[55].

His explication of the name Solomon may also be linked to chronology. As previously noted, following the Talmud, Rashi identifies the Solomon of the Song's superscription with God, the King of kings. The Talmud states that "Solomon" in the Song is always to be so identified, but it makes exceptions for two specific verses:

---

50. Rashi's source for the former is Song of Songs Rabba 4:12; for the latter, *Mekhilta, Yitro Baḥodesh* 8.
51. There is no known source for the second explanation.
52. Similarly, "My mother's house" (R 3:4), mentioned early in the composition, is identified with the Tabernacle in Shiloh, whereas the identical abode is synonymous with the Temple (R 8:2) in the closing chapter.
53. As discussed earlier, Rashi's explication of the twice-occurring phrase "When the day blows gently and the shadows flee away" (2:17, 4:6) reveals his concern for time order: the former depicting the sins in the desert period, the latter referring to the transgressions at Shiloh (after entering the Promised Land).
54. Similarly, see his gloss on 3:6.
55. See Genesis Rabba 55:7.

> All [mentions of the name] Shlomo that are stated in the Song of Songs… [are] sacred, meaning a song to [the] One for whom peace [*shehashalom*] is His, *except for this* [mention]: "My vineyard, which is mine, is before me; you, Solomon shall have the one thousand" (8:12)…. And some say: This [verse] too is non-sacred: "Behold, the bed of Solomon; sixty mighty men are around it" (3:7).[56]

Rashi, however, disregards both exceptions and consistently opts for the identification of Solomon with the King of kings. What could be prompting his choice? Perhaps positioning is the exegetical trigger. The first exemption (8:12) involves a verse in the Song's closing chapter, a section Rashi assigned to the period of redemption, rendering a Solomonic identification historically incongruous. Likewise, identifying the second exemption (3:7) with King Solomon is sequentially untenable given Rashi's anchoring of the immediately preceding verse in the desert period.[57]

Accounting for Out-of-Sequence Verses

Rashi occasionally employs various other features to explain verses that appear out of their expected sequence. For example, his characterization of the female protagonist as a lovesick "living widow" is a key interpretive tool. This portrayal allows him to account for verses that deviate from a strict chronological order,[58] as illustrated in the following instance:

---

56. Shevuot 35b. *Koren Talmud Bavli, Tractates Makkot and Shevuot, Commentary by Rabbi Adin Even-Israel Steinsaltz* (Koren Publishers, 2017), 365.
57. Already noted by *Siftei Ḥakhamim* (3:7). It is possible, though, that Rashi's consistent identification of Solomon with God is theologically motivated. As noted earlier, the name of God is completely absent in this composition; repeated identification of Solomon with the Divine helps fill this spiritual void.
58. As noted by Kamin, the primary motive for Rashi's innovative decision to turn the narrator into a "living widow" is connected to the Jewish-Christian debate. Depicting her as such indicates that the Temple's destruction and the ongoing exile were not a sign that God had *divorced* Himself from the Jewish people (as asserted by Christianity); rather, the ensuing exile was analogous to the status of *living widowhood*, which denotes separation but not severance of ties. See Kamin, *Rashi's Exegetical Categorization*, 247–50.

The beginning of the Song (1–2:6) contains, according to Rashi, a recital of events from the Exodus/wilderness period, including mention of the Exodus (1:10–11) *after* a description of the giving of the Torah (1:2–4) and the sin of the Golden Calf (1:5–6), an order which clearly reverses the true time sequence. This somewhat haphazard historical recounting culminates with the following statement:

> *And his right hand would embrace me* (R 2:6) – All this I remember now in my exile, and I am sick for His love.

Rashi's intent is that because the aforementioned historical description is emanating from the mouth of a lovesick widow, her words are exempt from any expectation of logic or order; i.e., the widow's fragile emotional state is utilized to "account for recalcitrant verses."[59]

In another instance, the repetition of themes stems from a more practical consideration, akin to a narrator picking up a dropped thread. Rashi explains:

> *The voice of my Beloved* (R 2:8) – The poet returns to the earlier topics, like a person who was brief with his words and returns and says, "I did not tell you the beginning of these events." He began by saying, "The king has brought me into his chambers" (1:4) but did not recount how He remembered them in Egypt with an expression of affection. And now he returns and says, "This pulling that I told you about, that my Beloved drew me and I ran after Him, happened as follows."

Indeed, chapter 2 revisits themes initially presented in the Song's opening chapter, where the protagonist reminisces about how her nascent bond with God was forged through potent forces of love. This repetition, therefore, is not a chronological break but a narrative technique.

Thus, it is clear that maintaining chronology was the decisive consideration governing Rashi's exegetical decisions on the Song. Whether by limiting midrashic material he deemed suitable for inclusion, by shaping

59. Kugel, "Two Introductions to Midrash," 155, n. 23.

his exegesis of repetitive phrases to conform with the unfolding timeline within the text, or by noting various emotional or practical considerations, time sequence trumps all other factors.

INTERIM SUMMARY

Rashi transforms the collection of seemingly disparate love poems into a cohesive narrative chronicling the sacred relationship between the female lover, representing the Congregation of Israel, and her beloved, God. Rashi's *dugma* surveys the historical record in sequence: a record typified by sin, resulting in estrangement from the Almighty, followed by reconciliation. Israel looks back from her present exile and desires once again to be reunited with her God.

This linear structure is reinforced by the recurring motif of the Divine Presence. The indwelling of God *(hashraat haShekhina)* is consistently depicted in spatial terms: Sinai, Tabernacle, Temple, houses of prayer and study, and future Temple. These spiritual centers form a continuum representing unbroken contact between God and His people throughout history; and they serve as the loci for the dissemination of Jewish law, Israel's sustaining force.[60] Consequently, exile is not a state of divine abandonment.

Drawing primarily from midrashic writings that can be categorized as atomistic, Rashi handpicks those that accord with his exegetical intent. He then adapts them and introduces original material, seamlessly interweaving the two into an organic whole.

60. Sinai: R 1:2; Tabernacle: R 2:4; 3:8; Temple (Sanhedrin/Chamber of the Hewn Stone): R 4:4–5, 7:3, 5; Houses of Prayer/Study: R 5:11, 6:9, 7:13, 8:10.

Chapter Three

Additional Manifestations of Symmetry and Wholeness

As noted earlier in our introduction, the Song raises questions of form: How many voices can be discerned within this composition, and to whom are they speaking? How can the abrupt transitions from singular to plural be explained? Upon searching for answers, we discover additional manifestations of wholeness and symmetry.

THE NUMBER AND IDENTITY OF THE VOICES

The Female Beloved's Companions

The Song's protagonists are undoubtedly the female and male lovers. Yet other actors also frequent the narrative stage, such as the "daughters of Jerusalem," who serve a supporting role. This female collective, mentioned seven times, ushers us through the narrative.[1] Sometimes

1. 1:5, 2:7, 3:5, 10, 5:8, 16, 8:4.

they silently observe the female lover; at other times they converse with her. She, in turn, addresses them three times in almost the same words:

> I adjure you, O daughters of Jerusalem, by gazelles, or by hinds of the field: Do not wake or rouse love until it please.[2]

Who is this female chorus sharing the limelight? Rashi identifies them with the nations of the world (R 2:7). This is surprising; why would inhabitants of the sacred city, Jerusalem, symbolize almost the polar opposite – the heathen nations? Rashi explains:

> *I am dark, but comely* (R 1:5) – [Scripture] calls the nations "the daughters of Jerusalem," because in the future she will become a metropolis for them all, as Ezekiel prophesied: "And I will give them to you as surrounding villages [though they are not of your covenant]" (Ezek. 16: 61).[3]

A metropolis is a "mother city"; hence, her surrounding villages are metaphorically deemed "daughters," or dependent towns. In the future the nations of the world will come on pilgrimage to Jerusalem to pay homage to God, and so their cities are considered Jerusalem's suburbs.

Rashi consistently interprets the addresses to the "daughters of Jerusalem," a recurring motif in the Song, as references to the nations:[4]

> *I adjure you* (R 3:5) – The nations, today, while I am exiled among you.

2. 2:7, 3:5, 8:4. Other refrains include the gazelle refrain (2:17, 4:6), the interrogation refrain (3:6, 8:5), and the embrace refrain (2:6, 8:3).
3. The Hebrew word in Ezekiel is *benot*, daughters, just like in the Song. Rashi's source is Song of Songs Rabba 1:5; similarly, see Exodus Rabba 23:11.
4. A fourth verse, with an identical first stich, concludes differently: "I adjure you, O daughters of Jerusalem! If you meet my beloved, tell him this: that I am faint with love" (5:8). Even in this verse, the identification is with the nations, but specific mention is made of Nebuchadnezzar's men.

> *I adjure you* (R 8:4) – Now the Congregation of Israel addresses the nations: "Even though I complain and lament, my Beloved holds my hand, and He is my support in my exile; therefore, 'I adjure you.'"

Rashi's use of the terms "today," "now," and "in my exile" makes it clear that he is referring to the nations of his own time.

In the following instance, however, Rashi veers from course:

> *By the daughters of Jerusalem* (R 3:10) – These are Israel, who fear and are complete [in their obedience] toward the Holy One, blessed be He.[5]

This explication is arrived at by an interpretive method known as *notarikon*,[6] which consists of dividing a word in two and expanding each component. Thus, *Yerushalayim=yere'im* (God-fearing) and *shelemim* (complete).

What can explain this deviation from his usual identification of the chorus with the nations?

Perhaps the partitive prefix *mi-* ("by" or "from") at the beginning of the word "daughters" (*mibenot*), indicates not all the nations, but only "a portion of," i.e., the Congregation of Israel.[7] Cohn raises the consideration of context in explaining this variance: Because this particular verse alludes to the Tabernacle rather than to the Temple, reference to the nations is inappropriate.[8]

---

5. See Numbers Rabba 12:4.
6. *Notarikon* is one of the thirty-two hermeneutical techniques used in interpreting the Bible in which a word breaks up into various components. See "Notarikon," *Encyclopedia Judaica*, vol. 12. (1971), 1231.
7. *Shir haShirim* (commentary by M. Zlotowitz, ArtScroll Series, Mesorah, 1977), 124; Gabriel H. Cohn, *Textual Tapestries: Explorations of the Five Megillot*, trans. D. Strauss (Maggid Books, 2016), 85–86.
8. Cohn, *Textual Tapestries*, 85. It is interesting to note that the anonymous scribe of the reliable medieval manuscript Lutzki 778 opposes Rashi's lack of consistency and appends his own explanation immediately following Rashi's gloss to this verse. He understands the letter *mem* at the beginning of the word "daughters" as comparative; thus, the meaning of the phrase is: "It was decked with love [of Israel] more than

In addition to the daughters of Jerusalem, other, more peripheral female characters, such as the "maidens/*alamot*," are similarly paired off with the nations of the world. The maidens who love "You" (1:3), i.e., God, correspond to Jethro and Rahab, who demonstrate their love for God through conversion to Judaism;[9] and the "innumerable" maidens of chapter 6 (v. 8) are identified with the family of nations branching out from Noah until Abraham.[10]

Note that whereas the "maidens" are identified with nations from the ancient past, the "daughters of Jerusalem" are primarily identified with those contemporary to Rashi. At any rate, the presence of the "nations" accompanies us throughout the narrative.

Unlike the "maidens," who remain silent, the "daughters of Jerusalem" raise their voices. Rashi identifies their speaking parts, which are not explicitly marked, based on clues in the text.[11] For instance, the seventh chapter begins: "Turn back, turn back, O Shulamite [an appellation for the Congregation of Israel[12]]; turn back, turn back, that we may gaze upon you" (7:1). The speaker of the request is plural: "We may gaze." What type of group would daringly desire to observe a woman in dance? Obviously, for Rashi, a female collective. Thus, Rashi attributes this appeal to the "daughters of Jerusalem," i.e., the nations. Likewise, he attributes the extensive description of her body which immediately

---

the daughters of Jerusalem." According to this explanation, the phrase "daughters of Jerusalem" is once again identified with the other nations. See alhatorah.org on the Song 3:10, note ר in the Rashi text; J. Rosenthal, ed., "Rashi's Commentary on the Song of Songs," in *Samuel K. Mirsky Jubilee Volume*, ed. S. Bernstein and G. Churgin (New York 1958), 153, n. י.

9. See Song of Songs Rabba 1:22. *Tanḥuma, Yitro* 3, connects our verse to Jethro only.
10. See *Shir HaShirim Zuta* 6:8.
11. The designation of their speaking part in verse 5:9 is based upon context. Because verse 5:8 mentions the "daughters of Jerusalem," Rashi understands 5:9 as their response. In addition, the verb "to take an oath" is used in both verses. Likewise, the last verse of chapter 5 is addressed to the "daughters of Jerusalem," and 6:1 is understood as their response.
12. Shulamite, from the root S-L-M, meaning complete or perfect, i.e., Israel, who is perfect in her faith. This is similar to Rashi's explication of the name Solomon (*Shlomo*), not as a proper noun but as an appellation describing God – the King to whom peace belongs (R 1:1).

follows (vv. 2–7) to them, although other exegetes attribute this praise of her physique to the male beloved.[13]

What is the nature of the nations' interaction with the Congregation of Israel? Confrontational, to say the least:

> *How is your beloved better than another* (R 5:9) – This is what the nations were asking Israel: "What is [it about] your God from all other gods, that you are ready to be burned and hanged for Him?[14]

> *Turn back, turn back, O Shulamite* (R 7:1) – They say to me: "Turn back, turn back" from after the Omnipresent. *Shulamite* – Perfect in your faith with Him, "turn back, turn back" to us.[15]

> *Where has your beloved gone* (R 6:1) – The nations taunt and provoke Israel, "Where has your Beloved gone?" Why has He left you abandoned like a widow?[16]

Thus they endeavor to create a wedge between Israel and her God. Yet she refuses to be swayed by their words and declares:

> *Do not wake or rouse love* (R 2:7) – That is between my Beloved and me, to change it or to exchange it, asking me to be enticed after you. *Until it please* – As long as it is lodged in my heart, *and He desires me.*[17]

> *Do not wake or rouse love* (R 3:5) – [Turning] *the love of my Beloved* away from me through seduction and enticement, *to abandon*

---

13. Hakham quotes the view espoused by Rashi, anonymously, and notes that it is contrived (*doḥak*). See *The Five Megillot: Daat Mikra Series* [in Hebrew] (Mossad HaRav Kook, 1973), p. נח, n. 3.
14. See *Mekhilta, Shira Beshallaḥ* 3.
15. See *Tanḥuma, Bemidbar* 11, explicitly noted by Rashi.
16. No known source.
17. No known source.

> *Him* and to turn away from following Him, "until it please" – as long as *He desires me.*[18]
>
> *I am my Beloved's* (R 6:3) – *You* [plural] *are not His.*

Stern has noted that on its most basic level the Song of Songs is a story about two passionate lovers – their presence and absence. This binary relationship forms the heart of the narrative. However, some rabbinic sources recast the narrative as a triadic relationship, with two females (Israel and the nations) competing for the same love, that of the Beloved (i.e., God).[19] Rashi, in essence, adopts this approach. The consistent character portrayal and significant role allocated to the "daughters of Jerusalem" subtly reframes the narrative as a conversation between three main actors – God, the Congregation of Israel, and the nations of the world, who for Rashi are primarily the Christians. Thus, the dialogue between the human actors, as molded by Rashi, expresses the ongoing theological tug of war between the two, with Israel stressing her unchanging and unalterable beloved nation status.[20]

Incidentally, another commentary, which some attribute to Rashbam, adopts the same narrative structure. That commentator, unlike Rashi, explicitly introduces the triadic relationship at the start of the commentary.[21]

---

18. No known source.
19. Stern, "Ancient Jewish Interpretation of the Song of Songs," 106–7.
20. Early church fathers claimed that the rejection of the Jews and the transfer of their chosen status to the Christians occurred at the time of the Golden Calf; see Rosemary Radord Ruether, "The *Adversus Judaeos* Tradition," in *Essential Papers on Judaism and Christianity in Conflict,* ed. J. Cohen (New York University Press, 1991), 177. See also Epistle of Barnabus 4:8.
21. Although in his introduction he mentions four participants: female beloved, male beloved, female friends, and maidens, throughout his commentary the application is to three only: Israel, God, and the nations; as noted by Sara Japhet, *The Commentary of Rabbi Samuel Ben Meir (Rashbam) on the Song of Songs* [in Hebrew] (World Union of Jewish Studies, 2008), 85. Regarding the question of authorship, see the discussion in the aforementioned source, pages 9–51.

The Male Beloved's Companions

In the text of the Song, the male Beloved's companions receive only fleeting mention; but in Rashi's commentary they gain a place of prominence.[22] Who are these friends who keep company with the Divine?

Rashi identifies the *re'im* with the priestly family:

> *Eat, friends* (*re'im*; R 5:1) – Aaron and his sons, in the Tent of Meeting, and all the priests, in the eternal Temple.[23]

However, this interpretation is exceptional; Rashi primarily sees the companions as celestial beings, Thus he takes the *ḥaverim* to be the ministering angels:

> *Companions* (*ḥaverim*), *listen to your voice* (R 8:13) – The ministering angels (*malakhei hasharet*), your companions.[24]

Similarly, the guardians of the walls are identified by Rashi as ministering angels (R 5:7).[25]

So too, when the male Beloved is described as being surrounded by myriads (*merevava*; 5:10), the intent is that he is encircled by many angelic armies (*beḥayalot*).[26] This is similar to the image found in the book of Daniel describing the multitudes surrounding the Divine: "Ten thousand upon ten thousand (*veribbo rivevan*) stood before Him" (Dan. 7:10). Note the identical root, R-B-B, employed in both texts to indicate an immense number.[27]

---

22. Mentioned a total of eight times: ministering angels: R 5:7, 8:13; celestial court: R 1:11, 8:5, 7; armies: R 5:10, 6:4, 7:9.
23. Song of Songs Rabba 5:1 identifies the companions with Moses and Aaron.
24. Song of Songs Rabba 8:13 connects our verse with the ministering angels.
25. The connection between "guardians of the walls" and angels is based on the verse in Isaiah (62:6) which describes Jerusalem as being constantly guarded, day and night, by watchmen placed by God.
26. R 5:10. Rashi understands the word *dagul* as "surrounded." Others, like NJPS, understand the phrase as meaning "preeminent among the myriads"; similarly, Koehler and Baumgartner, *HALOT*, vol. 1, 213, understand it to mean "outstanding."
27. See Koehler and Baumgartner, *HALOT*, vol. 3, 1175.

Rashi introduces celestial beings not only to identify anonymous characters, but also to resolve exegetical difficulties:

> *I say: Let me climb the palm tree* (R 7:9) – I boast of you among the heavenly armies (*ḥayalot shel malah*), that I will be elevated and sanctified through your actions in the lower abodes, when you will sanctify My name among the nations.[28]

According to Rashi, God is the speaker in this verse, and the palm tree stands for Israel. God is boasting to His heavenly companions that His nation's honorable actions cause Him to scale the tree (i.e., to become elevated, glorified). What prompts Rashi to mention this celestial group? Presumably, it is the fact that the text states, "I say," but does not reveal the addressee of God's words. "The heavenly armies" is added to fill this textual lacuna.

The following gloss is motivated by a grammatical consideration:

> *We will make wreaths of gold* (R 1:11) – I and My celestial court (*beit din*) decided before Pharaoh's arrival that I should entice him and harden his heart to chase you with all the best of his hidden treasures; so that we should make for you circlets of golden ornaments.[29]

The verse employs the plural verb form "we will add," which when identified with God could be misconstrued as implying multiple deities;[30] therefore Rashi glosses: God with His celestial court, thus preserving the oneness of God.[31]

---

28. No known source.
29. Song of Songs Rabba 1:54 and *Sifrei, Re'eh* 120, connect our verse to the Egyptian booty and the booty at the sea, but make no mention of His heavenly court.
30. Such as dualism (belief in two gods), or belief in a god that is divisible into different characteristics, such as trinitarianism; see E. Kanarfogel, "Trinitarian and Multiplicity Polemics in the Biblical Commentaries of Rashi, Rashbam, and Bekhor Shor," *Gesher* 7 (1979): 16–21. A similar concern is addressed in Rashi's commentaries on Genesis 1:26, 11:7.
31. Regarding the development of the motif of the heavenly tribunal as patterned after

The following glosses, found in close succession, resolve a similar issue:

> *Who is she* (R 8:5) – The Holy One, blessed be He, and His celestial court, say about the Congregation of Israel, "Who is she?" How very worthy is she, who ascended from the desert bearing all the good gifts.
>
> *He would be laughed to scorn* (R 8:7) – On all these [including the preceding parts of the verse] the Holy One, blessed be He, and His celestial court testify that to this extent the Congregation of Israel clings to her Beloved now.

What is prompting the invocation of God's celestial court? The reason, according to *Siftei Ḥakhamim*, is that verse 8:8 is stated in the plural form: "We have a little sister, whose breasts are not yet formed. What shall we do for our sister when she is spoken for?" Therefore, the previous verses, which are thematically continuous with this one, must be uttered by more than one character – God and His celestial court.[32]

Note that although Rashi's angelic pantheon delineates three distinct categories of celestial beings – ministering angels, heavenly armies, and the celestial court – they are all described as a collective and subject to the will of God, thus emphasizing God's sole governance of the world.[33]

In sum, Rashi's gloss to the Song introduces the angels primarily in order to address problems of language, yet their presence has enhanced the narrative balance. Just as the female beloved has primary

---

the human court, see E.E. Urbach, *The Sages: Their Concepts and Beliefs*, trans. I Abrahams (Magnes, 1975), 164–65.

32. It is noteworthy that the text does not require this connection between these verses; to the contrary, in the Masoretic tradition there is a gap of nine letters immediately preceding verse 8 (*parasha setuma*), often indicating a thematic switch. The joining of the verses is Rashi's own exegetical decision. Modern exegetes see verse 8 as the beginning of a new poem; so, too, the commentary attributed to Rashbam sees it as the start of a separate thematic unit.

33. This is a pronounced theme in Rashi's Genesis commentary; see Elazar Touitou, "Rashi's Commentary on Genesis 1–6 in the Context of the Judeo-Christian Controversy," *HUCA* 61 (1990): 174–78.

companions – daughters of Jerusalem – so, too, does her male counterpart with His celestial retinue. Both are also viewed as a collective. Yet since the angels have no speaking lines, the narrative preserves the narrative structure of only three main speakers.[34]

It is noteworthy that mention of His celestial court is found solely in the Song's opening and closing chapters, thus framing the narrative and adding a further sense of symmetry.

The Female Beloved

It is now time to examine the star of our story, the female beloved, i.e., the Congregation of Israel, because, after all, the greater part of the narrative is comprised of her words.[35] Who exactly is included in this assembly?

The key to unlocking her identity lies primarily in decoding what in Arabic poetry are known as the *wasfs*[36] – the extensive, fanciful descriptions of the protagonists' bodies. Each part of the body described represents a different group within the nation.

Let us begin with analyzing those parts of the woman's body that represent the national intellectual elite.

Regarding the female beloved's navel, compared to a "round goblet" (7:3), Rashi writes:

> It refers to the Chamber of Hewn Stone, which is situated in the "navel" of the world.[37] *Let mixed wine not be lacking* – Drink will not cease from there; i.e., from there, words of instruction will not fail.

34. It is noteworthy that the early church father Origen identifies four speakers in the Song: the female and male lovers, the female beloved's companions, and the companions of the male beloved, and allocates speaking lines to the male companions throughout. See Tamar Kadari, "'Friends Hearken to Your Voice': Rabbinic Interpretations of the Song of Songs," in *Approaches to Literary Readings of Ancient Jewish Writings*, ed. K. Smelik and K. Vermeulen (Brill, 2014), 190.
35. She speaks more than sixty verses, in contrast to about forty verses spoken by the male beloved. See Cohn, *Textual Tapestries*, 81.
36. *Wasf* is an Arabic term signifying "description." In *wasf* love poems, each part of the lover's physique is praised using far-fetched metaphors, similar to those used in the four extensive descriptions of the protagonists' bodies found in the Song (the female body: 4:1–7, 6:4–7, 7:2–8; the male body: 5:10–16).
37. See Sanhedrin 37a.

The Chamber of Hewn Stone was the seat of the Sanhedrin, the supreme legislative and judicial body, situated in the Jerusalem Temple at the end of the Second Temple period. This location was considered the center of the world, as the navel is the center of the body.

Similarly, her stately neck – synonymous with the Tower of David adorned with shields (R 4:4) – represents the same institution; for as the final arbiter of Jewish law and instruction, it provided spiritual strength and fortification.[38]

The brilliance of its members was manifest not only in Israel but also among the nations, as is gleaned from the comparison of the female protagonist's eyes to "pools in Heshbon by the gate of Bat-rabbim" (7:5):

> *Your eyes* – When your sages sit at the gates of Jerusalem, the city greatly populated, and are engaged in the calculation of the seasons and the constellations, their wisdom and understanding flow in the eyes of the nations like pools of water.[39]

The identification of her eyes with scholars sitting at the gates of Jerusalem is predicated upon explicating the proper noun "Bat-rabbim" not as a place name, but as a descriptive term meaning "the greatly populated city," i.e., Jerusalem (see Lam. 1:1). These sages are engaged in calculating the progression of the seasons and the positioning of the constellations – astronomical calculations that were deemed wise in the eyes of the nations – because of their universal relevance.

The members of Israel's premier legislative and judicial body comprise an important element within the Congregation of Israel; yet the Congregation of Israel comprises not only this top echelon, but also the middle tier, i.e., the disseminators and students of Torah. On her stately neck hang shields, understood as students of Torah (R 4:4). So too, the

38. Sanhedrin 37a considers the Sanhedrin the protector of not only Israel but the world.

39. Rashi appears to be combining two sources, which is not atypical. While Shabbat 75a links wisdom among the nations with calendric calculations but makes no mention of our verse, *Sifrei, Devarim* 41, links our verse to the sages and their calculations but makes no mention of its impact upon the nations.

eyes of the male beloved – "like doves by watercourses, bathed in milk and evenly set" – represent

> Torah scholars, whom the Holy One, blessed be He, designates as eyes to enlighten the world, just as the eyes enlighten a person. *Like doves* that wander from cote to cote in quest of their food, so do they go from the study house of one sage to the study house of another sage, seeking explanations of Torah. *By watercourses* – By study houses, which are the sources of the water of Torah. *Bathed in milk* – They brush themselves [i.e., glisten] with the milk of Torah and whiten its secrets and mysteries. *Evenly set* – They resolve the matters in their setting, i.e., appropriately. (R 5:16)[40]

Torah scholars, journeying from academy to academy, are like eyes that whiten, i.e., clarify, the mysteries of the Torah, thus enlightening the world with their erudition.

Elsewhere Rashi compares the three-stage ripening process of the pomegranate – budding, blossoming, and flowering – to the educational progression of a Torah disciple: beginning with study of the Torah, progressing to the learning of Mishna, and culminating with the analysis of Talmud (R 7:13). Thus, the text describes the student's intellectual development, mastering texts of increasing difficulty.

Membership within the fold, however, is not limited only to those who study; it is also attainable through religious practice. The pleasing scent of her garments (4:11) is likened to the precepts which are fulfilled through clothing, such as "ritual fringes, blue thread, the priestly garments, and the prohibition of *shaatnez* [the mixing of wool and linen]."[41]

Her head is compared to Mount Carmel, which symbolizes the phylacteries: The phylacteries sit prominently upon the head, just as this mountain rises high above the others (R 7:6).[42] And the locks of her

---

40. See Song of Songs Rabba 5:10. Although this explanation is not found in all manuscripts of Rashi's commentary, it is present in the more reliable ones, such as MS Lutzki 778 and MS Leipzig 1.
41. No known source; similarly, Rashi's commentary regarding "the maidens of Zion" (3:11) mentions circumcision, phylacteries, and ritual fringes.
42. No known source. Rabbinic sources (Berakhot 6a and *Targum Yonatan*) link the

hair symbolize the braided hair of the Nazirite,[43] beautiful with commandments as braided purple wool (R 7:6).[44]

So, too, "her feet in sandals" (7:2) are identified with the pilgrimage festivals.[45] Since the root P-A-M means both "step" (see Is. 26:6) and "time; occasion,"[46] the verse alludes to the pilgrimage to Jerusalem undertaken thrice yearly (see Deut. 16:16).[47]

Precepts govern their lives at all times – even during a state of war – as is gleaned from the description of the female beloved's unblemished teeth:

> *And [none are] blemished* (R 4:2) – The mighty of Israel, who cut down and consume their surrounding enemies with their teeth, and yet they distance themselves from robbing Israelites and from inappropriate sexual behavior, so that they should not become sullied by sin.[48]

Yet what about those who are spiritually incomplete both in study and in action? Are they disqualified from membership in the Congregation of Israel? Rashi, glossing the comparison of the female beloved's brow to a slice of pomegranate,[49] explains, "Even the *reikanin* (empty ones) among you are as full of precepts as a pomegranate."[50] This explanation

---

following proof text brought by Rashi to phylacteries: "And all the peoples of the earth shall see that the Lord's name is proclaimed over you, and they shall stand in fear of you" (Deut. 28:10). However, neither source establishes a connection with Mount Carmel or our Song's verse.

43. Presumably the uncut hair of the Nazirite would be gathered on the head like a mound (similar to a braid or crown). A further allusion to the Nazirite is seen in the second stich of the same verse: "A king is held captive in his tresses," i.e., the name of God [King] is bound to his tresses, because regarding the Nazirite it is written: "Hair set apart for his God is upon his head" (Num. 6:7).
44. *Argaman,* purple, was the color of royalty.
45. See Sukka 49b.
46. See Koehler and Baumgartner, *HALOT,* vol. 3, 952.
47. So too the linguistic connection between the word *ne'alim* (sandals) and *aliya* (ascension or pilgrimage), as noted in Rashi's commentary on Sukka 49b
48. See Song of Songs Rabba 4:5; *Shir HaShirim Zuta* 4:2.
49. "Your brow… [gleams] like a pomegranate split open" (4:3).
50. See Berakhot 57a.

is based upon the phonetic similarity between the words *rakatekh* (your brow) and *reikanim* (your empty ones), both sharing two root letters: *resh* and *kof*.[51] But what exactly are these "empty ones" lacking? What is the nature of their deficit?[52] Although Rashi's intent is somewhat obscure, he certainly intimates some type of spiritual deficit.

These same *reikanim* (empty ones) are also synonymous with the female lover's hair, "streaming down Mount Gilad" (4:1), thereby teaching:

> Even the empty ones among you are beloved to Me just like Jacob and his sons, who streamed down from Mount Gilad when Laban pursued them there.[53]

Thus even the spiritually compromised are beloved by God.[54] The Congregation of Israel incorporates all strata of society, from the intellectually rigorous to the ignorant, from the religiously scrupulous to the more lax.

THE ROLE OF WOMEN

But what about women? Where is their place within this congregation? After all, during Rashi's lifetime they did not receive a rigorous Torah education. As Baskin noted regarding women in medieval Christian Europe:

> The majority of Jewish girls were instructed at home. Mothers taught their daughters cooking, needlework, and household management, as well as the rules of rabbinic Judaism applicable to home and marriage; these were considered essential so that a woman would know how to observe dietary laws, domestic

51. "Empty" from the root R-Y-K (p. 1228–9), and "temple": R-K-H (p. 1288), Koehler and Baumgartner, *HALOT*, vol. 3.
52. English translations: "your worthless ones" (Judaica Press, p. 46); "your unworthiest" (ArtScroll, p. 129).
53. See Genesis 31:23.
54. Elsewhere in his gloss (R 7:14), Rashi even mentions the sinners of Israel and notes that "now" they seek God's presence.

> regulations pertaining to Sabbath and festivals, and the commandments relevant to her family life and relations with her husband.[55]

Therefore, they cannot be considered Torah disciples nor can they frequent houses of study. Moreover, the commandments Rashi highlighted are those primarily within the domain of men, such as ritual fringes, blue thread, priestly garments, and phylacteries, thus excluding women.

Perhaps an analysis of the most feminine body part, the breasts, will yield an application to women? Yet, here too, as noted by Kalman, they are consistently applied to men or male institutions:[56]

> *Your two breasts* (R 4:5) – Which nourished you. This refers to Moses and Aaron.[57]

> *Your two breasts* (R 7:4) – Another explanation, the king and the High Priest.[58]

> *Let your breasts be like clusters* (R 7:8) – Daniel, Hananiah, Mishael, and Azariah, who were for you like breasts to suck from.[59]

---

55. Judith Baskin, "Educating Jewish Girls in Medieval Muslim Spain and Christian Settings," in *Making a Difference: Essays in Honor of Tamara Cohn Eskenazi*, ed. D. Clines, K. Richards, and J.L. Wright (Phoenix Press, 2012), 27.
56. Jason Kalman, "The Beautiful Men of the Song of Songs? Replacing and Erasing the Female Beloved in Ancient and Medieval Jewish Interpretation," in *A Companion to the Song of Songs in the History of Spirituality*, ed. T.H. Robinson (Brill, 2021), 214.
57. See Song of Songs Rabba 4: 12.
58. No known source. *Midrash Lekaḥ Tov* brings a similar explanation: "These are the King Messiah and the righteous priest." Regarding the relationship between these two commentators, see Jonathan Jacobs, "The Allegorical Exegesis of Songs of Songs by R. Tuviah ben 'Eli'ezer – *Lekaḥ Tov*, and Its Relation to Rashi's Commentary," AJS *Review* 39/1 (2015): 89–92.
59. *Sifra, Aḥarei Mot* 13:13, compares Hananiah, Mishael, and Azariah to the palm tree mentioned in the very same verse, because they stood straight as a palm, refusing to prostrate themselves before the idol.

> *My breasts are like towers* (R 8:10) – These are the synagogues and the study halls, which nurture Israel with the words of Torah.[60]

The nourishing breasts, therefore, represent the male leaders or institutions that religiously sustain the Jewish people. This image of the nourishing sage, as noted by Marcus, builds upon Moses's complaint to God regarding his plight:

> Did I conceive all this people, did I bear them, that You should say to me, "Carry them in your bosom as a nurse carries an infant" (Num. 11:12).[61]

Nevertheless, Rashi's Song commentary does mention the contribution of women. Near the end of chapter 4, the female lover is compared to a locked garden and a sealed up spring (4:12), regarding which Rashi remarks:

> *A garden locked* (R 4:12) – Referring to the *tzeni'ut*/(modesty) of the daughters of Israel, who are not promiscuous in illicit relationships.[62]

Promiscuity and the danger of sexual temptation were serious concerns in rabbinic literature. Accepting the talmudic position that "women's minds are frivolous" and they are easily seduced, Rashi espouses in both his Bible and Talmud commentaries the strict enforcement of the laws of *tzeni'ut*,[63] a concept difficult to translate:

> Often translated as "modesty," but it connotes more than that English word might suggest, encompassing a range of halakhot

60. See Pesaḥim 87a and Bava Batra 7b.
61. Ivan Marcus, *Rituals of Childhood: Jewish Acculturation in Medieval Europe* (Yale University Press, 1996), 90.
62. See Yoma 75a, Song of Songs Rabba 4:24.
63. Grossman, *Rashi*, 281.

> [laws] and customs related to conduct, attire and interaction between men and women.[64]

In the aforementioned gloss, it is specifically the daughters of Israel who are lauded for their strength in not breaching the barriers between the sexes.

Rashi does not content himself with a gloss which praises their inaction but commends them, a few verses later, for the performance of a positive precept:

> *A garden spring* (R 4:15) – The *dugma* is: Regarding the immersions of purity which the daughters of Israel immerse themselves.

Jewish law deems a menstruant woman impure until she immerses in a ritual bath (*mikveh*). Rabbinic law teaches that the *mikveh* must be connected to a natural spring (or to a well of naturally flowing water). Hence this explication, original to Rashi,[65] seamlessly connects to the biblical text "a garden spring." Because immersion is the culmination of an intricate purification process, women are praised for the performance of this complicated precept.[66]

Let us appreciate the significance of Rashi's gloss. Although in ancient cultures, including Judaism, women were generally perceived as the passive partner and men the active one,[67] the inclusion of ritual immersion breaks this active/passive dichotomy. Women's performance

64. Ibid., 281, n. h.
65. Ibn Ezra explains this similarly.
66. This is one of the three commandments generally attributed to women in rabbinic literature: *nidda* (menstrual purity), *ḥalla*, and kindling the Shabbat candles. Mishna Shabbat 2:7 warns that a woman who is not careful with these precepts is apt to die in childbirth.
67. Ruth Mazo Karras, "Active/Passive, Acts/Passions: Greek and Roman Sexualities," *The American Historical Review*, vol. 105/4 (2000): 1255. With regard to Judaism, note the Talmud's exemption of women from positive, time-bound commandments; see Berakhot 20b; Kiddushin 29a. Additionally, one talmudic opinion exonerates Queen Esther for sleeping with the gentile king because she was "passive" during the sexual act; see Sanhedrin 74b.

of this positive precept transforms them into active players within the Congregation of Israel.

Thus God's beloved congregation is all inclusive – legislators and laymen, men and women, scholars and disciples, the devout and the impious.

THE VOICES: SUMMARY

In sum, an analysis of the identity and the nature of the Song's primary actors reveals an additional manifestation of narrative balance. Just as the female protagonist is flanked by a chorus – the daughters of Jerusalem – so too, the male beloved is surrounded by his celestial retinue. Whereas the former companions are foes, the latter are friends.

Yet when examining the actors who actually communicate, the number diminishes to three – God, the Congregation of Israel, and the nations – thus revealing the narrative's triadic structure. The conversation between the two human players reveals polemical motifs, such as the nations' (i.e., Christianity's) verbal attempts to sway Israel from her beloved God, and her stalwart refusal to be enticed by their treacherous words. Who is this assembly displaying such loyalty to the Divine? Here, too, Rashi's gloss develops a sense of wholeness. The Congregation of Israel represents the totality of the Jewish people – spanning both genders and all classes – each a vital component of the national whole.

FINAL SUMMARY

Serious questions arose regarding the canonization of Song of Songs due to its provocative subject matter and the absence of any spiritual dimension. Building upon rabbinic precedent, Rashi redeems the narrative through the implementation of the exegetical strategy of allegory, propelling the narrative to the spiritual realm.

In his allegorical reading called *dugma,* Rashi molds the loosely connected love poems into a coherent narrative depicting the sacred relationship between the female lover, the Congregation of Israel, and her beloved, God, over the course of history. Rashi explicates each verse as part of this developing plot, which extends from her inception as a nation at the time of the Exodus, through her development over the centuries both in the Promised Land and in the Diaspora until final redemption. Along this linear timeline one also detects a subtle pull on the vertical plane. Commenting upon the disparity between the female's praise of her beloved (5:10–15) working from His head down, in contrast to the male's praise recounted in the reverse direction, Rashi notes (R 7:2):

> Israel praises Him from the top to the bottom... to draw down His Divine Presence from the upper realms to the lower realms. But He enumerates their praise from the bottom to the top... for He comes to draw them toward Him.

Thus Rashi's narrative expresses the desire for connection between God and His people, a desire espoused by both parties, each one pulling in the direction appropriate to his sphere of existence, the Divine drawing up and the nation pulling down.

Practically speaking, "pulling down" is accomplished through the world of action: studying and disseminating His Torah and adhering to His commandments. This action is incumbent upon all segments of Israelite society, irrespective of gender, intellectual capacity, or religious affiliation.

This desire for divine-human connection is the narrative's primary leitmotif, ushering us along the linear timeline of Jewish history.

Culling from rabbinic writings that can be categorized as atomistic – explicating phrases or verses with no consideration of context – Rashi handpicks those that accord with his exegetical agenda and then edits them to fuse with the biblical text. When no appropriate source material is available, he introduces original explications to fill the exegetical vacuum and then seamlessly interweaves all into an organic whole.

His historical schema not only exhibits close affinity to the language and grammar of Scripture, but also resolves textual difficulties. Noting the abrupt changes of speaker from singular to plural and the elliptical nature of the biblical text, Rashi expands the role of the celestial retinue to meet these exegetical challenges.

Similarly, creation of the narrative framework addresses challenges of form. The delineation of the speaker and the demarcation of his/her speech unit and the time period being discussed greatly enhance the clarity of the narrative. So, too, his frame story resolves problems of chronology. Projecting the story forward and positioning the narrator as a "living widow" during Rashi's lifetime enables him to view the "problematic verses" which deviate from time sequence as her recollections or emotional flashbacks, thus excusing them from our expectation of order.

Beyond the textual questions, Rashi's *dugma* confronts a more menacing obstacle: the theological challenges posed by Christianity. Asserting that the church has superseded the nation of Israel, assuming their role as God's covenanted people, Christianity mobilized the Temple's destruction and the prolonged Roman exile as proof of this replacement theology. Rashi's allegorical reading refutes this fundamental claim. The *dugma*'s emphasis on the ongoing cyclical nature of Jewish history – divine pardon always following human sin – teaches that there is no transgression that is unforgivable, and therefore it is untenable that Israel forfeited her coveted status due to wrongdoing. The choice of the frame story continues this polemical thrust. Depicting the narrator as a "living widow" (Rashi's innovation), and not simply a "young lover," indicates that the Temple's destruction and the ongoing exile were not a sign that God had *divorced* Himself from the Jewish people. Rather the ensuing exile was analogous to the status of *living widowhood,* which denotes separation but not severance of ties. God's uninterrupted connection with Israel, as noted above, proves their ongoing chosen status.

Likewise, the commentary's emphasis on the centrality of the commandments negates the Christian tenet that with the coming of Jesus, the Law was abrogated.[68]

Rashi's *dugma* – a coherent chronological narrative, tracking the insoluble bond between God and His beloved nation along the timeline of history, in consonance with the language and form of Scripture – is certainly a holistic masterpiece.

68. For further discussion of this topic, see E. Touitou, "Rashi and His School," 231–51.

Rashi's Commentary on Proverbs

Chapter Four

Introduction

THE CHALLENGES OF THE BOOK OF PROVERBS

Genre and Content

Perusal of the book of Proverbs raises many an eyebrow: Are riches, honor, and success truly life's ultimate aspirations? Do descriptions of foreign women enticing innocent young lads align with the anticipated focus of a biblical book? What rationale justifies incorporating wisdom drawn from the animal kingdom – from the tiny ant to the towering bear – into the sacred text?

The key to unlocking this narrative hinges on its categorization as one of the biblical wisdom texts,[1] which, according to Segal, exhibit three distinguishing features. First, these texts focus on the individual ("you") rather than the collective, barely mentioning the names Israel, Judah, or communal institutions.[2] Second, they exhibit a utilitarian approach, seeking tangible benefits in the present life, focusing on the

1. This category is a modern one, beginning in the twentieth century; see *The Jewish Study Bible,* ed. A. Berlin and M.Z. Brettler (Oxford University Press, 2004), 1277. So, too, the books of Job and Ecclesiastes are considered wisdom texts.
2. In Proverbs, both Israel and Judah are mentioned only once, introducing Solomon as king of Israel (1:1), and the men of Hezekiah, king of Judah (25:1).

here and now. Third, they adopt a secular stance, concentrating on an individual's daily actions and offering pragmatic advice for success in the mundane spheres of life. While religious concepts like belief in God, divine providence, and reward and punishment lurk in the background, the admonitions about leading a moral and ethical life are not expressed in the name of God. Instead, they are framed as practical advice from one person to another, aiming for good reward in this world.[3]

Teasing out these distinctive features within Proverbs, we see that the book teaches that disregarding instruction leads to "poverty and humiliation" (13:18), while adhering to wisdom yields the tangible rewards of "riches and honor" (3:16). The diverse range of practical advice highlights its pragmatic orientation, including recommendations for proper table etiquette:

> When you sit down to dine with a ruler, consider well who is before you. Thrust a knife into your gullet, if you have a large appetite. (23:1–2)

It offers dietary advice, such as "Better a meal of vegetables where there is love, than a fattened ox where there is hate" (15:17) and cautions against overstaying one's visit, "Visit your neighbor sparingly, lest he have his surfeit of you and loathe you" (25:17).

The book's pragmatism occasionally clashes with Torah commandments, as when Proverbs advises against providing collateral for another, in contrast to Deuteronomy's command to lend to the poor without interest and with an "open hand":[4] "Harm awaits him who stands surety for another; He who spurns pledging shall be secure" (11:15).[5] Simi-

---

3. M.S. Segal, *Introduction to Scripture,* vol. 2 [in Hebrew] (Kiryat Sefer Press, 1987), 593–94. Similarly, as Brettler notes, "Wisdom books are thus in some ways a departure from the concerns of other biblical books. They share rather, as their focus, reflection on universal human concerns, especially the understanding of individual experiences, and the maintenance of ordered relationships that lead both to success on the human plane and to divine approval" (*The Jewish Study Bible,* 1277).
4. See Deuteronomy 15:8, 11.
5. Similarly, "Seize his garment, for he stood surety for another. Take it as a pledge [for he stood surety] for an unfamiliar woman" (20:16 and 27:13). So, too, see 17:18,

larly, although the Torah prohibits bribery, Proverbs acknowledges the effectiveness of this practice: "A gift in secret subdues anger, a present in private [subdues] fierce rage" (21:14).[6]

The secular nature of Proverbs is also shown by the near absence of any reference to Jewish ritual. While sacrifices are mentioned,[7] this composition lacks discussion of other central commandments like Shabbat, festivals, dietary laws, and circumcision. As noted by Gordis, even when God's unique name, YHVH (Hashem), appears, "it is often in stock phrases like 'the fear of YHVH,' 'the blessing of YHVH.'"[8] Toy even suggests that if we were to replace "Hashem" with the more generic name "God," "there is not a paragraph or a sentence in Proverbs which would not be as suitable for any other people as for Israel."[9]

For these reasons, the Sages grapple with the question of Proverbs' holy status:

> "These are the proverbs of Solomon which the men of Hezekiah king of Judah removed (*he'etiku*)"[10] (Prov. 25:1) – Not that they removed, but they took their time. Abba Shaul says: Not that they took their time, but that they interpreted them. Originally, they used to say: Proverbs, Song of Songs, and Ecclesiastes were withdrawn (*genuzim*), for they presented mere parables (*meshalot*) and were not part of Scripture. So they arose and withdrew (*veganzu*) them, until the Men of the Great Assembly came and interpreted them. (*Avot DeRabbi Natan* 1:4)

The question of the proposed fate of Proverbs (along with Song of Songs and Ecclesiastes) hinges on an understanding of the Hebrew

---

22:26.

6. Similarly, "Many court the favor of a great man, and all are the friends of a dispenser of gifts" (19:6).
7. Mentioned six times: 3:9, 7:14, 15:8, 17:1, 21:3, 27.
8. Robert Gordis, "Social Background of Wisdom Literature," HUCA 18 (1944): 90.
9. C.H. Toy, *Proverbs: The International Critical Commentary* (T & T Clark, 1970), xxi.
10. Jastrow's explication of the verb in this context; see Jastrow, *A Dictionary of the Targumim*, s.v. עתק, 1130.

root G-N-Z, signifying "to store away."[11] The question arises: Does this imply the removal of these biblical books from general circulation or their exclusion from the biblical canon?[12] In either case, this fate was averted through the reinterpretation of these texts. The nature of this reinterpretation will be explored below.

Challenges of Form

The book of Proverbs also presents challenges of form. The title *Mishlei* (Proverbs) is the plural form of the Hebrew root M-SH-L, which can refer to any one of several of literary forms, such as proverb, prophetic discourse, philosophical discourse, and lament.[13] The book's title thus indicates the wide range of material embodied in this composition – from extensive discourses to concise statements or aphorisms. This anthology of diverse literary genres displays, at times, a lack of organizational unity.

For example, Proverbs is composed of 915 verses, of which some 40 percent are one-line aphorisms that stand alone.[14] Other verses are grouped together in units with common themes or shared literary devices. Understanding the juxtaposition of the one-liners and the placement of the longer discourses poses a challenge. What logic guides the overall arrangement of verses and units in the composition?

Additionally, analysis of the material reveals the phenomenon of repetition. Heim notes that just over 24 percent of Proverbs' verses appear more than once.[15] Sometimes the repetition is in identical form;[16] in other cases there is a slight alteration, consisting of the change or addition of a letter or letters, which does not always affect the English translation.[17]

---

11. Sid Z. Leiman, *The Canonization of Hebrew Scripture, The Talmudic and Midrashic Evidence* (Connecticut Academy of Arts, 1991), 79.
12. Leiman, *The Canonization of Hebrew Scripture*, 86.
13. *The Bible, Proverbs with the Jerusalem Commentary*, ed. M. Zer-Kavod and Y. Kil, trans. A. Kanter and Y. Engelberg-Cohen (Mossad HaRav Kook, 2014), ix–x.
14. There are 375 single-line proverbs contained in chapters 10–22.
15. For a detailed analysis of this repetition, see Knut Martin Heim, *Poetic Imagination in Proverbs: Variant Repetitions and the Nature of Poetry, Bulletin for Biblical Research* 4 (Penn State University Press, 2013), 3–35.
16. E.g., 14:12 and 16:25, 18:8 and 26:22.
17. E.g., 9:4 and 9:16, 21:9 and 25:24.

קַח־בִּגְדוֹ, כִּי־עָרַב זָר; וּבְעַד נָכְרִיָּה חַבְלֵהוּ. (כז:יג)	לְקַח־בִּגְדוֹ, כִּי־עָרַב זָר; וּבְעַד נכרים (נָכְרִיָּה) חַבְלֵהוּ (כ:טז)
Seize his garment, for he stood surety for another. Take it as a pledge [for he stood surety] for an unfamiliar woman.	Seize his garment, for he stood surety for another. Take it as a pledge [for he stood surety] for strangers.

The Hebrew word translated "seize" is spelled with the letter *lamed* in one verse, and without it in another.

In other cases, the variation is a change of words and concepts:[18]

יִרְאַת ה׳ מְקוֹר חַיִּים - לָסוּר, מִמֹּקְשֵׁי מָוֶת. (יד:כז)	תּוֹרַת חָכָם, מְקוֹר חַיִּים - לָסוּר, מִמֹּקְשֵׁי מָוֶת. (יג:יד)
Fear of the Lord is a fountain of life, enabling one to avoid deadly snares.	The instruction of a wise man is a fountain of life, enabling one to avoid deadly snares.

What can explain this repetition?

The book of Proverbs also contains internal contradictions, which were an additional reason for seeking to suppress it:

> [The Sages] sought to suppress the book of Proverbs as well [because] its statements contradict each other.... And what [is the meaning of]: Its statements contradict each other? [On the one hand,] it is written: "Answer not a fool according to his folly, [lest you also be like him]" (Prov. 26:4), and [on the other hand,] it is written: "Answer a fool according to his folly, [lest he be wise in his own eyes]" (Prov. 26:5).

How does Rashi deal with the challenges of content and form? Does he grapple with all of them? In the following pages we will seek answers to these questions.

18. For all the various permutations, see Daniel C. Snell, *Twice-Told Proverbs and the Composition of Proverbs* (Eisenbrauns, 1993), 34–59.

RASHI'S PROGRAMMATIC STATEMENT

Rashi unveils his exegetical program in his comment on the "penultimate verse of the book's introduction – "For understanding proverb and epigram, the words of the wise and their riddles" (1:6):

> *For understanding proverb (mashal) and epigram (melitza)* (R 1:6) – That they should direct their attention to the verses through two methods: the allegory (*mashal*) and the image (*melitza*). They should understand what he alludes to with the image, but they should not neglect the image itself, for that too requires understanding. When he states: "It will save you from the strange woman, from the alien woman" (2:16), idolatry is meant; this is the allegory, but the image itself, the fact that he expressed his allegory through the image of a woman means that you shall beware of a harlot.

In this succinct introductory gloss, Rashi promises to explicate two levels of meaning, *mashal* and *melitza*. The former indicates the implied and deeper meaning, while the latter signifies the figurative meaning of the text.[19] It is noteworthy that Rashi's use of the term *mashal* aligns with our contemporary use of the term *nimshal*, representing the corresponding reality that is not written. Thus, his commentary on Proverbs follows a dual-track approach, as in his commentary on other biblical books.[20] Here, however, instead of his practice in other scriptural commentaries of employing the term *midrasho* for conveying deeper meaning and *peshuto* for introducing contextual explanations, he introduces new exegetical terms to elucidate the two levels of understanding: *mashal* and

19. *Melitza* literally means "figurative language"; see Koehler and Baumgartner, *HALOT*, vol. 2, s.v., 590, מליצה. Thus, in the statement "A rolling stone gathers no moss," the words "a rolling stone" constitute the *melitza*, whose *peshat* meaning is "something lacking stability or commitment."

20. Kamin, "Rashi's Exegetical Categorization," 16–32; Kamin, *Rashi*, 158–208; Benjamin Gelles, "Partnership of *Peshat* and *Derash* in Rashi's Exegesis," in *Rashi et la culture juive en France du Nord au moyen age*, ed. G. Dahan, G. Nahon, and E. Nicolas (1997), 97–102.

melitza.[21] While in Proverbs the terms *mashal* and *melitza* refer to two different types of sayings that we find in the text,[22] Rashi interprets the terms as two distinct ways in which we, the readers, should understand the words of Proverbs.

THE *MASHAL*: RASHI'S ALLEGORICAL EXPLANATION

Rashi's main interpretive strategy with Proverbs is to explain its multifarious references to wisdom as references to Torah. In Proverbs, *ḥokhma* (wisdom) and its numerous synonyms, including *bina* (understanding), *daat* (knowledge), *tevuna* (good sense), and *musar* (ethical teaching) represent human wisdom and understanding;[23] but in Rashi's *mashal*, all these terms simply mean the wisdom of Torah.

The identification of Wisdom with Torah is not limited to individual words or verses which present wisdom as an abstract term but also encompass substantial textual expanses where Wisdom is described as a living person. For instance, chapter 8 depicts Wisdom as a herald who publicly proclaims her message to those nearby, urging their acceptance of her moral instruction and substantiating her reliability by asserting her presence at the time of Creation. Furthermore, chapter 9 personifies Wisdom as a woman who constructs a house, prepares a lavish meal, and issues an open invitation to guide others toward understanding. Notably, Rashi interprets all these vivid portrayals as allusions to the wisdom inherent in the Torah.

Although precedence for the identification of Wisdom with Torah can be found in rabbinic literature which sporadically applies the Torah

---

21. *Mashal* is similar to the term *dugma* used in his commentary on the Song (see chapter 1).
22. A *mashal* is a proverb. The meaning of the term *melitza,* however, is uncertain. Some explain a sweet, pleasant saying, like its usage in Psalms 119:103: "How pleasing (*nimletzu*) is Your word to my palate." Others believe *melitza* is a wise but hard-to-understand statement due to its appearance in the text of Habakkuk 2:6, sandwiched between the words "parable" and "riddle," suggesting it might be something obscure. See Victor A. Hurovitz, *Proverbs: Mikra LeYisrael* [in Hebrew], ed. S. Ahituv, vol. 1 (Magnes, 2012), 136.
23. Of course, these wisdom terms are not identical; there are nuances of difference between them.

motif to individual proverbs and verse clusters, it is Rashi who systemically expands this spiritualization process, referring to Torah and the performance of its commandments more than 140 times.[24] Let us analyze the key themes within Rashi's *mashal* exegesis.

TORAH STUDY

A central preoccupation of Proverbs is the study of Torah. Rashi's treatment of this topic is comprehensive, covering incentives; guidelines for students, teachers, and scholars; decorum and discipline in the educational context; curriculum; techniques, and methods of study and learning; and the responsibility of parents.

Incentives

Rashi offers various incentives to Torah study. Engaging in Torah study leads to respect (R 13:4), popularity (R 19:4), and a good name (R 5:16). Comparable to a merchant ship, it brings blessing and sustenance to those who immerse themselves in its teachings (R 31:14)[25] and holds greater value than gold and silver because it enriches both the student and the teacher (R 3:14).

The emphasis on tangible future benefits stands in sharp contrast to Rashi's acknowledgment of the economic reality experienced by students throughout their prolonged years of study, which frequently meant enduring poverty and hunger pains (R 20:14, 31:20[26]). Rashi's depiction of this reality aligns with what is written in the Mishna:

> R. Yonatan said: Whoever fulfills the Torah out of a state of poverty, his end will be to fulfill it out of a state of wealth; and whoever discards the Torah out of a state of wealth, his end will be to discard it out of a state of poverty. (Avot 4:9)

---

24. The pronounced presence of these themes was first noted by Gelles, *Peshat and Derash in the Exegesis of Rashi*, 72.
25. This allegorical explanation, explicating the *eshet ḥayil* (capable wife) as referring to the Torah, is found at the end of the chapter after the contextual one (R 31:10).
26. This allegorical explication is found at the end of chapter 31.

Rashi himself had experienced these hardships. In a responsum penned during his later years, Rashi reflects on his earlier economic plight while studying in the renowned study halls in Germany and at the same time struggling to provide the necessities for his wife and young daughters: "For a lack of food and clothing were as a millstone around my neck, ruining the time I spent studying with my teachers."[27]

Torah illuminates the eyes of those immersed in study (R 15:30, 29:13) and brings happiness to a saddened heart (R 12:25). It gladdens both the student's biological father and the Father in heaven (R 10:1) and fortifies the student against the clutches of the evil inclination (R 25:21–22).

A Torah student is strengthened (R 10:15), assured longevity (R 3:2), and protected as though guarded by a shield (R 2:7).[28] Likewise, his possessions are protected, as Rashi gleans from the verse "Be infatuated (*tishgeh*) with love of her always" (5:19). He clarifies the nature of the intended love:[29]

> *Be infatuated always* – But the Rabbis (Eiruvin 54b) explain it [*tishgeh*] as the language of *mishgeh* [make a mistake, err] according to its literal meaning. Because of loving her [the Torah], you err in your other dealings because she [the Torah] protects them. It is said regarding Rabbi Elazar ben Pedat, who was preaching in the lower market, but his cloak was hanging in the upper market. Once a man came to take it, but a snake was coiled upon it.

27. Grossman, *Rashi*, 15. So, too, in Rashi's liturgical poem entitled *Torah Temima*, he describes the economic plight of the Torah student, "Bound up in study, / both young and elderly. / To aggrandize Torah and exalt it, / never departing from the study hall.... In hunger and thirst / and all their deprivations"; see Grossman, *Rashi*, 256.
28. Regarding protection, see also R 2:11, 18, 5:19.
29. His first explanation is drawn from the works of Rabbi Moshe HaDarshan (early eleventh century), who explains the verb *tishgeh* as "being engrossed," similar to its meaning in Arabic. Rabbi Moshe HaDarshan was one of Rashi's important sources for knowledge of Arabic; see Avraham Grossman, "The Treatment of Lexicon and Grammar in Rashi's Commentaries: Rashi's Ties with the Islamic Lands," *Lĕšonénu: A Journal for the Study of the Hebrew Language and Cognate Subjects* [in Hebrew] vol. 73, 3–4 (2011): 432–33.

Rabbi Elazar was so engrossed in preaching Torah that he overlooked his worldly possessions. Despite this negligence, the merit of his study protected them, as seen when a snake guarded his cloak from theft.

The reward for Torah study extends beyond the present world to the World to Come (R 12:14).[30] Furthermore, the Torah's commandments even afford protection after death, as Rashi highlights in reference to the description of the "capable wife" (*eshet ḥayil,* 31:10–31). She "is not worried for her household because of snow, for her whole household is dressed in crimson (*shanim*)" (v. 21):

> *From snow* (R 31:21) – Gehinnom, where the wicked are judged from fire to snow. *Dressed in crimson* – They are dressed in [commandments expressed in] double language: "Give to him readily" (*naton titen,* Deut. 15:10); "Rather, you must open your hand" (*patoaḥ tiftaḥ,* Deut. 15:8); "Furnish him (*haaneik taanik,* Deut. 15:14). All these save him from the snow of Gehinnom, as is expounded in *Tanḥuma.*

This explanation, drawn from *Tanḥuma,* explicates the word "crimson" (*shanim*) by changing the vocalization to get the word "two" (*shenayim*). Commandments expressed with a double verb (where the root is repeated for emphasis) afford protection. Perusal of Rashi's source provides additional detail regarding the weather patterns in Gehinnom:

> Hezekiah said, "The judgment of the wicked in Gehinnom [lasts] twelve months, six months in the heat and six months in the cold." At first the Holy One has an itch enter them,[31] and they say, "Is this the Gehinnom of the Holy One?" Then after that He brings them to the snow, where they say, "Is this the cold of the Holy One?"[32] (*Tanḥuma,* Buber, *Re'eh* 10)

---

30. Similarly, see R 13:2 and R 31:11, the allegorical explanation found at the end of the chapter.

31. The following source contains a more comprehensive explanation: "He brings them into Gehenna, *into the region whose heat eases the itch,*" *Pesikta de-Rab Kahana,* trans. W.G. Braude and I.J. Epstein (Routledge and Kegan Paul, 1975), p. 190 to *piska* 10:4.

32. *Tanhuma, S. Buber recension,* trans. J.T. Townsend (Ktav, 2003), 313.

It is noteworthy that Nicholas of Lyra, a medieval thirteenth-century Christian scholar heavily influenced by Rashi's Bible commentaries, cites Rashi in reference to our verse with the following addition:

> She shall not fear for her house in the cold of snow; this means from the punishment of Gehenna – which Rabbi Salomon says here, citing Job 24:19, "Let him pass from the snow waters to excessive heat, [and his sin even to hell]."[33]

This proof text, drawn from the book of Job, is not extant in our version of Rashi's text. Moreover, the sequence outlined in Job – snow to heat – reverses the order noted in Rashi's aforementioned gloss.

Guidelines for the Student

The student is required to study Torah, and if he cannot find an instructor to teach gratis, then he should pay for the service (R 23:23). Three times the directive is given to "buy" wisdom (R 2:6, 3:5, 4:7). It is emphasized that he should carefully seek out an upstanding teacher (R 23:3); but if the instructor is flawed, learning from his evil ways is prohibited (R 22:17).

The proper motivation and attitude are also addressed. One who is sated with Torah will "trample" even the logical, sweet reasoning akin to "honeycombs," in contrast to someone desiring Torah, who will perceive even intricate, "bitter" explications as "sweet" (R 27:7). Similarly, the study of Torah should be driven by the aim to fulfill its dictates rather than seeking to acquire a good name (R 17:16).

The pupil is encouraged not to postpone Torah study due to physical concerns like cold (R 20:4) or danger, as illustrated by the verse "There is a lion in the street; I shall be killed if I step outside" (R 22:13). Such concerns are considered flimsy excuses to conceal laziness or inactivity.

The student should not favor one explanation over another but should treat all material with reverence. This lesson is gleaned from the enigmatic verse "A man who loves wisdom brings joy to his father, but he

33. Herman Hailperin, *Rashi and the Christian Scholars* (University of Pittsburgh Press, 1963), 240, 354, n. 784.

who keeps company with harlots will lose his wealth" (29:3). What is the meaning of the second stich, and what logic connects the two parts of the verse? Rashi explains:

> *But he who keeps company* – But our Rabbis said (Eiruvin 64a): One who says, "This teaching is nice – so I will learn it, but this one is not nice – so I will not learn it," [he will lose his wisdom]. And support for their words [can be brought from the fact that] this is the only instance in the Bible where [the word] *zonot* (harlots) is written *plene*.[34]

This homiletical explication is predicated upon reading the Hebrew word *zonot* (harlots) as a contraction: *zo* (this), *not=naeh* (is nice), thus cautioning the learner not to selectively choose between interpretations, because such behavior diminishes the honor of the Torah. In this context, wisdom acts as the connecting link between both stiches.

Guidelines for Educators and Scholars

Proverbs also provides guidance for the teacher. Educators are advised to rise early and impart the assigned material to their students (R 31:15)[35] and to "sweeten" their explanations with clear reasoning in order to facilitate the learners' understanding (R16:21). Notably, both directives emphasize the necessity for advanced planning by the teacher and an awareness of the students' educational needs.

A teacher should not refrain from instructing a student due to the concern that his own personal study will be diminished (R 28:27). On the contrary, students contribute to deepening their teacher's knowledge, as Rashi elucidates in the following original gloss:

> *The tillage of the poor yields much food* (R 13:23) – Much grain comes to the world through the tilling of the poor people,

34. The proof provided is Rashi's original idea. He explains that in all other places, the word *zonot* is written defectively, without the letter *vav* after the *nun*, but here, because it is written *plene*, i.e., in full, it can be homiletically read as זונות=זו נאה.
35. Allegorical explanation found at the end of the chapter.

> meaning a lot of Torah emanates from students whose teachers learn from them through debating halakha.[36]

A similar message is gleaned from the world of oxen:

> *If there are no oxen the crib is clean* [i.e., empty] (R 14:4) – Meaning, in a place with no students,[37] there is no coming to the correct halakhic conclusion.

A teacher should withhold instruction if the student is evil and lacks the intention to fulfill the commandments (R 25:20).

Scholars are encouraged to study in pairs, because collaborative learning sharpens the knowledge of both partners, akin to the sharpening effect when rubbing together two pieces of iron (R 27:17). However, their conduct should align with their Torah studies; otherwise, they are likened to "a gold ring in the snout of a pig" (R 11:22).

Decorum and Discipline

The learning environment portrayed in Rashi's explanations is not one of equals; the teacher has the upper hand. This is exemplified in the following gloss that distinguishes between the speech of the pauper and the rich man:

> *The poor man speaks beseechingly* (R 18:23) – This one is accustomed to speak in this manner and that one in that manner. The verse teaches the rules of conduct (*derekh eretz*).[38] Even when "the rich man's answer is harsh," "the poor man speaks beseechingly"; so, too, regarding a teacher and student.[39]

36. This explanation is original to Rashi.
37. Standard editions read *talmidei ḥakhamim* (scholars) instead of students.
38. In mishnaic Hebrew, *derekh eretz* signifies the appropriate social norms and accepted human practice.
39. No known source.

Hence a student must respond respectfully even when confronted with a teacher's harsh words. And in an extreme case, where the incessant questioning of a student frays the teacher's nerves, Rashi does not condemn the instructor for embarrassing the student (R 30:32–33).

It is noteworthy that while beating children was an accepted mode of discipline in the medieval era, Rashi's commentary on Proverbs describes physical disciplining only within the family setting. For example, Rashi gleans from the famous verse "He who spares the rod hates his son, but he who loves him disciplines him early" (13:24):

> *He who spares his rod* (R 13:24) – Will eventually hate his child (*beno*) because he will see him eventually turn to evil ways. *Discipline him early* – Every morning discipline him.[40]

Thus, a parent should discipline his child daily.[41] While the first stich of the verse clearly describes beating, the intention of the second stich advocating "daily discipline" is unclear. The Hebrew word *musar* can denote both verbal chastisement and physical punishment.[42] It is noteworthy that Rashi does not explicitly expand his gloss to make it pertain to a classroom environment.

So too, regarding the couplet (3:11–12) which compares divine discipline with that of a father to a son, Rashi writes:

> *As a father [does to] the son whom he favors* (R 3:12) – He desires his son – to benefit and appease [him] – after smiting him with a rod; similarly, the good that follows the blow [divine punishment] will be pleasant to you.

40. See *Tanḥuma, Shemot* 1.
41. Rashi explains the word *shaḥar* (dawn) as every morning, in contrast to Gersonides, who explains it as meaning from the dawn of life, i.e., youth.
42. As noted by Fox, *musar* basically means "correction," verbal and physical. See M.V. Fox, *Proverbs 1–9: The Anchor Bible* (Yale University Press, 2009), 59. In Rashi's gloss to 1:8, the meaning is verbal.

Once more, Rashi is content with confining the act of smacking a child to the domestic setting and stresses the importance of reconciliation following the disciplinary action.[43]

Curriculum Considerations

The following proverb emphasizes the importance of order: "Put your external affairs in order, get ready what you have in the field, then build yourself a home" (24:27). According to Rashi, this establishes the proper sequence for studying Jewish texts:

> *Put your external affairs in order* (R 24:27) – This is Torah. *What you have in the field* – This is Mishna. *Then build yourself a home* – This is Talmud.[44]

This tripartite curriculum introduces texts of increasing complexity, enabling the student to progress gradually from one stage to the next,[45] mirroring the order outlined in the Mishna:

> He used to say: At five years of age the study of Scripture; at ten the study of Mishna; at thirteen [the child is obligated in] the commandments; at fifteen the study of Talmud. (Avot 5: 21)

However. some parts of Scripture should be excluded from the general curriculum, as Rashi deduces from the following verse, "It is the glory of God to conceal a matter, and the glory of a king to plumb a matter" (25:2):

> *The glory of God* (R 25:2) – Such as "the account of the Divine Chariot" and "the account of Creation." *And the glory of a king* – When you expound upon the honor due to the Sages and the fence that they placed around the Torah and the decrees they

43. However, Rashi's commentary on the Talmud seems to advocate moderate physical disciplining of students; see Gittin 36a and Makkot 16b. For further discussion, see A. Grossman, *Rashi: Religious Beliefs and Social Views* [in Hebrew] (Tevunot, 2008), 260–62.
44. See Sota 44a.
45. Similarly, see Rashi's commentary on Song of Songs 7:13.

> decreed, there you should investigate and search for the logic of the matter. But when you expound upon "the account of the Divine Chariot" and "the account of Creation," and the statutes written in the Torah, such as things that Satan denounces, like eating pork, mixing species in a vineyard, and *shaatnez* [the mixing of wool and linen], one should not investigate but conceal [the reasoning] and declare, "It's the decree of the King."[46]

"The account of the Divine Chariot" (Ezek. 1) and "the account of Creation" (Gen. 1) are biblical texts that serve as the foundation for mystical exegesis.[47] The former concentrates on describing the Deity and His celestial helpers, while the latter explores God's creation of the world. This esoteric subject matter is deemed suitable only for exemplary scholars due to the inherent dangers associated with its study, as described in the Talmud:[48]

> The Sages taught: An incident occurred involving a youth who was reading the book of Ezekiel in the house of his teacher, and he was able to comprehend the *mashal*, and fire came out of the electrum and burned him. (Ḥagiga 13a)

Therefore, this speculative literature faced severe restrictions within the educational curriculum, as did the study of *ḥukkim* (statutes that surpass human understanding).[49] By contrast, the Sages actively promoted investigation of the rationales for rabbinic laws and decrees. Rashi reiterates both directives – for the study of rabbinic decrees and against the analysis of mystical texts – in a gloss to the following verse describing the consumption of honey: "It is not good to eat much honey, nor is it honorable to search for honor" (25:27):

---

46. See Y. Ḥagiga 2:1; *gezeirot*: Yoma 67b.
47. Regarding the impact of Ezekiel 1 on Jewish mysticism, see Meira Polliack, "Ezekiel 1 and Its Role in Subsequent Jewish Mystical Thought and Tradition," *European Judaism* 32, no. 1 (Spring 1999): 70–78.
48. See also Mishna Ḥagiga 2:1.
49. Similarly, see Rashi's commentary on Genesis 26:5 and Leviticus 19:19 regarding the unfathomable nature of *ḥukkim*.

> *It is not good to eat much honey* (R 25:27) – Excessive, a hint to expounding upon "the account of the Divine Chariot" and "the account of Creation" and revealing it to the masses; the uneducated will mock the words and ask, "What is above and what is below" (M Ḥagiga 2:1). But what is worthy of inquiry? The words of the Sages; it is honorable to investigate their honor [i.e., their thinking]. Regarding their decrees, one should ask why they decreed; what is the reasoning for the safeguard in each decree.[50]

The connection between honey and esoteric speculation is already made in the Talmud:[51]

> Ben Zoma glimpsed the Divine Presence and was harmed, i.e., he lost his mind. And with regard to him the verse states: "Have you found honey? Eat as much as is sufficient for you, lest you become full from it and vomit it" (Prov. 25:16).

The analogy suggests that while honey is beneficial in moderation, excessive consumption should be avoided, just as esoteric speculation should be pursued with restraint. By contrast, the rationale behind rabbinic enactments should be thoroughly investigated, as such analysis brings honor to the Sages.

Studying and Learning Techniques

Rashi also provides practical tools to optimize the acquisition of knowledge.

1. Subdividing Material

Confronting large amounts of material poses a significant obstacle and deterrent for less intelligent students. In such cases, Rashi recommends dividing the information into smaller, more manageable units (R 17:24). Similarly, those seeking to save time by tackling extensive material all at once are discouraged from doing so; a lesson Rashi gleans from the

50. Rashi combines two sources: Mishna Ḥagiga 2:1 and Ḥagiga 14b.
51. Ḥagiga 14b.

following proverb: "Wealth gotten through vanity will dwindle, but he who gathers by hand increases it" (13:11):[52]

> *Wealth gotten through vanity* (*mehevel*, R 13:11) – One who makes his study in bundles (*ḥavilot*) will dwindle [as he will forget it]. [But if he gathers] by hand – little by little [it will grow].[53]

By swapping out the initial consonant,[54] Rashi reads the word *hevel* (vanity) as *ḥavila* (bundle), thereby teaching that studying too much material simultaneously, as if bundling it together, is ineffective, because it leads to forgetfulness and erroneous decisions (R 24:31).

2. *The Power of the Question*

The question is the most powerful learning tool at the disposal of both student and teacher. A student is encouraged to pepper his teacher with questions and doubts even if incessant questioning leads to embarrassment and shame. Rashi gleans this lesson by comparing the learning process with the production of butter! Proverbs states:

> If you have been put to shame, you will be in your ascendancy; if you have been a schemer, then clap your hand to your mouth. As milk under pressure produces butter, and a nose under pressure produces blood, so patience under pressure produces strife. (30:32–33)

Explicating these enigmatic verses, Rashi writes:

> Our Rabbis explain (Berakhot 63b): "*If you have been put to shame*" – because of words of Torah, by seeking and asking your teacher about everything that is unclear to you, and even if you appear in his eyes like a mindless fool, ultimately you will ascend in the end. But if you muzzled (*ve'im zamota*) – placed

52. So, too, see R 19:15, 23:4.
53. See Eiruvin 54b; Avoda Zara 19a.
54. The letters *heh* and *ḥet* are interchangeable for homiletical purposes.

> a muzzle on your mouth and closed it, refraining from asking everything [that was unclear to you]– eventually when you are asked to render halakhic decisions, you will "*place your hand on your mouth*" – and you will be dumb. Because "just as milk under pressure produces butter," so, too, "pressing anger" – when your teacher is angry with you for not understanding quickly, and you are put to shame [for asking many questions], eventually, from your mouth will emanate halakhic decisions and directives.

Thus, Rashi stresses that even in an extreme case in which the pupil's inquisitiveness leads to personal embarrassment, he should keep on asking, because probing leads to profound understanding. However, when a student recognizes that his instructor is incapable of providing an answer, he should "thrust a knife into" his "gullet" (23: 2), meaning he should remain silent, to avoid embarrassing his teacher.[55]

A teacher is encouraged to respond to an inquisitive student because such questioning significantly enhances the teacher's own knowledge, as depicted in the following original gloss that draws a parallel between the magnate and the poor man:

A rich man thinks himself wise, but a perceptive poor man will probe him (R 28: 11) – Scripture is describing a teacher and student, that the student probes him (*ḥokro)* and through this [investigation] the teacher becomes wiser.

This rigorous intellectual exchange makes for a learning environment conducive to free thinking and creativity, mirroring the atmosphere that characterized Rashi's own *beit midrash*. Grossman notes regarding the tremendous literary output – both in quantity and scope of material – produced by Rashi and his students:[56]

What accounts for Rashi's success in producing this valuable material? Among the important factors, one may cite his openness, critical

---

55. See Ḥullin 6a.
56. The illustrious Babylonian yeshivot of the *Geonim*, spanning some five hundred years, produced literature more limited in scope than that of Rashi and his students in two generations. See Grossman, *Rashi*, 54.

approach, encouragement of creativity, thorough analysis, and cordiality. . . .[57]

> His guiding principle was the pursuit of truth, and any method that could promote it was proper and desirable. This openness underlay Rashi's encouragement of his students to investigate things – even customs and written prayer books – and not accept them as settled.[58]

3. *Incremental Learning: Memorization, Analysis, and Formulation*

As noted above, the tripartite division of study – Scripture, Mishna, and Talmud – promotes the gradual mastery of texts of increased complexity. Rashi frequently distinguishes between the initial stage of memorization (*ḥokhma*), and the subsequent, more sophisticated phase of discernment (*bina*):[59]

> *The wise (leḥakham) of heart shall be called discerning* (R 16:21) – Who learned wisdom from his teacher. *Shall be called discerning* (*navon*) – Eventually he will be discerning in matters and subtle (*mefulpal*) in his wisdom and will be considered discerning (*navon*).

Likewise, this progression is clearly articulated in the following gloss:

> *The beginning of wisdom is [to] acquire wisdom (ḥokhma)* (R 4:7) – The beginning of your wisdom is learning from others, acquiring knowledge from the mouth of a teacher. *Afterward*, "With all your acquisitions, acquire discernment (*bina*)" – Focus it [the wisdom you have already acquired] independently so that you will understand the reasons and discern one thing from another.

57. Grossman, *Rashi*, 54.
58. Ibid., 60.
59. See R 1:5.

Incremental learning culminates in the rendering of halakhic decisions. Rashi drives this lesson home in his interpretation of Proverbs 5:15–17:

> *Drink water from your own cistern* – From the cistern that the Holy One, blessed be He, gave you for your share, the Torah of Moses. *Your cistern* – Gathered water. *Your own well* – Spring water. Meaning, initially [what you learned is] like gathered water, but at the end [the water is] flowing and moving. *Your springs will gush forth* – At the end you will acquire students, render decision for the community, and achieve fame in the public squares.

The water sources mentioned – cistern, well, and spring – are metaphors for the progressive stages within the learning process.[60] As Rosenberg explains:

> The study of Torah first involves learning and remembering. This process is symbolized by the cistern in which rainwater is stored. It is usually cemented with lime to prevent leakage, which symbolizes the preservation of studies in the student's memory. As the student advances, his Torah becomes like running water, gushing out of a spring. The student develops original ideas and interpretations of the subject matter, thus constantly increasing his knowledge.[61]

Notice Rashi's penultimate phrase: "Render decision for the community"; making halakhic decisions is the pinnacle of the learning process.

Parental Responsibility

Up to this point, our examination has centered upon the responsibilities of the teacher and student. What is the role of parents within the educational dynamic? Rashi offers insight into this question in the following comment:

---

60. The verses that follow (5:18–19) speak of loyalty to the wife of one's youth, for which "drinking from one's own cistern" was possibly intended as a metaphor.
61. *Proverbs: A New English translation,* trans. and notes A.J. Rosenberg, 29.

> *Train a lad* (R 22:6) – According to what you teach your son and educate him, whether in good or bad ways,[62] "he will not swerve from them even in old age."[63]

It is noteworthy that while the biblical verse advises to "train a lad," Rashi replaces "lad" with "your son."[64] This substitution reflects Rashi's view that the initial phase of education takes place within the home, involving parents.[65] According to Rashi, children are malleable and can be molded either positively or negatively, "for good or for bad." If parents fall short in their educational responsibilities and the child veers off course, undesirable habits acquired are not attributed to inherent inclinations in the child but rather to the neglect of parental guidance.[66] Thus, the educational journey commences in the home, guided by parents, and is later complemented by the involvement of an external educator.

INTERIM SUMMARY

In sum, Rashi's allegorical exegesis delves into the diverse facets of Torah study. His comprehensive *mashal* analysis considers the human players involved, proper decorum, motivational aspects, curriculum insights, and essential pedagogical tools. Through this allegorical reading, Rashi skillfully unifies the varied array of proverbs found in the book of Proverbs under one thematic umbrella, thereby creating a cohesive, holistic narrative.

---

62. Printed editions erroneously read "in words/בדברים."
63. See *Midrash Mishlei* 22:6.
64. Printed editions erroneously read *lanaar*, "to the lad," instead of "to your son."
65. Although the word "son" is mentioned twenty-two times in Proverbs and often is synonymous with not only a biological son but also a student, and in Rashi's commentary on Deuteronomy 6:7 he clearly states that all instances of "son" mean "student," our case is different. Here the verse states "lad," and Rashi constricts its meaning to "son" only.
66. Cooper notes a later interpretation that views the nature of a child in a darker light; it assumes a child's natural predisposition toward evil. See Alan Cooper, "On the Social Role of Biblical Interpretation: The Case of Proverbs 22:6," in *With Reverence for the Word*, 180–93.

RASHI'S EDUCATIONAL PROGRAM: A REFLECTION OF HIS INNER VALUES?

It is time to explore a complex question: Does the educational guidance provided by Rashi in Proverbs authentically mirror his intrinsic educational values, or is it largely influenced by his role as an exegete, driven by the need to clarify specific biblical words or phrases?

Our search for an answer will lead us to consider his other writings, since examining the consistency of his educational advice across various contexts may provide insight.

One last thought before we begin. Rashi did not gloss every verse; his commentary covers 77 percent of the verses in Proverbs.[67] Hence, if he disagreed with a rabbinic explanation, he simply could have ignored it and brought no comment at all.

Commencing with his commentary on other biblical books, we discover that many educational motifs outlined in Proverbs, such as the love of Torah, the virtues of Torah study, and proper study methods, receive comprehensive treatment elsewhere in his biblical commentaries, thus hinting at their significance in his eyes.[68]

Expanding our investigation to include his responsa literature yields valuable insights. As a distinguished rabbinic leader, Rashi addressed inquiries from both local and distant sources, formulating answers known as responsa. Some of these responses touch on matters related to education, as evidenced in the following examples.

Correspondence with Rabbi Samuel of Auxerre

Rabbi Samuel, a scholar from the French town of Auxerre, submitted sixteen intricate questions to Rashi regarding Rashi's commentaries on Jeremiah and Ezekiel. Rashi's response illuminates aspects of his pedagogical approach.[69]

---

67. He commented on 704 of 915 verses.
68. See Grossman, *Rashi*, 208–21.
69. For the full text of responses that Rashi wrote to questions about his commentary on Jeremiah and Ezekiel, see *Mikraot Gedolot HaKeter – Ezekiel*, ed. and notes J.S. Penkower (Bar-Ilan University, 2000), [320]–[321].

In answering his questioner, Rashi prioritizes sequence by explicitly stating: "I will answer this first because it was asked first,"[70] thereby enhancing his reader's understanding by maintaining a logical flow of information.

When queried about the physical layout of Ezekiel's Temple,[71] Rashi writes: "I don't know what I can add to my explanation found in the *kuntres*,[72] but I will draw it and send it to him."

Rabbi Samuel's difficulty with the complex subject matter prompts Rashi to present the information in an alternative format – making a drawing of the Temple according to the text in Ezekiel. This visual aid aims to enhance the questioner's comprehension. Despite the disappearance of this drawing, and others, from standard editions of the rabbinic Bible (*Mikraot Gedolot*), they are preserved in medieval manuscripts.[73] Rashi's inclination to draw reflects his commitment to addressing the specific educational needs of the student. Thus, from both aforementioned examples, we gather that Rashi aimed to present his answers in a format that would maximize understanding.

Another question from Rabbi Samuel points out an internal inconsistency in Rashi's commentary on Ezekiel,[74] prompting Rashi to acknowledge the error and respond:

---

70. Question number 8.
71. Question number 9.
72. *Kuntres* means a type of pamphlet or notebook in which explanations were written. Rashi uses this term elsewhere to describe the notebook of his own teacher (Rashi on Gittin 82a, s.v. "Which accords with the view of Ben Nanas"), and later in history Rashi's own commentary will be nicknamed "the *kuntres*."
73. A copy of the drawing is found in *Mikraot Gedolot HaKeter – Ezekiel* [322]. Rashi also drew maps of the Holy Land, as attested to by his grandson, Rashbam (commentary on Num. 34:2): "My grandfather, our teacher [Rashi], explained [this text] and drew [maps of] boundaries." Translation taken from *Rashbam's Commentary on Leviticus and Numbers, an Annotated Translation*, ed. and trans. M.I. Lockshin (Brown Judaic Series, 2001), 295. For a discussion of these and other drawings of Rashi, see Mayer I. Gruber, "What Happened to Rashi's Pictures?" *Bodleian Library Record* 14 (1992): 111–24, and Gabrielle Sed-Rajna, "Some Further Data on Rashi's Diagrams to His Commentary on the Bible," JSQ 1(1993/94): 149–57.
74. Question number 10.

> In any event, I erred in this explanation.... And my words contradicted each other – and now I dealt with it with our brother Shemaiah and edited it.

Rabbi Shemaiah was Rashi's intimate disciple who aided him in revising and correcting his commentaries. He was not Rashi's biological brother; rather, the term signifies the strong bond and feeling of closeness between the two.[75] Rashi's admission of error and collaboration with Rabbi Shemaiah to rectify the inconsistency underscore his humility and the importance of accuracy in his eyes.[76] This incident exemplifies how a student's probing question can enhance his or her teacher's knowledge, a key theme in Rashi's commentary on Proverbs.

Correspondence with Rabbi Meir ben Shmuel

Another responsum written to his son-in-law, Rabbi Meir ben Shmuel, sheds further light on his educational philosophy. In this correspondence, Rashi recounts the dispute with his teachers regarding the *kashrut* of an animal's lung:

> I, Shelomo, your beloved, inform you that I have not recanted and will not recant. The words of my teachers are not clear to me; they have responded to my arguments only superficially and still I will reveal them only to those who will respect their privacy. Were it not for the great tragedy that has befallen us, I would repeat myself to them even if they would not listen. *I am relying upon the great sage, Rabbi Yaakov b. Yakar. Despite the fact that I never heard this from him personally, in any case my inclination, my reasoning and my comprehension emanate from him.* They [my opponents] too are not arguing from either tradition or the Talmudic text but from their own understanding. If they would

75. So too, he responds to Rabbi Samuel in a warm and endearing fashion, calling his questioner both "my brother" and "my friend/*habibi*," utilizing both terms twice.
76. Humility is an outstanding quality of Rashi; the phrase "I do not know" is found more than fifty times in his Bible commentary. Similarly, the pursuit of truth is sacrosanct to Rashi; see Grossman, *Rashi*, 24–25.

> only respond to me appropriately, I might reconsider, but it is difficult for me to cause Jews to suffer monetary loss in a case such as this for which there are several appropriate reasons to issue a sanction (*heter*) [legal permission].[77]

Rashi states that his teachers are unable to offer a satisfactory explanation for their strict decision, which results in substantial financial loss. He reaches a different conclusion by relying on his own reasoning, which, he notes, is based on prior learning with his revered teacher, Rabbi Yaakov ben Yakar: "My reasoning and my comprehension emanate from him."[78] Goldberg and Sokolow elucidate the pedagogical process unfolding in this text:

> By basing himself not on an actual ruling *transmitted* by his teacher, Rabbi Yaakov b. Yakar, but on the "inclination, reasoning and comprehension" that he had *constructed* based upon earlier studies with Rabbi Yaakov, Rashi was able to stake a legitimate claim to a position that was no less authoritative in spite of the fact that it had no explicit precedent.[79]

This exchange, according to Goldberg and Sokolow, exemplifies Rashi's orientation toward a constructivist theory of education. In this pedagogical approach, the student, drawing from active engagement with a teacher in the past, possesses the capability to construct new understanding in the present.[80] In this process the learner actively constructs meaning through engagement with the world, with the teacher assuming

77. Responsum number 59. Translation: Scott Goldberg and Moshe Sokolow, "Sages on Stages, or Guides on the Side? Rashi, Ramban, Radak and Constructivist Educational Theory," in *Between Rashi and Maimonides: Themes in Medieval Jewish Thought, Literature and Exegesis*, ed. E. Kanarfogel and M. Sokolow (Yeshiva University Press, 2010), 292.
78. Rabbi Yaakov ben Yakar was Rashi's teacher for approximately six years in the Mainz Yeshiva and had a profound impact on both Rashi's personality and learning style; Rashi called him "my venerable Rabbi." See Grossman, *Rashi*, 15–16.
79. Goldberg and Sokolow, "Sages on Stages, or Guides on the Side?" 293.
80. Ibid., 292–93.

the role of a facilitator. The teacher guides the student in this endeavor, gradually withdrawing assistance as the individual gains more competence – a concept referred to as "scaffolding."[81]

Viewing students as active participants in their own learning and teachers as guides or facilitators is a recurring theme in Rashi's commentary on Proverbs. The rigorous classroom give-and-take, guided by the teacher, along with the interfacing with texts of escalating complexity, nurtures analytical thinking. This process culminates in the student's ability to construct independent decisions.

In sum, after investigating Rashi's writings beyond the immediate context of Proverbs, we identify recurring themes and principles that characterize his approach to education. Thus the educational philosophy revealed in Rashi's interpretation of Proverbs does indeed appear to reflect his personal overarching beliefs.

THE IDENTIFICATION OF WISDOM WITH TORAH

What motivated Rashi to identify "wisdom" (*ḥokhma)* with the Torah and not simply attribute it to the power of human intelligence? Grossman poses this fundamental question and proposes two potential answers, viewing the latter explanation as more plausible.[82]

First, he points in the direction of the Iberian Peninsula and suggests that Rashi is concerned about the influence of Spanish rationalist philosophy. Grossman speculates that along with the teachings of the medieval Spanish grammarians, Menahem and Dunash,[83] the philo-

---

81. Saul Mcleod, "Constructivism Learning Theory & Philosophy of Education," Simply Psychology, June 15, 2023, www.simplypsychology.org/constructivism.html.
82. Avraham Grossman, "The Tension Between Torah and Hokhmah (Wisdom) in Rashi's Commentary on the Bible," in *Teshura LeAmos: Asufat Meḥkarim BeFarshanut HaMikra Muggeshet LeAmos Hakham,* ed. Moshe bar Asher et al. [in Hebrew] (Tevunot, 2007), 13–27; Avraham Grossman, "Rashi's Rejection of Philosophy: Divine and Human Wisdoms Juxtaposed," *Simon Dubnow Institute Yearbook* 8 (2009): 95–118.
83. Menahem ben Saruq (910–970) compiled the first complete dictionary written in the Hebrew language. In his commentary on the Bible, Rashi relies heavily upon this dictionary, entitled the *Maḥberet,* quoting from it more than two hundred times. Dunash ben Labrat (ca. 920–ca. 990) compiled a list of 180 criticisms of Menahem's

sophical thoughts of Spanish sages had also penetrated the Ashkenazic zone. Afraid of the possible impact of this speculative thinking upon his philosophically inexperienced readers, Rashi took pains to emphasize that there is no wisdom other than the wisdom of the Torah.

Alternatively, he posits a local stimulus – the emerging monastic method of study in northern France known as scholasticism. The "twelfth-century Renaissance," which actually commenced in the middle of the previous century, during Rashi's lifetime, placed emphasis on man's reason and manifested itself in a new learning style which utilized dialectic reasoning to rigorously analyze theological beliefs.[84] Christian propagandists adopted this method of analysis in their fight against Judaism, and Rashi feared their impact because of the Jews' inexperience with this new learning style. Therefore, he identified "wisdom" with Torah and not with human reason in an effort to discourage his coreligionists from entering into dialectic-style religious conversations or debates.

Grossman's theories posit external influence, and Berger introduces two key questions for assessing externally motivated stimuli. First, can the exegetical position be accounted for by the exegete's own tradition or milieu? Second, how compelling is the external argument? Berger advocates that historians should prioritize internal motivations unless they are inadequate to comprehensively explain the phenomenon under discussion,[85] a perspective previously acknowledged by Soloveitchik:

> An historian has no right to claim extraneous influences unless he or she can show that the conclusion arrived at by the thinker

---

work in a composition entitled *Tehuvot al Menahem* and Rashi draws also from this work approximately fifty times. For a detailed analysis of both compositions and the epic debate between them, see Angel Sáenz-Badillos, "Early Hebraists in Spain: Menaḥem ben Saruq and Dunash ben Labrat," in *Hebrew Bible/Old Testament: The History of Its Interpretation*, vol. 1: *From the Beginnings to the Middle Ages*, part 2: *The Middle Ages* 96–109.

84. Rashi's descendants, the Tosafists, will apply the dialectic method to the study of Talmud. Regarding the nature of this learning style and its potential abuses, see Haym Soloveitchik, "Three Themes in Sefer Hasidim," *AJS Review* 1 (1976): 339–57.

85. David Berger, "Polemic, Exegesis, Philosophy, and Science: Reflections on the Tenacity of Ashkenazic Modes of Thought," in *Cultures in Collision and Conversation* (Academic Studies Press, 2011), 160–61.

> is so atypical that unless something impinged, consciously or unconsciously, upon his thought he could never have arrived at the conclusion that he did.... If, however, the line of reasoning is a valid one... the historian has no right to attribute it to outside forces.[86]

In our case, with regard to the first question, the Jewish interpretive tradition abounds with connections between "wisdom" and Torah, as noted by Berger:

> Even a casual look through the midrashic and other rabbinic materials reveals that the equation of the Torah and *ḥokhma* is simply overwhelming... and is treated as virtually self-evident.[87]

Moreover, the Proverbs text itself links "wisdom" with Torah, as in the following verses:

> My son, heed my words; And store up my commandments (*mitzvotai*) with you. Keep my commandments (*mitzvotai*) and live my teaching (*torati*), as the apple of your eye. Bind them on your fingers; write them on the tablet of your mind. Say to Wisdom (*ḥokhma*), "You are my sister," and call Understanding a kinswoman. (Prov. 7:1–4)

Regarding the second question, there is little or no evidence that Rashi himself was aware of Spanish rationalism; therefore, there would be no reason for him to try to protect his readers from such influence. Similarly, regarding the dangers of scholasticism, this type of concern is reflective of a later period within the Jewish-Christian debate.[88]

---

86. Haym Soloveitchik, "Halakhah, Hermeneutics, and Martyrdom in Medieval Ashkenaz (part 1 of 2)," *JQR* 94/1 (2004): 77.
87. Berger, "Polemic, Exegesis," 160–61.
88. Ibid., 163–64.

Thus, Berger concludes that it is unnecessary to look for external motivations, given the strength of the internal Jewish consideration – an argument we find more compelling.

Irrespective of the stimulus, Rashi embraces the equation "wisdom= Torah" using it as the means to create thematic unity.

JUDAIZING PROVERBS

It is now time to revisit our initial question. The Sages desired to withdraw the book of Proverbs from general circulation due to its utilitarian and "secular" nature until the Men of the Great Assembly came and interpreted the verses.[89] What is the nature of this interpretation?

Presumably, it consisted in a spiritualization of the narrative, a process that began with the Rabbis and culminates with Rashi. Systematically identifying more than 140 verses with the concept of Torah and its related notions, Rashi thoroughly "Judaizes" the book of Proverbs.

This process of Judaizing has an added dimension. The Rabbis frequently associate biblical verses that express general ideas with specific characters or events mentioned elsewhere in the Bible. As noted by Fraenkel, this practice is rooted in the concept of "the unity of the Bible," which perceives the entire biblical corpus as a cohesive living organism, with all its parts intricately interconnected and mutually nourishing. Consequently, the influence of one organ can extend to another, even when they are distant from one another.[90] These rabbinic connections are established based on identical words (*gezeira shava*) or similar ideas.

Rashi expands this tradition and associates approximately eighty phrases with specific biblical incidents or personalities.[91] Through these historical identifications, he notes the behavior of men, such as that of King Saul:

89. *Avot DeRabbi Natan* 1:4.
90. Yonah Fraenkel, *Midrash and Aggada*, vol. 1 [in Hebrew] (Open University, 1996), 163.
91. In comparison, Rabbi Yosef Kimhi identifies four verses only.

> *A prudent man keeps his silence* (R 11:12) – When one devoid of sense degrades him, as it states regarding Saul, "And they scorned him and brought him no gift; but he was one who keeps his silence" (I Sam. 10:27).

King Saul is praised for remaining silent when he was scorned shortly after his coronation. This association, original to Rashi, is based upon the presence of the root Ḥ-R-SH (remain silent) in both verses.[92]

Rashi also assesses the actions of women, as illustrated in the following gloss:

> *The wisest of women* (R 14:1) – Build their homes, for they are preserved by them, like the wife of On ben Pelet, as is explained in the chapter "*Ḥelek*."[93] *[But a foolish one tears it down] with her own hands* – This is Korah's wife.

The Talmud attributes wisdom to On ben Pelet's wife, crediting her with steering her husband away from the rebellion against Moses's authority. By contrast, the wife of Korah is accused of encouraging her husband's rebellious actions (Num. 16); hence, the former is deemed "the wisest of women," and the latter is considered "the foolish one."[94]

Approximately one-third of Rashi's identifications in Proverbs are either original or are drawn from rabbinic sources that are no longer extant.[95] These identifications not only enhance the composition's religious dimension but also serve as a pedagogical tool, assisting the delivery of the proverbs' messages through concrete examples.

---

92. Rabbinic sources link our verse with other examples of silence, such as Jacob's lack of verbal response after the rape of Dinah; see *Tanḥuma*, Buber, *Vayishlaḥ* 13.
93. *Ḥelek* is chapter 10 in Tractate Sanhedrin.
94. See Sanhedrin 109b.
95. For example, in Rashi's commentary on 13:8 he explicitly states: "The Midrash Aggada interprets it as speaking of the half shekel," but this source, linking the Proverb's verse to the half shekel, is no longer extant.

SUMMARY

Rashi's commentary on Proverbs unites hundreds of diverse proverbs under one thematic roof. Applying the proverbs to all facets of Torah acquisition – student, teacher, curriculum, motivation, rewards, and pedagogical methods – Rashi transforms this composition into a holistic narrative, an "Educational Manual for Torah Student and Teacher."[96]

Exploration of Rashi's works beyond the immediate context of Proverbs reveals consistent themes that represent his educational approach. This broader examination indicates that Rashi's general philosophy of education, as expressed in Proverbs, aligns with his personal overarching beliefs.

Rashi's application of the "secular" proverbs to the world of Torah spiritualizes the composition, thus affirming its rightful place in the canon. He further underlines its religious nature by associating dozens of proverbs with specific biblical personalities and events. Thus he thoroughly "Judaizes" what appeared to be a compendium of worldly wisdom.

96. In a somewhat similar vein, with an emphasis on education, some scholars view the original setting of wisdom literature as schools connected to the royal court. The proverb collections were used to train children of the upper class for official positions; see Fox, *Proverbs 1–9: The Anchor Bible*, 7.

Chapter Five

Additional Manifestations of Symmetry and Wholeness

Further analysis of Rashi's Proverbs commentary uncovers additional manifestations of symmetry and cohesiveness.

OPPOSITES

The book of Proverbs depicts a world of black-and-white character types – ranging from the fool and the wise to the wicked and the righteous, the poor and the rich, the sluggard and the diligent. This tendency to deal in dichotomies is a hallmark of wisdom literature. Based on rabbinic sources, Rashi consistently relates these polar opposites to the pursuit or nonpursuit of Torah knowledge. Thus, the "fortress" of the rich man is the wealth of Torah knowledge that he amasses. Conversely, the poverty of the poor man is his lack of Torah study, which leads to "ruin" (R 10:15).[1]

1. Similarly, see R 13:8, 18:23, 22:7, 28:11.

Similarly, the indolence of the sluggard, whose failure to tend his vineyard leads to the overgrowth of thorns and nettles, along with the collapse of its supporting walls, is synonymous with the dissipation of a Torah disciple's knowledge when the subject matter is not properly reviewed (R 24:30–34). Opposed to the sluggard is the industrious ant:

> Lazybones, go to the ant; study its ways and learn. Without leaders, officers, or rulers, it lays up its stores during the summer, gathers in its food at the harvest. How long will you lie there, lazybones...a bit more sleep...a bit more hugging
> yourself in bed, and poverty will come calling upon you. (6: 6–11)

In Rashi's eyes, the key lesson here extends beyond mere industriousness in worldly matters; it is a call for diligence in the pursuit of Torah knowledge (R 6:11). The ant's meticulous preparation during favorable seasons serves as a metaphor for the gathering of wisdom, emphasizing the importance of continuous effort and learning.

Rashi's tendency to portray things in terms of opposites extends to his treatment of women.[2]

Archetypes: *Isha Zara* and *Eshet Ḥayil*

While employing a range of terms to depict both positive and negative female figures,[3] the central focus in Proverbs is on the opposition of the "strange woman" (*isha zara*) to the "capable wife" (*eshet ḥayil*).[4] The former is extensively described on four occasions near the beginning

2. The analysis below of the *eshet ḥayil* and *isha zara* also incorporates some of Rashi's comments regarding "Madame Folly," who, in his *mashal*, is likewise associated with Christianity.
3. Positive women: the wife of your youth (5:18); a graceful woman (11:16); beautiful woman (11:22); capable wife (19:14). Negative woman: nagging/contentious wife (19:13, 21:9, 19, 25:24, 27:15); harlot (6:26, 7:1, 23:27); evil woman (6:24); adulteress (30:20).
4. The term *eshet ḥayil* has been translated in a variety of ways; we have adopted the translation "the capable wife" (*Tanakh, New Jewish Publication Society,* 1564). Other translations include "the woman of strength" (Fox, *Proverbs 10–31: The Anchor Bible,*

of the book,[5] while the latter merits a comprehensive depiction in the closing chapter.[6] Who are these women, and what broader concepts or ideals do they represent?

Let us commence with the "strange woman." The term *isha zara* presents challenges in translation, with interpretations including "foreign woman," "strange woman," and "the woman who belongs to another."[7] Rashi generally deems her a *zona* (prostitute)[8] and provides an allegorical interpretation as follows:

> *It will save you from a strange woman* (R 2:16–19) – From the *knessiya* (assembly; congregation) of idolatry,[9] which is *minut.* It cannot be said that he spoke only of an actual adulteress, for what is the praise of the Torah, that he says here, "Will save you from a strange woman," and not from any other sin? Rather, this is *minut,* idolatry, the casting off of the yoke of all the commandments. *Her house sinks down to Death* – This refers back to "will save you, etc." (v. 16), for whoever comes to her house will sink and slip as if down an incline that leads to death, and the Torah will guard you from this fall. Hence, it is a great thing for you. *The dead* – Those who neglect the way of goodness and are forsaken without support until they fall into Gehinnom. *Cannot return* – To them it seems difficult to leave it and to repent.

According to Rashi, the *isha zara* is an allegory for idolatry or *minut* (heresy), but what type of heresy or idolatry is intended?

---

888); "a woman of valor" (Abraham Cohen, *Proverbs,* Soncino Series [Soncino, 1967], 211). The term *eshet* (the construct form of *isha*) is occasionally translated as "woman" and at other times as "wife."

5. 2:16–19, 5:1–14, 6:24–35, 7:5–27.
6. 31:10–31; the capable wife is also briefly mentioned in 12:4.
7. Roger N. Whybray, *The Book of Proverbs – A Survey of Modern Study* (Brill, 1995), 73; Fox, *Proverbs 1–9: The Anchor Bible,* 134–41.
8. R 1:6, 5:3–6 (twice), 6:24–26 (twice), 7:8–10.
9. Standard printed editions read *apikorsut* due to censorship.

The following episode, recounted in the Talmud, may provide the answer. R. Eliezer was arrested by secular authorities and later released. In an attempt to comprehend the reason behind this troublesome event, R. Akiva suggests that it might be due to his inappropriate thoughts:

> [R. Eliezer] said to him: Akiva, [you are right, as] you have reminded me [that] once I was walking in the upper marketplace of Tzippori, and I found a man [who was one] of the students of Jesus the Nazarene,[10] and his name was Yaakov of Kefar Sekhanya. He said to me: It is written in your Torah, "You shalt not bring the payment to a prostitute… [into the house of the Lord your God]" (Deut. 23:19)…. [Is it permitted] to make from [the payment to a prostitute for services rendered] a bathroom for a high priest [in the Temple?] And I said nothing to him [in response]. He said to me: Jesus the Nazarene taught me the following…. "For of the payment to a prostitute she has gathered them, and to the payment to the prostitute they shall return" (Mic. 1:7). [Since the coins] came from a place of filth, let them go to a place of filth…. And I derived pleasure from the statement, [and] due to this, I was arrested for heresy… [because] I transgressed that which is written in the Torah…. "Remove your way far from her" (Prov. 5:8); this [is a reference to] heresy (*minut*), "and do not come near the entrance of her house"; this is [a reference to] the ruling power (*reshut*).[11]

The talmudic discussion culminates with identifying the "strange woman" in Proverbs chapter 5 with *minut* (heresy) and specifically with the teachings of Jesus. Rashi extends this identification to encompass all

10. In standard editions of the Talmud the name Jesus the Nazarene has been removed by censors.

11. Avoda Zara 17a; *Koren Talmud Bavli, Tractates Avoda Zara and Horayot, Commentary by Rabbi Adin Even-Israel Steinsaltz* (Koren Publishers, 2017), 86. For a comparison of this version of the story with parallel versions recounted in rabbinic literature, see Joshua Schwartz and Peter Tomson, "When Rabbi Eliezer Was Arrested for Heresy," *JSIJ* 10 (2012): 145–81, jewish-faculty.biu.ac.il/sites/jewish-faculty/files/shared/JSIJ5/schwartzandtomson.pdf.

verses in Proverbs referring to the strange woman. As we shall see, Rashi consistently aligns *Minut* with Christianity (the teachings of Jesus) and *Minim* with Christians in his commentary on the Later Prophets and Writings.[12] In Rashi's uncensored gloss to Daniel 12:10, he explicitly states: "For example, the heretics (*haMinim*), the students of Jesus (*Yeshu*)."[13]

Rashi's aforementioned gloss (2:16) begins with an unusual phrase: "*knessiya* of idolatry," where *knessiya* denotes an assembly or congregation specifically associated with idolatry (*minut*). This term *knessiya* appears eleven times in Rashi's commentary on the Bible, with all instances save one referring to a gathering of the Jewish people.[14] The exception lies in our gloss, where *knessiya* takes on the distinct meaning of a gathering convened for idolatry or Christianity. Baer suggests that Rashi might have been influenced by the Latin term *ecclesia,* widely used in Christianity to describe the mystical connection between the Messiah and his church.[15] Most scholars note, however, that Rashi probably did not understand Latin,[16] and any awareness of the term would have come through oral communication.[17]

---

12. Judah Rosenthal, "Anti-Christian Polemic in Rashi's Bible Commentary" [in Hebrew], in *Meḥkarim UMekorot,* 1 (Rubin Mass, 1967), 105–8 and n. 24; Elazar Touitou, "Answering the Heretics" [in Hebrew] *Sinai* 99 (1985): 145–48; Avraham Grossman, *The Early Sages of France* [in Hebrew] (Magnes, 2001), 477–79; Shaye J.D. Cohen, "Does Rashi's Torah Commentary Respond to Christianity? A Comparison of Rashi with Rashbam and Bekhor Shor," in *The Idea of Biblical Interpretation – Essays in Honor of James Kugel,* ed. H. Najman and J. Newman (Brill, 2004), 458–72.
13. See *Daniel, Ezra-Nehemiah* [*Mikraot Gedolot HaKeter*] [in Hebrew], ed. M. Cohen (Bar-Ilan University Press, 2019), 84.
14. Jeremiah 9:1; Hosea 2:7; Micah 1:11; Zephaniah 3:10; Ezekiel 23:2; Psalms 45:14, 68:7; Proverbs 10:1–2; Song of Songs 1:8, 6: 9.
15. Yitshak F. Baer, "Rashi and the World Around Him," in *Jewish Intellectual History in the Middle Ages,* ed. J. Dan (Praeger, 1994), 112–13.
16. Sarah Kamin, *Jews and Christians Interpret the Bible* [in Hebrew], 55, n.121; David Berger, "Mission to the Jews and Jewish-Christian Contacts in the Polemical Literature of the High Middle Ages," *The American Historical Review* 91:3 (1986): 590, n. 68.
17. Esra Shereshevsky, "Rashi's and Christian Interpretations," *Jewish Quarterly Review* 61 (1970): 76–86; Kamin, *Jews and Christians Interpret the Bible,* 55, n. 121.

A second notable feature in Rashi's commentary on the strange woman is the elevation of idolatry to a graver sin than others in the Bible. According to Rashi, a person who draws near to idolatry (Christianity) forsakes the entire Torah.[18]

The third distinctive characteristic is the connection between engaging with the *isha zara* and the peril of falling into Gehinnom (the netherworld) – a rabbinical motif introduced by Rashi to elucidate the biblical text.[19] Rashi repeats this cautionary motif three times within the context of the strange woman, thereby emphasizing the severity of the consequences and issuing a strong warning to the reader.[20]

The *isha zara* holds such pivotal significance in Rashi's commentary that when, in his introductory programmatic statement, he chooses one allegory to typify the essence of the entire book, he opts for the strange woman:

> *For understanding proverb (mashal) and epigram (melitza)* (R 1:6) – That they should direct their attention to the verses through two methods: the allegory (*mashal*) and the image (*melitza*).... When he states: "It will save you from the strange woman, from the alien woman" (2:16), idolatry is meant; this is the allegory, but the image itself, the fact that he expressed his allegory through the image of a woman means that – You shall be aware of a harlot.

Thus, in Rashi's commentary on Proverbs, the *isha zara*, identified with Christianity, emerges as a central polemical figure.

Now let us turn our attention to her antithesis, the capable wife (*eshet ḥayil*). The passage on the *eshet ḥayil* is a self-contained poem, structured as an alphabetic acrostic that spans the twenty-two letters of the Hebrew alphabet (31:10–31). Rashi provides a comprehensive gloss to this poem, explicating the majority of its verses.[21] His commentary follows

18. Similarly, see R 6:24. The comparison between idolatry and all the other commandments can be found in *Mekhilta Bo DePesaḥiyah*, 5/15.
19. Claude G. Montefiore and Herbert Loewe, *A Rabbinical Anthology* (Jewish Publication Society, 1960), xlvi–l.
20. R 2:18, 5:9, 6:26.
21. Rashi's contextual explanation is shorter than his allegorical one. He gives brief

a two-tiered approach, initially presenting the *melitza* – the contextual explanation – and then delving into the allegorical one. Transitioning to the second tier of his commentary, the *mashal*, Rashi commences with the following comment:

> *And let her works praise her in the gates* (R 31:31) – This is the contextual meaning, which I explained, but according to the allegory – it is explained as referring to the Torah and those who study it.

In his allegorical commentary, Rashi applies the verses of the poem to the Torah and those dedicated to its study. Thus, the *eshet ḥayil*, who "rises while it is still night" (31:15), is the dedicated teacher who begins instruction early in the morning. The commitment to Torah promises material rewards, like a merchant fleet bringing blessing and sustenance (R 31:14), as well as spiritual rewards in the World to Come (R 31:11).[22] Study and performance afford protection not only from the day of judgment (R 31:25) but also from Gehinnom (R 31:21).

The promised benefits extend beyond the individual to the nation, with the anticipation of Christianity's defeat:

> *She sets her mind on a field* (R 31:16) – [The Torah] muzzles Esau, "the man of the field" (Gen. 25:27), with a muzzle and a bridle. *And takes him* – From the world, to destroy him.

This gloss is grounded in the hermeneutical principle of *gezeira shava,* which employs analogical reasoning. The term *sadeh* (field) appears both in our verse and in Genesis 25: 27, where it is associated with Esau.[23] Therefore, Rashi concludes that our verse also refers to him.[24] Furthermore, Rashi interprets the verb *zamema* as derived from the root Z-M-M,

contextual explanations of twelve verses (55 percent); and allegorical interpretations of sixteen verses (73 percent).

22. Similarly, see R 12:14, 13:2. This idea is found in Mishna Pe'ah 1:1.
23. See *Tanḥuma,* Buber, *Re'eh* 4:17.
24. This application is original to Rashi.

to muzzle, suggesting that our verse refers to the muzzling of Esau, symbolizing his ultimate destruction. The downfall of Esau, i.e., the Christians, is a recurring motif in this commentary.[25]

While envisioning the destruction of Esau, the Torah protects Israel:

> *From the fruit* (R 31:16) – Of her deeds. *She plants a vineyard* – Israel, to keep them alive for eternal life.[26]

The contrast between Esau's demise and Israel's redemption is brought out by the use of the Hebrew word *olam*, which means both "world" and "forever." Whereas Esau is destined to be taken "from the world (*min ha'olam*)" for destruction, Israel, through righteous deeds, is destined to endure "for eternal life (*leḥayei olam*). This deliberate comparison, pitting the downfall of Esau (Christianity) against the preservation of Israel, instills hope for a brighter future in the hearts of medieval Jews and subsequent generations.

Historical precedent buttresses Rashi's assurance of national protection and deliverance:

> *Her lamp never goes out at night* (R 31:18) – [The word] night [is written ליל] without the [final letter] *heh* (ה), [alluding to] "the night [ליל] of vigil" (Ex. 12:42), when the Egyptians were plagued; [on that night,] she shone for Israel and protected them.

Just as in the night before the Exodus the Torah protected Israel while the Egyptian firstborn died, Rashi says that a similar safeguarding will occur in the future. Midrashic sources connect our verse to the "night of vigil" and the protection afforded to one individual, Bithiah, Pharaoh's daughter.[27] Rashi's interpretation extends this protection to encompass the entire nation of Israel.

---

25. See R 14:14, 21:12.
26. The identification of the vineyard with the nation of Israel is found in the *Tanḥuma-Yelammedenu, Ḥayei Sara*, par. 4, but the conclusion of the comment, "To keep them alive for eternal life," seems original to Rashi. Israel is allegorized as a vine in Psalms 80:9 as well as in other passages.
27. See *Pesikta DeRav Kahana*, "And it came to pass at midnight," *piska* 7. See also

In Rashi's allegorical commentary on *eshet ḥayil,* he comments on sixteen out of the twenty-two verses. I have identified sources for only six of Rashi's comments (38 percent), with three of these connections being somewhat general in nature. Consequently, it becomes evident that Rashi's *mashal* commentary on the capable wife is predominantly original.[28] While the glosses connecting the capable wife with the individual student of Torah align with traditional sources, what takes one by surprise are the glosses that extend the poem to a national scale and reference Esau (Christianity). By incorporating the downfall of Esau and the concept of eternal life for Israel, Rashi introduces polemical material into his gloss on *eshet ḥayil.*

Rashi has deliberately molded certain glosses on the *eshet ḥayil* to counterbalance the description of the *isha zara.* The capable wife brings blessing, prosperity, and life; the strange woman brings poverty and death.[29] While the strange woman leads her victims to abandon the yoke of commandments and descend into Gehinnom,[30] the capable wife (representing Torah) protects those who adhere to her commandments from such misfortune. The strategic placement of these contrasting elements within the biblical text serves to accentuate the contrast between these two women. The detailed description of the *eshet ḥayil* is located in the closing chapter of Proverbs, whereas the extensive descriptions of the *isha zara* are found in the opening collection of proverbs as well as in Rashi's introductory programmatic statement. Thus, these contrasting women, with polemical underpinnings, emerge as thematic bookends, framing our narrative.

CHRISTIAN ENTICEMENT

The Role of Speech

Closely linked to the theme of Christianity is the theme of speech. Anti-Christian polemic is not confined to the periphery or edges of

---

Pesikta Rabbati, piska 17.

28. Rosenberg, *Proverbs: A New English Translation,* 206, draws a similar conclusion.
29. R 6:26.
30. R 2:16–19.

this composition; rather, it pervades the entire text. A comprehensive examination of Rashi's uncensored commentary on Proverbs reveals over fifty comments referring to Christianity, with speech emerging as the most prominent theme.

About 20 percent of the proverbs in chapters 10–29 are related to the theme of speech, and the opening chapters 1–9 "are almost entirely about the spoken word."[31] The significant role of speech in Proverbs has long been acknowledged.

Rashi connects the "speech" aphorisms in Proverbs with the Christian missionizing efforts and employs a variety of terms to describe verbal enticement, with a predominant focus on the Hebrew root S-U-T (to entice),[32] used sixteen times to denote such behavior.

The identity of the enticer is not specified in the following gloss:

> *The impious man destroys his neighbor through speech* (R 11:9) – *The impious*, who entices (*mesit*) his friend on an evil way, destroys him with his mouth.

However, in the remaining cases (fifteen in number), the proximity of *sut* to other phrases connects the enticement to Christianity. For example, the combination of the terms *sut* and "idolatry" provides such specificity.

---

31. Whybray, *The Book of Proverbs*, 141.
32. Traditional biblical dictionaries translate *sut* as "to incite" (HALOT, 2, s.v. 749, סות). However, in contemporary usage, "to incite" may imply encouraging to act in a violent way (*Concise Oxford English Dictionary*, ed. C. Soanes and A. Stevenson [Oxford University Press, 2004], 719), unlike "entice," which conveys persuasion or allurement by offering pleasure or advantage (*Concise Oxford English Dictionary*, 476). Given this differentiation, moving forward, we will interpret the root S-U-T as "to entice, persuade, allure, or seduce."

Sut and Idolatry

Rashi viewed Christianity as a form of idol worship, labeling it with the term *avoda zara*.[33] In his Proverbs commentary, he links the root S-U-T with idolatry six times,[34] as exemplified in the following example.

Proverbs 26, verses 4 and 5, present a contradiction, with the former advising against answering a fool in his foolishness, while the latter enjoins the opposite: Answer a dullard! In classic rabbinic literature, this famous contradiction was cited as grounds for removing the book of Proverbs from widespread circulation. Rashi reconciles the contradiction in the following way:

> *Do not answer a dullard* – With words of quarrel and contention, lest you become like him. *Answer a dullard* – Who comes to allure you to idolatry (*lehasitkha le'avoda zara*); let him know his folly, *else he will think himself wise*. The meaning of these two verses is explained in [the verses] themselves: *Do not answer* – In a matter in which you will become like him if you answer him. *Answer a dullard* – in a matter in which if you do not answer him, *he will think himself wise*.

According to Rashi, each verse is associated with a distinct type of quarrel. The former describes a senseless dispute conducted in an argumentative manner. In response to this, the text cautions against answering, as it would result in both parties being deemed foolish. On the other hand, the latter verse, which advises to "answer, else he will think himself wise," applies when one person is attempting to lure another to idolatry, which for Rashi in his Proverbs commentary means Christianity. In this scenario, it is imperative to respond appropriately and effectively

33. Israel Elfenbein, "Rashi in His Responsa," in *Rashi: His Teachings and Personality*, ed. S. Federbush (1958), 90; *Teshuvot Rashi*, ed. I. Elfenbein [in Hebrew] (1942), 337 (no. 327); Rosenthal, "Anti-Christian Polemic," 110; Katz, *Exclusiveness and Tolerance: Studies in Jewish-Gentile Relations in Medieval and Modern Times* (Oxford University Press, 1961), 24–36.
34. In four cases, he supplements it with additional references to Christianity, such as Esau and *min*, while in the remaining two instances, only the term idolatry is used.

to prevent the "dullard," the enticer, from perceiving himself as correct. This comment is original to Rashi.

Although the above contradiction was noted by the Talmud (Shabbat 30b), Rashi ignores the resolution proposed there:

> [The Sages] sought to suppress the book of Proverbs as well [because] its statements contradict each other. And why did they not suppress it? They said, [in the case of] the book of Ecclesiastes, didn't we analyze it and find an explanation...? Here too, let us analyze it. And what is [the meaning of]: Its statements contradict each other? [On the one hand,] it is written: "Answer not a fool according to his folly, [lest you also be like him]" (Prov. 26:4), and [on the other hand,] it is written: "Answer a fool according to his folly, [lest he be wise in his own eyes]" (Prov. 26:5). [This is] not difficult: [as] this... [is referring to a case where the fool is making claims] about Torah matters; [whereas] that... [is referring to a case where the fool is making claims] about mundane matters.[35]

According to the Talmud, the initial verse cautioning against answering the fool pertains to discussions on worldly matters, while the subsequent verse encouraging an answer is directed at a fool discussing words of Torah.

It is surprising that Rashi, despite his focus on Torah as the primary motif in his *mashal* commentary on Proverbs, disregards the talmudic resolution. It appears that his desire to ward off the danger of enticement to Christianity takes precedence over the theme of Torah in his gloss to these verses.

Sut, Idolatry, and Esau

Proverbs 14:10–16 is composed of seven verses that initially appear to lack a thematic connection. Rashi presents two original explanations to elucidate these verses in succession. This is an unusual occurrence. While occasionally linking adjacent proverbs, Rashi generally does not

35. *Koren Talmud Bavli, Tractate Shabbat, Part One, Commentary by Rabbi Adin Even-Israel Steinsaltz* (Koren Publishers, 2012), 143.

offer thematic connections within larger units of aphorisms.[36] His first explanation expounds the verses as distinguishing between the righteous and the wicked, while the latter distinguishes between Esau and Jacob. The following is Rashi's second explication:[37]

> Another explanation:[38] *The heart alone knows its bitterness* – Israel, who are of embittered heart in exile, for they are killed for the sanctification of the name; *in their joy* – In the future [no stranger shall mingle]. *The house of the wicked will be demolished* – The house of Esau. *A road may seem right to a man* – The road of idolatry seems right in the eyes of Esau, "a man of the field" (Gen. 25:27), *but in the end,* etc. *Even in laughter* – That the Holy One, blessed be He, causes them to laugh in this world. Their hearts will ache in the future.... *An unprincipled man reaps the fruit of his ways* – Esau. *A good man of his deeds* – Jacob. *A simple person believes* – Their words and is enticed after them; *a clever man ponders* – And will not be enticed.

Rashi's gloss posits that the word "wicked" refers to Esau, as does the generic word "man."[39] Esau is viewed not only as the biological son of

36. By contrast, Rabbi Moshe Kimhi excelled in this area, connecting units composed of two to seven verses no less than ninety times. See J. Klein, "The system of adjacent verses in R. Moshe Kimhi's commentary on Proverbs," in *Studies in Bible and Exegesis* 1, ed. U. Simon and M. Goshen-Gottstein [in Hebrew] (Bar-Ilan University Press, 1980), 209–28.
37. The precise location of this second explanation varies among manuscripts and early printed editions, suggesting that Rashi may have added it later, possibly after the First Crusade.
38. Rashi introduces this second explanation with the neutral term *davar aḥer*. Generally, this term connects elucidations originating from the same exegetical category, mainly midrashic. See Kamin, *Rashi*, 158, n. 1; Amnon Shapira, "Does '*Davar Aḥer*' in Rashi Present Two Alternate or Similar Explanations?" in *Pirkei Neḥama, Professor Nechama Leibowitz Memorial Volume*, ed. M. Ahrend, R. Ben-Meir, and G.H. Cohen [in Hebrew] (Elinor Library, 2001), 292–96.
39. The exception is when the word "man" is described as "good" (v. 14); in this case, he is identified as Jacob.

Isaac and Rebecca but also as the progenitor of the Roman Empire and, subsequently, of the Christian Church.[40]

The above gloss presents a sharp contrast between Jews (Jacob) and Christians (Esau). During Rashi's lifetime, the heart of the Jewish people is embittered in exile because they are being killed for the sake of Heaven, in contrast to the Christians, whom God is allowing to laugh. Yet, in the future, the tables will be turned: The Jews will be joyful and Christian hearts will ache.[41] Cognizant of the fleeting nature of the present, the clever man will not be enticed by the words of the Christians, whereas the simple man will be.

The commentary challenges the familiar Christian assertion that the Jews' lowly state in exile signifies the transfer of the Chosen People status from Jews to Christians due to their rejection of Jesus. According to this Christian claim, their own success serves as evidence of their replacement as the *verus Israel* (true Israel). Rashi's response takes on this notion, asserting that the current state is only transitory; in the future, the Jews will experience joy while the Christians will endure sorrow.

Sut and *Min*

The noun *min* is coupled with the root S-U-T numerous times in Rashi's Proverbs commentary. As discussed in our exploration of the *isha zara,* in Rashi's commentary on the Later Prophets and Hagiographa, the word *min* serves as a code name for Christianity and Christians. Let us examine a number of examples.

Proverbs 6:12–15 describes the deceitful ways of a cunning individual, and Rashi explains:

> *Walks with a crooked mouth* – He walks with crooked lips. *Winking his eyes* – Winks of deceit. *Pointing his finger* – They are all expressions of hinting: One applies to the eye, one to the foot, and one to the finger, but the main idea is that it is speaking of *haMinin,* who entice (*hamesitim*) people to idolatry.

40. Gerson D. Cohen, "Esau as Symbol in Early Medieval Thought," in *Jewish Medieval and Renaissance Studies,* ed. A. Altman (Cambridge University Press, 1967), 18–48.
41. Similarly, see R 14:13.

Rashi's original gloss evokes the comprehensive nature of Christian enticement, where all bodily organs are mobilized to persuade a Jew to abandon his faith.[42]

The Proverbs text (17:12) reads: "Sooner meet a bereaving bear than a fool with his nonsense," and Rashi glosses:

> *Sooner meet a bereaving bear* – It is better for a person that a bereaving bear encounter him than one of the foolish *Minim*[43] who entice (*hamesitim*) him to idolatry.[44]

In *Bereshit Rabbati*, a midrash attributed to Rabbi Moshe HaDarshan of Narbonne (eleventh century), the verse is linked with Esau, although it remains unclear if Rashi was familiar with this specific work.[45]

What were the *Minim* saying and why were they deemed so perilous? Rashi's original gloss supplies the answer:

> *Who speak duplicity* (R 2:12) – These are *haMinim*[46] who entice (*hamesitim*) Israel to idolatry and distort (*umehapkhim*) the Torah to evil.

Rashi establishes a linguistic connection between the actions of Christian enticers and the biblical text through the use of the root H-P-K (overturn, distort); "men who speak duplicity (*tahpukhot*)" (Prov. 2:12) refers to the Christian enticers who distort or overturn/*umehapkhim* the Torah.

Similar allegations of the Christian distortion of the Torah can be found in Rashi's uncensored glosses to the Talmud, marked by the repeated use of the verbs with the root H-P-K.

---

42. Similarly, see R 10:10, 11:9.
43. The word *haMinim* is missing from standard printed editions.
44. Due to censorship, standard printed editions replace the word "idolatry" with the phrase "to veer from God and His Torah."
45. See Hananel Mack, *The Mystery of Rabbi Moshe Hadarshan* [in Hebrew] (Bialik, 2010), 188–94, 223–39.
46. Due to censorship, in standard printed editions this word is replaced with *haapikorsin*.

> Rosh HaShana 17a: *HaMinim* – The students of Jesus Nazareth, of who distorted/ *hafkhu* the words of the living God to evil/*leraa*.[47]
>
> Berakhot 12b: *Minut* – The students of Jesus the Nazarene, who distort (*hahofkhim*) the true meaning of Torah (*taamei haTorah*) to preach [theological] error and idolatry (*midrash ta'ut ve'elil*).[48]

What Christian "distortion" of the Torah "to evil" is intended? Rashi is alluding to the bringing of scriptural proofs from the Old Testament by Christian scholars and polemicists to prove the truthfulness of Christian beliefs. Scholars like Blumenkranz and Funkenstein have demonstrated that in the early Middle Ages, the arguments put forth by Christian scholars were repetitive and largely involved the reiteration of points from earlier church fathers.[49] While Rashi's knowledge of Christianity was limited,[50] he was well acquainted with the basic technique of twisting the meaning of the Old Testament"("*mehapkhim* the Torah") to bolster Christian doctrine.

Jewish Comportment: Between Rashi's Commentaries to Proverbs and the Song of Songs

How did the Jews respond to Christian propaganda? Proverbs 9:7 describes the danger of rebuking a wicked man: "To correct a scoffer or rebuke (*mokhiaḥ*) a wicked man for his blemish is to call down abuse on oneself." Rashi provides insight into this verse:

47. Similarly, Rashi's commentary on Berakhot 12b.
48. An alternative explanation for the word *elil* is not idol, but rather "nought"; similar usage can be found in Rashi's glosses to Jeremiah 14:14; Zechariah 11:17.
49. Bernard Blumenkranz, "The Roman Church and the Jews," in *Essential Papers on Judaism and Christianity in Conflict*, ed. J. Cohen (New York University Press, 1991), 193–230; Amos Funkenstein, "Changes in Christian Anti-Jewish Polemics in the Twelfth Century," in *Perceptions of Jewish History* (University of California Press, 1993), 172–78.
50. Daniel Lasker, "Rashi and Maimonides on Christianity," in *Between Rashi and Maimonides, Themes in Medieval Jewish Thought, Literature and Exegesis*, ed. E. Kanarfogel and M. Sokolow (Yeshiva University Press, 2010), 3–21.

> *And he who reproves (mokhiaḥ) a wicked man, [that is] his blemish* (R 9:7) – It is a blemish to the one who reproves [a wicked man], for he [the wicked man] berates him (*meḥarpo*) and does not heed him. This is a warning not to speak with those who entice *(hamesitim)*, not even to reprove them (*lehokhiḥam*) or to draw them near (*ulekorvam*).

Rashi's application of this verse to enticers is an original interpretation, asserting the prohibition against communication with them. The gloss is linguistically linked to the biblical text through the use of the root Y-K-H (to reprove).[51] Let us compare this comment with Rashi's gloss to *Song of Songs* (7: 9–10), which also discusses communication with an enticer:

> *Let your breasts be [like clusters]* (v. 9) – And now, defend the truth of My Words, so that you will not be enticed (*titpati*) after the nations. May the good and wise among you be steadfast in their faith, to respond (*lehashiv devarim*) to those who entice you (*lamefatim*), so that the lesser ones among them [i.e., the Jews] will learn from them [from the good and wise among you]. *And your mouth* will be *like choicest wine* (v. 10) – Be careful (*hizahari*) with your answers (*biteshuvotayikh*) that they should be like the choicest wine. *That glides down smoothly to my beloved* – I am careful (*zehira*) to answer.

Let's explore the commonalities and distinctions between the two glosses. Both comments discuss how to respond to enticement. The Proverbs gloss employs the root S-U-T to depict the seducers, while the Song of Songs gloss uses the synonymous root P-T-H (to entice).[52] Moreover, both glosses feature the root Z-H-R (caution, warning) – once in the former and twice in the latter.[53] Rashi's consistent use of this term

51. Koehler and Baumgartner, *HALOT*, vol. 2, 410, s.v. יכח, "to rebuke, to reproach."
52. Ibid., vol. 3, 984–85, s.v. Iפתה, "to persuade, entice."
53. In the Proverbs gloss, the meaning of the root Z-H-R is "to warn" against doing something. By contrast, in the Song gloss, the same root implies "being careful" when doing something.

underscores the perceived danger associated with conversing with the enticers.

However, a notable difference emerges. While the Proverbs commentary explicitly declares that it is forbidden to speak with the seducers, the Song commentary encourages and guides the elders, the wisest of minds, on how to respond. Their answers are to be as refined as fine wine, in order to teach the laymen. Another distinction lies in the verbs used to describe speech: the former employs the verb "to speak" while the latter uses the verb "to answer."

The two glosses appear contradictory. In one, we are told to speak; in the other, not to speak. One can propose that the two sources are intended for different groups within the nation. The Song of Song's gloss is directed to the elders and scholars of the generation, instructing them to respond to enticers with effective answers. On the other hand, our Proverbs gloss is aimed at the laymen, explicitly warning them not to respond.

However, the Song of Songs gloss concludes with the phrase "So that the small ones among you will learn from them." In this context, "the small ones" refers to the laymen, who are expected to learn from the responses of the scholars. But why must they learn if it is forbidden for them to respond? By closely examining both texts, we shall propose a different distinction between the glosses.

The comment on Song of Songs, with its emphasis on the verb "to respond," pertains to the classic scenario in medieval times where a Christian enticer confronts a Jew with a claim, and the Jew needs effective responses.[54] Rashi directs the greatest minds of the generation to

54. Touitou has noted that in the writings of the northern French exegetes from the school of Rashi (Rashbam, Bekhor Shor), the phrase *teshuva laMinim,* in contrast to the phrase *teshuvat haMinim,* can mean a challenge posed to the *Minim,* i.e., a Jew directly confronting a Christian and not simply responding to a Christian claim. This does not apply to the Song gloss for two reasons. First, the phrase *teshuva leMinim* does not appear, and in its place is written: *Lehashiv devarim lamefatim;* the term *Minim* is not even mentioned. Second, the "smaller ones" are supposed to learn from the answers of the "elders," and Rashi would certainly not be encouraging the "small ones" to challenge Christian enticers. See Touitou, "Answering the Heretics" [in Hebrew], 144–48.

provide high-quality answers that can be disseminated among the less knowledgeable. On the other hand, the Proverbs gloss depicts a different situation. The warning against "speaking" describes a scenario where the Jew initiates contact with the enticer, making the first move. Promoting this type of conversation is strictly prohibited. The closing phrase, "even to rebuke them and to draw them near," suggests that at times Jews were initiating discussions with Christians to persuade them of the truthfulness of Judaism.

Does this gloss accurately reflect historical reality? Were Jews, during Rashi's lifetime, sometimes on the offensive?

"The Jewish Challenge"

Berger has shown that a substantial number of anti-Jewish treatises produced by Christian theologians in the eleventh and twelfth centuries state that the impetus for their writing was the Jewish challenge.[55] This term denotes situations where Jews posed questions to Christians regarding their Christian faith. Berger contends:

> The evidence, moreover, does not allow the assumption that these discussions were necessarily initiated by proselytizing Christians.... Whether Jews or Christians initiated these exchanges, the indications are overwhelming that they were real and frequent.[56]

Berger concludes that prior to the thirteenth century, in the absence of an organized, full-scale Christian missionizing movement, there were "lively, regular, often friendly debates between Jews and Christians, which were sometimes begun by the Jewish participant."[57]

Rashi's Proverbs gloss (R 9:7) appears to caution against this type of interfaith encounter initiated by a Jew. However, the tone of the exchange Rashi describes is not amicable. Rashi prohibits speaking to the enticer

55. Berger, "Mission to the Jews," 585–91.
56. Ibid., 586.
57. Berger, "Mission to the Jews," 591; Daniel Lasker, "The Jewish Critique of Christianity: In Search of a New Narrative," in *Studies in Christian-Jewish Relations,* Council of Centers on Jewish-Christian Relations, vol. 6 (2011), 1–9.

because he will taunt you and not listen. Rashi's use of the root H-R-P (to taunt)[58] employs sharp language akin to the Bible's description of the speech of Israel's enemies, such as Goliath (I Sam. 17:36) and Rav-Shakeh (II Kings 19:4). Rashi also uses this term to describe warring families seeking his mediation.[59]

What was the objective of these discussions initiated by Jews? Katz suggests a proselytizing component, noting that medieval Judaism "dares to hope to win adherents from other faiths, and sometimes even to take action with that aspiration in view."[60] However, Berger points to a different objective. He sees no indication that Jews engaged in religious discussions with Christians with the pragmatic aim of converting them. Instead, Jews challenged Christians as a manifestation of pride, seeking to boost their own morale and unsettle their adversaries.[61]

Regardless of the motive, Rashi unequivocally warns his readers not to initiate this type of discussion. This particular gloss is the only one that hints at a Jewish initiative; the remaining fifteen describe the Christian as making the first move.

The Impact

Given the understanding that in eleventh-century northern France (a) there is ongoing enticement to Christianity, and (b) Jews occasionally initiate interfaith discussions, can we assess the effect of these interactions upon the Jewish community? Two glosses in Rashi's commentary shed light upon the consequences.

Proverbs 9:13–18 describes the behavior of Madame Folly, personifying foolishness as a woman who attempts to entice youths into her home. She allures them by saying, "Stolen waters are sweet, and bread eaten furtively is tasty" (9:17). Regarding this verse, Rashi writes:

> *Stolen waters are sweet* – There is no pleasure from intimacy as great as the pleasure from intimacy with a married woman. And

58. Koehler and Baumgartner, *HALOT*, vol. 1, 355, s.v. I חרף, "to annoy, taunt."
59. Elfenbein, *Teshuvot Rashi*, 81–82 (no. 70).
60. Jacob Katz, *Exclusiveness and Tolerance*, 81.
61. Berger, "Mission to the Jews," 590–91.

> also, regarding the *minut*,[62] *stolen waters are sweet*, for they were afraid to do it [i.e., practice *minut*] in public, but did it in secret.

Drawing from the Talmud (Sanhedrin 26b), Rashi interprets our verse as a metaphor for adultery, suggesting that intercourse with a married woman is especially pleasurable. His second explanation then extends the metaphor to spiritual adultery – to the worship of other gods. In this context, "stolen waters" refers to individuals involved in *minut* clandestinely due to fear of doing so in public.[63] This explanation is original to Rashi. Applying it to Christians is difficult, since their majority status allowed them to worship openly. Consequently, the verse perhaps refers to Jews practicing Christianity privately.

Rashi acknowledges the existence of Jewish apostasy. In Proverbs 23:26–28, a warning is issued against the dangers of the strange woman. The warning concludes with the verse "She, too, lies in wait as if for prey, and she will increase the unfaithful among men." On this verse, Rashi writes:

> *And she will increase the unfaithful among men* (R 23:28) – Increasing in Israel those who are treacherous to God. The text is speaking about *minut*.[64]

Once again, there is no known source for Rashi's comment. Here Rashi implies that large-scale conversion to Christianity was occurring in his lifetime.

Does this comment reflect historical reality? Was there large-scale conversion to Christianity during Rashi's lifetime? Historians stress the difficulty of conclusively determining the number of Jews in Ashkenaz who embraced Christianity during the Middle Ages. The prevailing consensus suggests that this was a limited phenomenon.[65] The large number

62. Standard printed editions read "mitzva" instead of *minut.*
63. Use of the word "secret (*beseter*)" links the gloss to the text of Proverbs: "And bread eaten furtively (*setarim*)."
64. The closing phrase, "The text… *minut*," is absent from standard printed editions due to censorship.
65. Grossman, *The Early Sages of France* [in Hebrew], 500–503; David Malkiel, "Jews

of rabbinic responsa dealing with questions of Jewish apostasy does not necessarily reflect the frequency of such incidents, as even the isolated case required attention from rabbinic authorities.[66]

Although Rabbeinu Tam, Rashi's grandson, wrote in his *Sefer Ha-Yashar* that "more than twenty bills of divorce involving apostates were executed in Paris and [Île-de-] France,"[67] Katz believes that this figure was an aggregate from different time periods rather than a singular event.[68] Grossman, on the other hand, contends that this number is indicative of widespread apostasy, considering the small size of medieval Jewish communities in the twelfth century.[69]

The numerous warnings against Christian enticement in Rashi's Proverbs commentary (a non-halakhic work) and even the acknowledgment of widespread apostasy in one comment align with the view that apostasy was more common than previously thought. Berger draws a similar historical conclusion:

> In the last generation, arguments have been presented for a variety of theses that would have seemed implausible thirty years ago; that Northern European Jews discussed biblical texts with Christians in non-polemical contexts... that sharp polemical exchanges, sometimes initiated by Jews, took place on the streets and even in homes, that Jews were sorely tempted by Christianity and converted more often than we imagined.[70]

---

and Apostates in Medieval Europe – Boundaries Real and Imagined," *Past and Present* 194 (2007): 7–9.

66. J. Katz, *Exclusiveness and Tolerance*, 67; Jeremy Cohen, "The Medieval Jewish Apostate: Peter Alfonsi, Hermann of Cologne, and Pablo Christiani," in *Jewish Apostasy in the Modern World*, ed. T. Endelman (Holmes and Meier, 1987), 23.
67. Translation taken from Malkiel, "Jews and Apostates," 8.
68. Katz, *Exclusiveness and Tolerance*, 67.
69. Grossman, *The Early Sages of France* [in Hebrew], 503; Haym Soloveitchik, "Can Halakhic Texts Talk History," *AJS Review* 3 (1978): 172. According to Soloveitchik, the Jewish communities during Rashi's era were "generally tiny, averaging from a handful to a score of families," which was approximately two generations before the period described by Grossman.
70. David Berger, "A Generation of Scholarship on Jewish-Christian Interaction in the Medieval World," *Tradition* 38:2 (2004): 5.

In sum, we have identified the centrality of enticing speech in the Proverbs text and noted that Rashi consistently applies it to ongoing Christian missionizing efforts. Thus, Christian enticement emerges as the dominant polemical theme within Rashi's Proverbs commentary, further unifying the composition from start to finish.

AUTHORSHIP

The cohesiveness of Rashi's commentary is also tied to the question of authorship. Proverbs' introductory superscription ascribes authorship to "Solomon, son of David, king of Israel" (1:1), a claim reiterated in two other chapter headings:

> The proverbs of Solomon. (10:1)
>
> These too are proverbs of Solomon, which the men of King Hezekiah of Judah copied. (25:1)

It makes sense to attribute this genre of literature to Solomon, given that elsewhere in the Bible he is credited with composing three thousand proverbs (I Kings 5:12). To explain why there are only 915 proverbs in this book, Rashi offers an explanation:

> *Three thousand proverbs* – Three studies (*alafim*) of proverbs. "The proverbs of Solomon" is written three times in the book of Proverbs.[71]

Rashi interprets the Hebrew word *alafim* not as thousands but as "studies."[72] Thus, the phrase "three thousand proverbs," means three "studies" of proverbs, alluding to the three units in the book of Proverbs that begin with the heading "Proverbs of Solomon."

Other Proverbs verses, however, suggest the involvement of additional contributing writers, such as the Sages:

71. No known source.
72. Such as the meaning of the same root in Job 33:33.

> Incline your ear and listen to the words of the Sages. (22:17)

> These also are by the Sages. (24:23)

The book also introduces named personalities, including: "Agur son of Yakeh… the speech of the man Ithiel, to Ithiel and Ucal" (30:1), and "Lemuel, king of Massa"(31:1). Who are these individuals, and is it possible that Solomon drew material from their compositions?

Agur and Lemuel

Contemporary scholarship views Proverbs as a collection of wise sayings culled from various authors, including those enumerated above.[73] This notion is not entirely new; already Saadia Gaon (tenth century) wrote:

> The simple meaning of the text, which our Sages[74] refer to as *peshuto shel mikra*, is that there was a man named Agur who had a teacher named Ithiel. This student received and transmitted the teachings of his teacher… and Lemuel received and transmitted the ethical teachings of his mother. He (Agur) was famous among the people.[75]

Similarly, Ibn Ezra posits that Agur was an esteemed and knowledgeable figure, a contemporary of Solomon, from whom Solomon collected words of wisdom.[76]

---

73. Fox, *Proverbs 1–9: The Anchor Bible,* 6.
74. "Sages" in this context refers to *Ḥazal,* rabbinic scholars, as opposed to the mention of Sages in the Proverbs text, which, according to modern scholarship, refers to secular wise men.
75. M. Zer-Kavod and Y. Kil, *Mishlei with the Jerusalem Commentary,* (Mosad HaRav Kook, 2014), 374 n. 1a. Rashi was not familiar with Saadia's commentary on Proverbs, which was written in Arabic. However, Rashi does mention seeing certain explications of Saadia on the book of Daniel, quoted by other authors; see Rashi's commentary on Daniel 7:25, 8:14, 11:14.
76. Comment on Proverbs 30:1. He viewed the name Lemuel as an epithet for Solomon.

By contrast, based on rabbinic writings, Rashi views the names Agur, Yakeh, Ithiel, and Ucal – enumerated together in one verse (30:1) – as pseudonyms for Solomon. Rashi explains:

> *The words of Agur son of Yakeh* (R 30:1) – The words of Solomon, who gathered (*agar*) understanding and vomited it (*heikia*); this is how the Rabbis interpreted it.[77]
>
> *The speech of the man to Ithiel* – The man Solomon said this speech about himself because of "Ithiel" [*iti El*; i.e., God is with me] – because he relied upon his wisdom to amass much gold and silver, and many horses and many wives, all of which he was warned not to do (Deut. 17: 16–17). But he said: *Iti El* [since God is with me] – I will have many wives and they will not sway my heart, I will amass gold and not turn away, and I will amass horses and not return the nation to Egypt. "To Ithiel and Ucal" – because I said: God is with me (*iti El*), and I will be able (*ukhal*) to do [all this] and [still I] will not falter.

Rashi connects the name Agur with the Hebrew root A-G-R (to gather), referring to the extensive wisdom that Solomon gathered.[78] However, metaphorically, Solomon "vomited" this wisdom, as suggested by the term Yakeh, related to the root letters K-Y-A (to vomit). Solomon believed himself exempt from the three restrictions placed on a Jewish king, because he felt "Itiel," a combination of *iti* (with me) and *El* (God). Solomon reasoned that with God's presence and his own above-average wisdom, he would be shielded from any negative consequences. Rashi then explicates the name Ucal as a verb: "I can" [do it and not be harmed]. However, Solomon later realized the flaw in his reasoning. This homiletical explanation skillfully links the names Agur, Yakeh, Ithiel, and Ucal with Solomon's folly.

77. See *Tanḥuma, Va'era* 5.
78. Note also the similarity between the Hebrew words *ben* (son) in the phrase "ben (the son of) Yakeh" and *bina* (understanding).

Rashi employs a similar technique to elucidate the name Lemuel (31:1), which he views as a fusion of two words: *lemu,* meaning "for the sake of," and *El,* meaning "God."[79] Solomon recounts his mother's reprimand "for the sake of God," indicating that he acknowledges his foolish behavior before the Almighty. This behavior was his marriage to the daughter of Pharaoh and his lack of discretion on their wedding night:

> *A speech where his mother rebuked him* (R 31:1) – When he married [the daughter of] Pharaoh on the day of the dedication of the Temple, she brought for him many musical instruments, and he was awake all night, and he slept the next morning until the fourth hour, as is explained in the *Pesikta.*[80] And the keys of the Temple were under his head. Regarding that time, we learn: "About the morning offering that is offered at the fourth hour" (Eduyot 6:1) – and his mother entered and chastised him with all this speech.

Solomon's nighttime levity caused him to oversleep, resulting in a delay in the morning sacrifice on the Temple's inaugural day.

Accordingly, in both cases, the named individuals are interpreted as epithets for Solomon, thereby excluding the involvement of external authors in the composition of Proverbs.

The Sages and the Men of King Hezekiah

Nevertheless, the words "These also are by the sages" (24:23) suggest that various sages contributed. Did Solomon borrow from their writings?

The answer hinges upon the meaning of the prepositional letter *lamed* preceding the word "the sages"(*laḥakhamim;* 24:23). This letter encompasses various meanings, such as "to," "of," and "for." Rashi clarifies as follows:

---

79. Rashi brings a similar example from the book of Job (40:4), in which two words are combined into one: *lemofi* (40:4) – *lemo* (into), *fi* (my mouth).
80. This allegorical explanation is not extant in the version of the *Pesikta* that we have today. However, it is present in Leviticus Rabba 12:5.

> *These also are (la) the sages* (R 24:23) – All the issues in the following section are directed to the sages who sit in judgment, that they should not show favoritism in judgment because it is not good.[81]

Rashi reads the letter *lamed* as "to" rather than "by," teaching that Solomon provides guidance "to" the wise men on the principles of proper judgment. Thus, the Sages, like the named personalities mentioned above, are not involved in the writing of Proverbs.

What role did the men of King Hezekiah play in the book's composition? After all, the text explicitly mentions their direct involvement:

> These too are proverbs of Solomon, which the men of King Hezekiah of Judah *he'etiku.* (25:1)

The key lies in understanding the Hebrew verb *he'etiku.* While its precise meaning is uncertain, possibilities include "copy," "transcribe," and "collect,"[82] suggesting some form of participation in the editing process.[83] Rashi, however, explains differently and interprets the verb as "to strengthen" and "to return to expound" (R 25:1). Although his exact intention is unclear, he seems to be speaking of the reinterpretation or dissemination of the proverbs, thereby strengthening their presence within the biblical canon. Abba Shaul gives a similar explanation:

> "These are the proverbs of Solomon which the men of Hezekiah king of Judah *he'etiku*" (Prov. 25:1) – Not that they removed, but they took their time [deciding whether to remove the book from the canon]. Abba Shaul says: Not that they took their time, but that they interpreted. (*Avot DeRabbi Natan* 1:4)

According to Rashi's reading, King Hezekiah's men are not engaged in the editing process but rather in a subsequent stage of reinterpretation.

81. See *Tanḥuma, Mishpatim* 4.
82. See Fox, *Proverbs 10–31: The Anchor Bible*, 777–78.
83. The Talmud (Bava Batra 15a) interprets the verb as "to write."

One notes a recurring pattern in Rashi's commentary: Aside from Solomon, no one is involved in the composition of the Proverbs text.

Solomon – Between Rashi's Commentaries on Proverbs and the Song of Songs

A comparison between Rashi's commentaries on Proverbs and Song of Songs reveals an interesting contrast in the treatment of the name Solomon. In the former, all references to Solomon (and other named personalities) are equated with Solomon, the king of Israel. In the latter, every mention of Solomon is linked to the King of the Universe. Though each commentary takes a different approach, they share a common aim – to enhance the holiness of the composition. In Proverbs, this is achieved by attributing sole authorship to Solomon, while in Song of Songs the narrative is elevated through dedicating the composition to the Almighty. This divergence underscores Rashi's deliberate effort to infuse each text with heightened spiritual significance, appropriate to the theme and context of each composition.

To sum up: Rashi's commentary on Proverbs encounters a number of verses that imply the involvement of multiple contributors, both individuals (Agur, Yakeh, Ithiel, Ucal, Lemuel) and collectives (Sages, King Hezekiah's men). However, he explains these verses so as to insist that Solomon was the sole author. This exclusive emphasis on Solomonic authorship forms yet another dimension of cohesion within the narrative.

FINAL SUMMARY

The book of Proverbs presents fundamental questions regarding its content and structure. Why was this seemingly secular, utilitarian, and randomly organized narrative deemed worthy of inclusion in the biblical canon? What criteria could possibly justify its selection as holy writ?

Rashi answers these questions with a *mashal*, an allegorical explanation. Through his allegoric lens, scores of aphorisms in Proverbs portraying human and animal behavior are elevated to a higher spiritual plane. By applying nearly 150 verses to the world of Torah study, he transforms this collection into an educational Torah manual for student and teacher. This comprehensive guidebook explores components vital for successful

Jewish education, including insights into curriculum planning, factors affecting motivation, and an understanding of essential pedagogical tools and methods. Thus, his *mashal* unifies the rich tapestry of proverbs found in the book of Proverbs, weaving them together under a singular thematic umbrella.

Analysis of Rashi's educational approach in his other works reveals a correlation with his teachings in Proverbs, suggesting that his educational beliefs transcend specific textual contexts and reflect his overarching view on education.

The transformation of Proverbs into a Jewish educational manual achieves an important objective beyond cohesion: It "Judaizes" the composition. This process of "Judaization" is furthered through Rashi's interpretation of the archetypes found in Proverbs, which are portrayed as stark character contrasts – the foolish and the wise, the wicked and the righteous, the impoverished and the affluent, the lazy and the diligent. Rashi consistently relates these oppositions to the quest for Torah knowledge.

Analysis of Rashi's treatment of the two main opposing female figures – the strange woman and the capable wife – reveals an additional layer within his commentary. The former, prominently featured in the early chapters of the text, is equated with Christianity, whereas the latter, her antithesis, depicted in the final chapter of Proverbs, represents Torah. Rashi shapes his glosses on the *eshet ḥayil* (Torah), to counterbalance the dangers posed by the strange woman (Christianity). The capable wife brings blessing, prosperity, and life, while the strange woman brings poverty and death. While the strange woman leads her victims to forsake the yoke of commandments and descend into Gehinnom, the capable wife shields those who adhere to her commandments from such calamity. Thus, Rashi's glosses on these contrasting female figures, whose placement within the text frames the narrative, reveal his polemical motives.

Similarly, recognizing the significant role of speech in the book of Proverbs, Rashi relates the "speech" aphorisms to Christian missionizing efforts. Applying more than fifteen verses to their rhetoric that aims to persuade, he exposes their deceitful intentions and techniques and cautions against engaging in any form of interfaith dialogue. Rashi's focus on this motif suggests that Jewish apostasy was more prevalent than previously believed. Thus the motif of Christian enticement emerges as the dominant polemical motif spanning the composition from beginning to end.

In sum, the holistic nature of Rashi's commentary on Proverbs is manifested on several levels. Overall, it unifies the diverse range of proverbs, weaving them together beneath a cohesive thematic framework, thereby imbuing the narrative with spiritual depth and strengthening internal Jewish values. In particular, it leverages the proverbs as a tool to counteract foreign, external challenges, bolstering Jewish resilience against the allure of Christianity.

Rashi's Commentary on Ecclesiastes

Chapter Six

Introduction

Perplexing, troubling, thought provoking, the book of Ecclesiastes[1] examines the world and the nature of human existence with stark honesty. What is the purpose of human toil? Why does wickedness often go unpunished while the righteous suffer? In contrast to the pragmatic wisdom found in the book of Proverbs, Ecclesiastes offers a speculative approach to wisdom. Rather than prescribing how one should live, it engages in a profound exploration of the meaning and significance of life itself.

As Kohelet wrestles with life's fundamental questions, his existential journey poses serious challenges. First, some of his statements appear to contradict fundamental tenets of Judaism, for instance by suggesting that the fate of man is the same as that of the animals and questioning the ascent of the human soul to an afterlife (3:19–21).

Furthermore, his statements sometimes contradict one another. For instance, he asserts, "Anger is better than laughter" (7:3), yet he also

1. The term "Ecclesiastes" will designate the work itself, while the name "Kohelet" will represent both the author and the work.

acclaims laughter, stating, "Of laughter I said, 'It is to be praised,'" (2:2). How can these opposing views coexist in the same text?

Similarly, he presents contrasting views on wisdom, now depicting wisdom as a shelter (7:12) that protects those who possess it, now expressing a sense of its futility: "For as wisdom grows, vexation grows; to increase learning is to increase heartache" (1:18).

He also expresses contradictory views of life's pleasures. He insists that there is nothing better for man than "to eat, and drink, and enjoy himself" (8:15) in his toil, suggesting that life's simple pleasures are its ultimate purpose; yet he also declares, "All such things are wearisome" (1:8). Life, in this view, is an exhausting and ultimately unfulfilling endeavor.

Why was Ecclesiastes selected to be incorporated within the Holy Scripture? How does Rashi make sense of this composition?

Unlike his commentaries on Song of Songs and Proverbs, Rashi's commentary on Ecclesiastes is not introduced by any preface or programmatic statement. Nevertheless, two fundamental observations will help clarify his approach. First, Rashi's commentary follows a two-tiered structure, consistent with his commentary on the other biblical books. Second, his analysis of key terms and phrases at the outset of his commentary assists in unraveling this narrative.

KEY TERMS AND PHRASES

Hevel

The term "vanity" (*hevel*) occurs frequently throughout the book of Ecclesiastes, appearing thirty-eight times – almost as many times as it occurs in the rest of the Bible. Such repetition emphasizes the term's pivotal role in understanding the core message of this narrative.

Although Rashi does not define the term, his understanding of its general meaning can be inferred from context. For instance, in the following examples the meaning appears to be "futility:"

> *This too is hevel* (R 2:19) – This too is one of the *havalim* that were created in the world, that the wise man labors, and the fool inherits.

> *This too* (R 2:26) – This is one of the *havalim* that were given to creatures, that they labor, and someone else takes.

> *This too* (R 8:10) – This is one of the *havalim* that were given to the world to weary mankind, for the Holy One, blessed be He, does not hasten to mete out retribution, and then people think that there is neither judgment nor Judge.

Sometimes Rashi's explication of the word seems to convey other meanings. It can suggest transience:

> *The few days of the life of his hevel* (R 6:12) – Which are limited in number.

It can denote meaninglessness:

> *For there are many things* (R 6:11) – With which he occupied himself during his lifetime, such as the games of the kings, monkeys, elephants, and lions. They increased his *hevel,* and what remains for him after he dies?

It can indicate falsehood:

> *For despite many dreams, etc.* (R 5:6) – For [despite all that] dreams, prophets of *hevel,* "and many words" – tell you, to part with the Omnipresent.

Only in one instance does Rashi provide a direct definition of the word:

> *All that comes* (R 11:8) – Upon him will be *hevel* and darkness. The word *hevel* sometimes refers to misfortune and troubles, as in, "For he [the stillborn child] comes into *hevel* and departs into darkness" (Eccl. 6:4).

Thus, the word *hevel* carries a range of meanings, from negative connotations such as "futility" and "falsehood" to more neutral interpretations like "transience" and "void of meaning." Its precise definition is contingent upon the specific context in which it appears.

"Havel Havalim! **All Is** *Hevel!"*

The motto of this composition, which frames the entire narrative, consists of repeating the term *hevel*: "*Havel havalim*! All is *hevel*!" (1:2, 12:8). Rashi interprets:

> *Havel havalim, all is hevel, said Kohelet* (R 1:2) – Kohelet complains about all that was created in the seven days of Creation, that it is "*havel havalim*, all is *hevel*".... Seven *havalim* [are mentioned], corresponding to the seven days of Creation.[2]

And in a shorter version near the book's closing:

> *All is hevel* (R 12:8) – All that was created during the six days of Creation."

Rashi proposes that the sevenfold reference to H-V-L in the second verse of the book subtly alludes to the seven days of Creation.[3] His introduction of the Creation motif is connected to the subsequent verses of Ecclesiastes, wherein Kohelet describes the unchanging laws of nature established at the world's creation: the daily cycle of the sun rising and

2. See *Kohelet Zuta* 1:2; Ecclesiastes Rabba 1:2. There are two extant versions of the Midrash on Ecclesiastes: Ecclesiastes Rabba and a briefer rendition, *Kohelet Zuta*, also known as "Minor Ecclesiastes." When Rashi refers to the Midrash on Ecclesiastes, scholars have concluded that he is drawing from the latter, shorter version. For further insights into this determination, see Marc Hirshman, *Midrash Kohelet Rabbah 1–6* (The Schechter Institute of Jewish Studies, 2016), 73–74, www.schechter.ac.il/flipbooks/midrash-kohelet-raba/search-1.pdf. Consequently, when citing Rashi's source from the Midrash on Kohelet, I will initially indicate *Kohelet Zuta*.
3. The number seven is derived as follows: The first word of the verse, *havel*, is singular, therefore equaling one; the second word, *havalim*, a plural form, equals two; the fifth word, *havel*, equals one; the sixth word, *havalim*, equals two; the eighth word, *havel*, again equals one. This yields a total of seven.

setting (1:5–6)[4] and the perpetual flow of water back to its sources (1:7). Interpreting these verses metaphorically, Rashi writes:

> *The words of Kohelet* (R 1:1) – [Is followed by] "The sun rises" (v. 5), "All the rivers flow into the sea" (v. 7). He refers to the wicked as the "sun," the "moon," and the "sea," which receive no reward. So it was taught in *Sifrei* (Deut. 1). I learned from there that the section refers to the wicked and compares them to the rising sun, which ultimately sets.[5]

And a few verses later, Rashi continues in a similar vein:

> *Round and round goes* (R 1:6) – Also the wicked, no matter how much their sun rises, they will ultimately set. No matter how much they gain power, they will ultimately return to their stench. "From filth they came, and to filth they will go."[6]

According to Rashi, what is *hevel* is not creation itself but rather the prosperity of the wicked, which, like the sun in its cycle, will eventually set.

Rashi's inclusion of the phrase "From filth they came, and to filth they will go" in his gloss is a deliberate act with a subtle polemical intent. This phrase mirrors a statement found in Tractate Avoda Zara 17a concerning a conversation between R. Eliezer and a student of Jesus of Nazareth. By incorporating this phrase, Rashi subtly suggests a parallel between the prosperity of the wicked, a message he gleans from the text of Ecclesiastes, and the prosperity of Christians during his lifetime. He implies

---

4. For insights into the interpretive history of verse 6, which describes the *ruaḥ* – whether it pertains to the sun or the wind – see Sara Japhet's article "'Goes to the South and Turns to the North, (Ecclesiastes 1:6): The Sources and History of the Exegetical Traditions," *Jewish Studies Quarterly* 1 (1993/1994): 289–322.
5. The celestial bodies are metaphorically interpreted as representing the wicked. This interpretation aligns with the overall negative tone established by the term *divrei* at the beginning of the book, a word which, according to the Midrash, implies harsh words or reproof.
6. The quotation is from Avoda Zara 17a.

that just as the sun eventually sets, so too will the power and influence of Christians ultimately decline.

Thus, Rashi employs the mechanism of metaphor to uncover deeper meaning within the description of the luminary and primal elements at the beginning of Ecclesiastes.

Yitron

Kohelet frequently explores the concept of "value," often employing the term *yitron*[7] (as well as *sakhar* and *revaḥ*) to convey this idea, with the term introduced as early as verse 3. Rashi provides insight into its meaning:

> *What yitron* (R 1:3) – Reward (*sakhar*) and gain (*motar*).[8]

While *yitron* typically denotes "greater" when comparing two objects or parts,[9] within the context of our verse it signifies profit or benefit.[10] Rashi implies that meaning or value is measured through gain and reward, a notion which M.V. Fox defines as follows:

> We say that an action or quality is meaningful when it accomplishes something external to and appropriate to the action.[11]

The recurring presence of this term and its synonyms throughout the text seems to suggest that Kohelet is deeply concerned with the notion of benefit and its significance in life.

"Beneath the Sun"

In the very same verse, we encounter the phrase "beneath the sun" (1:3), which is a hallmark expression appearing twenty-nine times in

---

7. Similarly, *yeter* and *motar.*
8. In Ecclesiastes 3:19 the term *motar* means superiority.
9. See *Siftei Ḥakhamim* ad loc.
10. Koehler and Baumgartner, *HALOT*, vol. 2, p. 453: "1. What comes of, result (Qoh. 1:3), 2. Profit, advantage (Qoh. 10:11)."
11. M.V. Fox, "The Inner Structure of Qohelet's Thought," in *Qohelet in the Context of Wisdom*, ed. A. Schoors (Peeters, 1998), 225.

Ecclesiastes and absent from all other biblical books. Rashi explains the phrase as follows:

> *[What reward does a man have] beneath (taḥat) the sun* (R 1:3) – Equivalent to the Torah, which is called light, as it states, "And the Torah is light" (Prov. 6:23). All the labor which he does instead of engaging in Torah, what reward does it yield?[12]

Later on, he notes more succinctly:

> "*Beneath (taḥat) the sun* (R 4:1) – Instead of the Torah."

The preposition *taḥat,* which in these verses is usually understood as "beneath," can also mean "instead of" or "equivalent to," and Rashi chooses this meaning. Rashi metaphorically interprets the "sun" as the light of the Torah, drawing on the statement in Proverbs "And the Torah is light" (Prov. 6:23).[13] This interpretation asserts that any pursuit undertaken in lieu of Torah will ultimately yield no gain or reward. Thus, Rashi urges us to choose engagement with Torah over worldly occupations.

The Talmud also links this phrase to the world of Torah, but slightly differently:

> And the school of R. Yannai said: Under the sun is where [man] has no [profit from his labor; however,] before the sun, [i.e., when engaged in the study of Torah, which preceded the sun,] he does have profit. (Shabbat 30b)

---

12. See *Kohelet Zuta* 1:3; Ecclesiastes Rabba 1:3.
13. A similar comparison between Torah and light is found in a later verse: "*And the light is sweet* (R 11:7) – The light of Torah is sweet. *And it is good for the eyes to behold the sun* – And fortunate are the students whose eyes see a legal opinion whitened and clarified thoroughly. So is it expounded in *Aggadat Tehillim*." However, in his commentary on 4:7, Rashi notes that the phrase "beneath the sun" is interchangeable with "beneath the sky"; this observation reveals an inconsistency in his explanations.

Based upon the notion that the Torah preceded the creation of the sun and the physical world (Pesaḥim 54a), the school of R. Yannai explicates the phrase "*taḥat* the sun" as "after the sun," thus asserting that the Torah, which existed before the sun, indeed brings profit. Why did Rashi favor his interpretation ("equivalent to") over that of the Talmud ("after") when both interpretations lead to the same conclusion? Rashi's choice is likely due to its stronger alignment with Hebrew grammar. In general, the preposition *taḥat* can mean "underneath" or "in place of,"[14] but not "after," lending linguistic legitimacy to Rashi's homiletical interpretation.

Rashi warns against engaging in mundane chatter, which ultimately leads to exhaustion and frustration:[15]

> *All things are wearisome, etc., the eye shall not be sated from seeing, nor shall the ear be filled* (R 1:8) – This refers back to "What profit [has man]" if he exchanges the study of Torah to speak wasteful words? They are only wearisome, and he will not be able to acquire them all, and if he comes to engage in the vision of the eye, it will not be satisfied, and if in the hearing of the ear, it will not be filled.

By contrast, Torah study not only brings satisfaction but also fosters creativity and innovation:

> *Only that shall happen which has happened, etc.* (R 1:9) – In whatever he learns, concerning a matter that is other than the sun, there is nothing new. He will see only that which already was, which was created in the six days of Creation. But one who engages in Torah, constantly finds new insights therein, as the matter is stated, "Let her breasts satisfy you at all times" (Prov. 5:19) – this breast, whenever the infant touches it, he finds taste

14. Koehler and Baumgartner, *HALOT*, vol. 4, 1722–23: "Below, in place of, instead of."
15. M.V. Fox supports Rashi's interpretation that our verse refers to speech, asserting that the Hebrew word *dabar* (plural: *debarim*) is never used for physical entities, like the sun or wind, but specifically denotes words. See M.V. Fox, *A Time to Tear Down and a Time to Build Up: A Rereading of Ecclesiastes* (W.B. Eerdmans, 1999), 167.

> in it. Thus, we find in Tractate Ḥagiga (14b), that R. Eliezer b. Hyrcanus said things that no ear had ever heard before concerning the account of the Divine Chariot.

Rashi supports his assertion about the innovative nature of Torah study with a reference to the book of Proverbs, as it was interpreted in the Talmud:

> "Let her breasts satisfy you at all times" (Prov. 5:19) – Why were matters of Torah compared to a breast? Just as with a breast, whenever a baby touches it, he finds milk in it, so too, with matters of Torah. Whenever a person meditates upon them, he finds new meaning in them. (Eiruvin 54b)

By likening Torah learning to the constant nourishment a baby receives from its mother's breast, the Talmud emphasizes the continuous discovery of new knowledge in Torah study. While the Talmud introduces this metaphor, it does not explicitly connect it to the verse in Ecclesiastes; this connection is an original suggestion by Rashi.

Rashi illustrates the creativity connected with Torah study by bringing a quotation from Tractate Ḥagiga, likely referring to the following incident:

> The Sages taught: An incident involving Rabban Yoḥanan b. Zakkai, who was riding on a donkey and was traveling along the way, and R. Elazar b. Arakh[16] was riding a donkey behind him.... [R. Elazar] said to him: My teacher, allow me to say before you one

16. Note the discrepancy regarding the identity of the Rabbi. While Rashi identifies him as R. Eliezer b. Hyrcanus, the Talmud recounts the episode as involving R. Elazar b. Arakh. Moreover, R. Eliezer b. Hyrcanus prided himself on never stating anything that he had not heard from his teachers (see Sukka 27b), raising questions about Rashi's identification of the Sage. In the notes on this verse in mg.alhatorah.org, Hillel Novetsky notes that Rashi seems to have mixed two sources: Ḥagiga 14b and *Avot DeRabbi Natan* 6:4. The former mentions R. Elazar b. Arakh, whereas the latter mentions R. Eliezer b. Hyrcanus. The former discusses the Divine Chariot, whereas the latter refers to an explanation that "no ear had ever heard before."

> thing that you taught me.... He said to him: Speak.... Immediately, R. Elazar b. Arakh began [to discuss] the Design of the [Divine] Chariot and expounded, and fire descended from heaven and encircled all the trees in the field, and all [the trees] began reciting song.... Rabban Yoḥanan b. Zakkai stood and kissed [R. Elazar b. Arakh] on his head, and said: Blessed be God, Lord of Israel, who gave our father Abraham a son who knows [how] to understand, investigate, and expound the Design of the [Divine] Chariot.[17]

This supernatural incident illustrates the innovative nature of Torah Study.

Rashi's interpretation of the pivotal terms *hevel, havel havalim, yitron,* and "beneath the sun" at the beginning of Ecclesiastes sets the stage for his commentary on the entire text. The reading of the text as an allegory about Torah and its benefits and rewards is the guiding principle in his exposition of this book. Let us examine this core theme.

TORAH

At the center of Rashi's interpretation of Ecclesiastes is the equation of "wisdom" with Torah:

> *I set my mind to study* (R 1:13) – Torah, which is the wisdom [referred to in this verse].
>
> *And my heart conducted itself with wisdom* (R 2:3) – Even when my body was being indulged with wine, my mind prevailed to hold onto wisdom – Torah.
>
> *My thoughts also turned to consider wisdom* (R 2:12) – I turned away from all my affairs to delve into Torah.
>
> *I tried with wisdom* (R 7:23) – With Torah.

17. Ḥagiga 14b.

By contrast, the state of "foolishness" is understood as wickedness (R 2:13), which presumably means disregard for the teachings of the Torah.

Likewise, Rashi interprets the term "wise" in Ecclesiastes as referring to the "righteous" individual, whereas "fool" signifies the "wicked:"[18]

> *So I reflected, etc.* (R 2:15) – Perhaps I will think in my heart from now on that as it happens to the [fool=] *wicked* man, so will it happen to me, so why should I be more [wise=] *righteous*...?

In a similar vein, mundane activities are reinterpreted through a spiritual lens, with "eating and drinking" equated with engagement in Torah study (R 5:17, 8:15), and inactivity and laziness associated with those who abandon the Torah (R 10:15).

Torah Study

Rashi's interpretation deals both with the individuals involved in Torah study and the characteristics of the sacred texts themselves.

Individuals Involved in Study: The Importance of Numbers

The book of Ecclesiastes (4: 8–12) stresses that Torah is not meant to be a solitary pursuit. First acknowledging the disadvantage of being alone, having "neither son nor brother" (v. 8), Rashi explains:

> *Who has neither son nor brother* (R 4:8) – If he is a Torah scholar, he neither acquires for himself a disciple, who is like a son, nor a companion, who is like a brother... *there is no end to his labor* – He toils in study... *and his eye is never satisfied with riches* – He will not feel satisfaction with the insights of Torah, for a person learns much Torah from his students.... *For whom do I labor* – Since I do not develop students.[19]

---

18. Similarly, regarding the fool, see R 4:5, 5:3.
19. See *Kohelet Zuta* 4:9; Ecclesiastes Rabba 4:9. Rashi brings two additional explanations, applying the verse to a bachelor and a merchant.

Despite this scholar's accumulation of extensive Torah knowledge, he could have acquired even more if he had nurtured students. Moreover, he now has no one to whom he can transmit the fruits of his labor.

Kohelet proceeds to extol the advantages of companionship:

> Two are better off than one, in that they have greater benefit from their earnings. For should they fall, one can raise the other; but woe to him who is alone and falls with no companion to raise him! (4: 9–10)

Elucidating these verses, Rashi initially provides a literal explanation before offering the following allegorical interpretation:

> *For should they fall* (R 4:10) – And regarding studies, if his studies are too difficult for him, his partner will restore them to him, or if he errs and is not exact in what he heard from his teacher, his partner will come and set him straight.[20]

In his explanation, Rashi emphasizes the educational benefits of collaborative study pairs,[21] wherein the stronger student can support and complement his partner's learning process, leading to a more thorough and precise grasp of the material.

Continuing, the text uses the metaphor of a three-ply cord, which Rashi explains literally before drawing a metaphorical connection to Torah study:

> *A threefold cord is not readily broken* (R 4:12) – Another explanation: Whoever is a Torah scholar, as well as his son and his grandson, the Torah will never cease from his seed.[22]

---

20. See *Kohelet Zuta* 4:9–10; Ecclesiastes Rabba 4:9.
21. Makkot 10a delineates the pitfalls of solitary study.
22. See Ketubot 62b.

Three generations of study firmly establish the Torah within that household, because as Rashi notes elsewhere, "The Torah naturally returns to its own home."[23]

Rashi then brings a third explanation, also connected to the realm of Torah:

> Another explanation: "The threefold cord," [i.e., one well versed] in Scripture, Mishna, and proper conduct (*derekh eretz*), will not quickly sin.[24]

A signature feature of Rashi's Bible commentary is his tendency to offer dual explanations for a given word or phrase, with triple interpretations being exceedingly rare. Amnon Shapira, discussing the double explanations connected by the phrase "another explanation" in Rashi's Genesis commentary, notes that where three explanations are provided, the third is typically a variant of the second, thus upholding the general principle of duality within Rashi's commentary.[25] This observation finds support in Rashi's triple explanation of our verse in Ecclesiastes, wherein both the second and third interpretations relate to the world of Torah study.

The importance of numbers is highlighted in an additional explanation of Rashi; Kohelet states:

> Sow your seed in the morning, and don't hold back your hand in the evening, since you don't know which is going to succeed, the one or the other, or if both are equally good. (11:6)

23. Rashi on Bava Batra 59a.
24. See Mishna Kiddushin 1:10.
25. Amnon Shapira, "Does *Davar Aḥer* Present Two Alternative or Complementary Explanations?" [in Hebrew], 292. Likewise, Shapira observes that when Rashi presents three explanations, with the first aligned with the contextual interpretation (*peshuto*) and the second with the midrashic interpretation (*midrasho*), the third explanation (connected by the term "another explanation") is typically a variant of the second one. See Amnon Shapira, "Rashi's Twofold Interpretations (*Peshuto* and *Midrasho*): A Dualistic Approach?" in *The Bible in the Light of Its Interpreters: Sarah Kamin Memorial Volume,* ed. S. Japhet [in Hebrew] (Magnes, 1994), 292.

Regarding this verse, Rashi explains:

> *Sow your seed in the morning, etc.* (R 11:6) – You learned Torah in your youth; learn Torah in your old age. You had students in your youth; have students in your old age. You married a child-bearing woman in your youth; marry a childbearing woman in your old age.

Rashi metaphorically interprets the terms "morning" and "evening" to symbolize the stages of life, signifying youth and old age, respectively. To reinforce his message, Rashi offers historical evidence:

> *Since you don't know which is going to succeed* (R 11:6) – Whether the students and children of your youth will survive you, or perhaps only those of your old age will survive. We find that R. Akiva had twenty-four thousand students from Gabat to Antipatris, and they all died between Passover and Shavuot, and he came to our Sages in the south and taught them.[26]

Ultimately it was the students whom R. Akiva taught in his later years who carried on his legacy.

Individuals Involved in Torah Study: Their Influence

Rashi's commentary emphasizes the influence of individuals dedicated to Torah study, both personally and within the community at large. As we examine his explanations, observe Rashi's focus on "reward" or "gain," aligning with the themes prevalent in the book of Ecclesiastes.

Kohelet asserts that even if an iron tool is blunt and has not been sharpened, it increases the strength of armies (10:10). Rashi extends this analogy to an impoverished Torah scholar: Even if he is hungry and looks miserable next to the rich, his wisdom can strengthen armies. There is no known source for this interpretation.

Toward the conclusion of the book, Kohelet turns to causes and effects in the natural world, whose events are beyond human control:

26. See Yevamot 62b.

> If the clouds are filled, they will pour down rain on the earth; and if a tree falls to the south or to the north, the tree will stay where it falls. (11:3)

Taking the tree as a metaphor for a Torah scholar, Rashi explains:

> *Likewise, know that "if a tree falls, etc."* (R 11:3) – If a wise and righteous man resides in a city or in a country, then in the place where the wise man resides, there his wisdom, his exemplary traits, and his bestowal of goodness upon the inhabitants of that place through his good custom that he guided them on a straight road will remain discernible after his death.... *Tree* – Torah scholar, who with his merit protects like a tree, which provides shade over the earth.[27]

The scholar or righteous individual who leads his community members along the proper path continues to protect them even after his death, as a tree shades the earth.

What about a scholar who reneges on his communal responsibilities? Rashi compares him to a wicked snake charmer! Kohelet states, "If the snake bites because no spell was uttered, no credit is gained by the trained charmer" (10:11), and Rashi metaphorically explains:

> *No credit is gained* (R 10:11) – By the wicked charmer who could have charmed it but did not. So, if the people of your city stumble over prohibitions because the wise man did not preach to them or teach them the statutes of the Torah, he gets no credit because of his silence, and he will not profit.

Rashi asserts that a scholar who withholds guidance from his community, thereby causing them to sin, will not reap any personal gain from his silence. There is no identified source for this interpretation.

---

27. The linkage between a tree and the protective capacity of a righteous individual is drawn from Bava Batra 15a. Similarly, see Rashi's commentary on Numbers 13:20. Rashi's innovation lies in connecting this idea to the text in Ecclesiastes.

SACRED AND REVERED TEXTS

A significant portion of Rashi's glosses relates words of Ecclesiastes directly to Jewish sacred texts. While some of these glosses refer to the Written Law (R 12:10–11), the majority refer to the Oral Law.

Talmud

Rashi consistently emphasizes the primacy of talmudic study, as we see in his interpretation of verses 5:8 and 5:9. In 5:8, Kohelet extols the benefits of the earth, on whose produce even the king depends. The next verse warns that accumulating wealth does not lead to contentment. Rashi provides an allegorical interpretation for these seemingly unconnected verses:[28]

> Another explanation: *The profit of the earth is desired by all* (R 5:8) – The reward of Israel is in all aspects of Torah, be it in Scripture, in Mishna, or in Gemara. *The king himself is subject to the field (sadeh)* – If the king is well versed in Scripture and Mishna, he must still be subservient to the one well versed in Gemara, because he harrows (*mesadded*) and arranges before him the decisions regarding prohibition and permissibility, ritual impurity and purity, and civil laws.
>
> *[He who] loves money* (R 5:9) – Torah, will not be sated with it. *And he from the multitude who loves abundance* – Of Torah, will *have no produce* – One who has Scripture and Mishna, but has no Gemara, what benefit does he have? All these explanations are in Leviticus Rabba [22:1].

Drawing on the Midrash, Rashi interprets both verses symbolically, equating the terms "soil" (*sadeh*, v. 8) and "produce" (*tevua*, v. 9) with the study of sacred texts, particularly talmudic study. While the study of

28. While these two verses belong to separate thematic units – praising authority in the first (vv. 7–8) and addressing greed in the second (vv. 9–20) – Rashi's explanation bridges the gap between them.

Scripture and Mishna are valuable, talmudic study is deemed primary due to its clear practical relevance.

A similar lesson is gleaned from a verse that speaks of one who accumulates riches, wealth, and honor, but "God does not permit him to enjoy it"; instead, a stranger ultimately reaps the benefits (6:2). Rashi allegorically explains:

> *But God does not permit him to enjoy it* (R 6:2) – However, the Midrash Aggada [explains it as referring to] the words of Torah. *Wealth, possessions, and honor* – Scripture, Mishna, and Aggada. *Does not give him the power* – Because he did not achieve Gemara, therefore, he has no benefit from his studies in any practical Torah decision. *For instead a stranger will enjoy them* – The one who is versed in Gemara.[29]

Rashi notes that the three terms "riches," wealth," and "honor" correlate with the study of three distinct types of Jewish texts – Scripture, Mishna, and Aggada. But only the one who studies Gemara can "enjoy it," i.e., apply it in practice. This is reserved for the "stranger," interpreted as the one who has studied Gemara.

Rashi was cognizant of the difficulty in mastering the Talmud, as illustrated by the following gloss:

> *One human being in a thousand* (R 7:28) – It is customary in the world, [that out of] a thousand who enter [a school] to [learn] Scripture, only one hundred of them emerge successful and capable of learning Mishna. And of those hundred who enter [to study] Mishna, only ten of them emerge successfully as able to study Gemara. And of those ten who enter to [study] Gemara, only one emerges who is capable of rendering decisions, the result being one out of a thousand.[30]

Mastery of the Talmud is achievable by only a select few.

29. See Ecclesiastes Rabba 6:2.
30. See Leviticus Rabba 2:1; Ecclesiastes Rabba 7:28.

Human Legislation

In keeping with its emphasis on the Talmud, Rashi's commentary on Ecclesiastes also stresses the ordinances established to safeguard biblical law. These legal enactments, which form a protective fence around the Torah, originate from diverse human sources.

Moses

Kohelet compares the words of the wise with those of a foolish ruler:

> The words of the wise are heard [when spoken] softly, more than the shout of a ruler of fools (9:17).

Rashi elucidates this verse in the following manner:

> *Are heard [when spoken] softly* (R 9:17) – Even though they are spoken softly, they are heard and accepted by mankind. *More than the shout of a ruler of fools* – The kings of the nations. Moses passed away many years ago, yet his decrees are still accepted by Israel, and how many kings of the nations issue harsh decrees, but their words do not endure.[31]

Rashi equates the "words of the wise" with the "decrees" of Moses, which were universally accepted and continue to endure. This requires some clarification.

Moses is traditionally credited with transmitting not only the Written Torah but also a set of oral traditions. The latter are known as "the laws given to Moses at Sinai" (R 12:10); Rashi uses the term "his decrees (*gezeirotav*)." The Talmud attributes four *gezeirot* to Moses, but states that "four prophets came and revoked them" (Makkot 24a).This contradicts Rashi's statement that Moses's degrees are still accepted.

The Midrash (Ruth Rabba 3:2) uses a different verse from Ecclesiastes to draw a comparison between a decree issued by Moses and one by a non-Jewish ruler. The exposition proceeds as follows: Hadrian, a tyrannical ruler, boasted to R. Yehoshua b. Ḥananya that he surpassed

31. No known source.

Moses because he was alive while Moses was deceased. Hadrian bolstered his claim by quoting the verse "For a live dog is better than a dead lion" (Eccl. 9:4). R. Yehoshua then challenged Hadrian to issue a decree prohibiting the lighting of fires for three days, to which Hadrian agreed. Later, smoke was seen in the distance. Hadrian explained that this was because the governor was sick and a doctor had recommended hot water for him. R. Yehoshua pointed out to Hadrian that his decree had already been violated during his lifetime. By contrast, Moses's decree regarding not lighting a fire on the Sabbath had been faithfully observed by Jews for generations, thus proving Moses's superiority.

In that midrash, the decree attributed to Moses – the prohibition against kindling a light on the Sabbath – is a biblical law. Moses is treated as the author of this legislation because he serves as the conduit through which the law is communicated. The same logic could apply to Rashi's use of the term "decrees" in our verse: The decrees are biblical laws, which are attributed to Moses because he conveyed them to the nation.[32]

Solomon

Solomon is also credited with instituting a small number of ordinances. This acknowledgment is based upon the identification of Kohelet with Solomon, a connection that will be explored in more detail later. Rashi infers Solomon's legislative role from the characterization of Kohelet as a wise individual who "listened to (*izzen*) and tested the soundness of many maxims" (12:9).

From the root A-Z-N, Hebrew forms the verb "to listen,"[33] and also the noun "ear," which can also denote a handle. Thus Rashi interprets:

> *He listened* (R 12:9) – He made handles for the Torah, like a basket which has no handles with which to grasp it, and he came along and made handles for it, for he instituted "Eiruvin" as a safeguard for the observance of the Sabbath, and the ritual washing of the

32. Similarly, *Lekaḥ Tov* links our verse (9:17) with the Mosaic prohibition against lighting a fire on the Sabbath.
33. Koehler and Baumgartner, *HALOT*, vol. 1, 27: "To use one's ears; to listen."

> hands as a safeguard for purity, and secondary forbidden marriages as a safeguard for the prohibitions against incest.[34]

The Talmud speaks of "handles of the Torah."[35] Just as handles on a basket ensure secure holding without touching or dropping its contents, Solomon's preventive rules across three realms of Jewish law ensure observance of the Torah.

The Rabbis

The majority of ordinances originate with the Rabbis:

> *He who breaches a stone fence* (R 10:8) – A fence of the Sages, by transgressing their ordinances. *Will be bitten by a snake* – Death at the hands of Heaven.[36]

Rabbinical ordinances serve as a protective barrier, preventing the Jewish people from transgressing biblical laws. Anyone who breaches these safeguards is subject to divine punishment. Rashi even states that upholding the words of the Sages is more crucial than upholding the words of Scripture:

> *And furthermore, my son, be careful* (R 12:12) – More than the uprightness of the words of truth, the words written in the book [Torah]. *Be careful my son* – To observe the words of the Sages.[37]

People must be extra vigilant in upholding the words of the Sages, because whereas biblical transgressions lead to punishments of varying degrees of severity, violating rabbinic ordinances always warrants

34. See Song of Songs Rabba 1:8; Shabbat 14b; Yevamot 21a.
35. Eiruvin 21b.
36. See Avoda Zara 27b. Similarly, Rashi writes later in this commentary, "*The sayings of the wise* (R 12:11) – The "fence" that they made for the Torah with decrees in order to distance a person from sin, e.g., eating hallowed things [is permitted] until dawn, but they declared '[only] until midnight.'"
37. See Eiruvin 21b.

the death penalty, as in the aforementioned verse about the snakebite (10:8). In his Talmud commentary, Rashi makes this explicit:[38]

> *Positive and negative commandments* – Some biblical laws do not carry the death penalty. But [violation of] the words of the Sages are all punishable by death. As the verse states, "And he who breaches a fence will be bitten by a snake" (Eccl. 10:8).

Kohelet also compares "the sayings of the wise" (12:11) to a goad (because "just as a goad directs a cow to its furrows, so do their words direct a person to the ways of life"; R 12:11) and to nails:[39]

> *Like well-fastened (netu'im) nails* (R 12:11) – Just as this nail is permanent, so are their words permanent, and just as a sapling (*netia*) is fruitful and multiplies, so are their [the Rabbis'] words fruitful and multiply [thus making it easier] to find a reason for them.[40]

The word *netu'im* (fastened), used to describe the nails, means, literally, "planted." The word translated "sapling" is formed from the same root. This prompts Rashi, following the words of the Sages,[41] to offer a dual interpretation: Rabbinic legislation is permanent and unchanging, like nails, yet also fruitful like the sapling, allowing for multiple interpretations and elucidations.

Regarding the heads of the nails, Rashi writes:

> *With asuppot* (12:11) – Nails that have a large and thick head; *grose* in Old French. So did Dunash the son of Labrat explain it.

Following the explanation of the medieval Spanish grammarian Dunash,[42] Rashi explains that the term *baalei asuppot* refers to the large head of a

38. Rashi's commentary on Eiruvin 21b.
39. See *Tanḥuma, Vayelekh* 1.
40. Ibid.
41. Koehler and Baumgartner, *HALOT*, vol. 2, 694: "1. To plant, 2. To drive in nails."
42. Many are familiar with his famous liturgical poem *Dror Yikra* traditionally sung around the Sabbath table.

nail.[43] A glimpse into the commentary of Rashi's close colleague Rabbi Josef Kara helps elucidate Rashi's intent:

> *With asuppot* (12:11) – Meaning, with big and thick heads, where the majority of the metal is gathered, so, too, you should not move from the words of the Sages.

Thus, the large and thick heads of the nails emphasize the permanent and authoritative nature of the Sages' words.

Rashi further points out that the word *masmerot* (nails) is spelled here with the letter *sin* for the s sound, instead of the usual *samekh.*[44] This substitution enables him to read the word as *mishmarot,*[45] or "watches," alluding to the twenty-four watches of the priests and Levites in the Temple, and by extension, the twenty-four books of the Bible.[46] Thus he hints at equating the words of the Sages with the written Scriptures.

According to traditional rabbinic thought, these oral traditions of the Sages emanate from God Himself, as Rashi notes:

> *All were given from one shepherd* (R 12:11) – All their words are the words of the living God, He said them; and one shepherd gave them, Moshe from the Almighty.[47]

---

43. Alternatively, Ibn Ezra, based on the explanation of Menahem ben Saruq, views the term as describing the words of the wise, which are gathered from various books and joined together as a nail joins two boards.
44. See Isaiah 41:7 and Jeremiah 10:4, where the word "nails" is spelled with a *samekh.*
45. The letters *sin* and *shin* are distinguishable only by a dot above the letter: for *sin,* the dot is above the left-hand side, and for the letter *shin* it is above the right-hand side; thus, homiletically, מִשְׂמֶר (nail) = מִשְׁמֶר (watch).
46. Rashi uses the word "Torah" to signify the twenty-four books of the Bible, as does his source, *Tanḥuma, Vayelekh* 1.
47. See *Tanḥuma, Vayelekh* 1.

Moshe is the shepherd,[48] the conduit through which both the Written and Oral Laws are transmitted to the Jewish people from the same divine source.[49]

If the words of the Sages are indeed so significant, why were they all not written down? Rashi explains:

> *The making of many books is without limit* (R 12:12) – If we would attempt to write, we would be unable to do so.

The sheer volume of their teachings is so vast that committing their words to writing is impossible.

The Torah Way of Life

Rashi's commentary promotes not only Torah study but also the fulfillment of its teachings.[50] Upholding the commandments shares center stage in his commentary with Torah study, and often the two themes are intertwined, such as in the following glosses:

> *And get enjoyment* (R 3:13) – In the Torah and the commandments.

> *He gives wisdom, knowledge, and joy* (R 2:26) – A heart [i.e., mind] to engage in Torah and in the commandments.

> *To receive his share* (R 5:18) – After his death, because God made it possible for him to engage in Torah and in commandments during his life, so that he would receive reward [after death].

48. Isaiah alludes to Moses as a shepherd: "Where is the One who brought them up from the sea along with the shepherd of this flock?" (63:11).
49. *Siftei Ḥakhamim* notes that the Hebrew term "from one shepherd" (m-r-'-h) is written defective, without a *vav*, thus serving as an acronym for ***Moshe Rabbeinu alav hashalom*** (Moses our teacher, of blessed memory).
50. The prevalence of these themes has already been noted by Gelles, *Peshat and Derash in the Exegesis of Rashi*, 85–87.

> ***Yissakhen** by them* (R 10:9) – I.e., will be warmed, as in "And be his warmer (*sokhenet*)" (1 Kings 1:2). So will one who engages in Torah and in commandments ultimately benefit from them.

In the last example, the word *yissakhen* is usually translated as "will be endangered," which fits the context ("He who removes stones will be hurt by them, and he who splits logs will be endangered by them"). However, Rashi finds the same root in the passage where Abishag is summoned to warm the aged King David, and interprets the verse in that sense.

General Mention

References to the commandments are sometimes of a general nature, for example:

> *That men revere Him* (R 3:14) –Therefore, there is nothing better for a man to occupy himself with other than the commandments and fearing Him.

> *Who loves money will not be satisfied with money* (R 5:9) – [Whoever] loves the commandments never has his fill of them. *Nor one who loves abundance* – Many commandments.

> *For who knows* (R 6:12) – What good deeds a man should do during his life, so it should be good for him in the everlasting world.

Note the elegance of Rashi's style in employing a range of terminology to depict God's instructions: "commandments," "good deeds," and elsewhere in this commentary: "goodness," "kindness." and "charity."

Let us now delve deeper into specific commandments noted in his commentary.

SPECIFIC COMMANDMENTS

Speech

Rashi often links verses to the realm of speech. For instance, the Torah underscores the gravity of making vows (Deut. 23: 22–24), a sentiment echoed by Kohelet when he urges, "'Obey the king's orders!' because of the oath to God" (8:2).

But which "king" is meant here, and what "oath to God" is being alluded to? Rashi clarifies:

> *I obey the king's orders* (R 8:2) – The reason why I am prepared to observe the commandment of the King of the Universe, which is the best of them all, is *because of the oath to God* (8:2) – Which we swore to Him at Ḥoreb [i.e., Sinai], to keep His commandments.[51]

Rashi's explanation spiritualizes this verse and applies it to the nation as well as to the individual. He identifies the "king" as none other than God, the King of the Universe, and explains that the obligation to obey His commandments stems from the communal covenant made at Mount Sinai.[52] According to Jewish tradition, this covenant was not limited to the generation of the Exodus but extends to all future generations.[53]

Kohelet also stresses the seriousness of fulfilling personal vows:

> It is better not to vow at all than to vow and not fulfill. Don't let your mouth bring you into disfavor, and don't plead before the messenger that it was an error, but fear God; else God may be angry by your voice and destroy the work of your hands (5:4–5).

Rashi sheds light on the nature of this vow and the role of the messenger:

> *And don't plead before the messenger* (R 5:5) – The representative who comes to demand of you the charity that you pledged publicly. *[By saying] that it was an error* – In error, I pledged it; I thought that I would have the ability to give. *And destroy the work of your hands* – The commandments you had in your hands, as you

---

51. See *Kohelet Zuta* 8:3; Ecclesiastes Rabba 8:2.
52. Rashi brings an alternative explanation that explicates the two parts of the verse as relating to different kings: The obligation to obey a human king (first stich) applies only if it doesn't conflict with the commands of the divine King (second stich).
53. See Deuteronomy 29:14 and Rashi's commentary ad loc.

> had already performed them; they will be lost. It is expounded in this manner in the Midrash. [Why should God be angry] *by your voice* – Because of your voice.[54]

The vow mentioned is a public commitment to give charity, with the donor later failing to uphold his promise. Rashi stresses the importance of honoring one's commitments, especially when made in a public setting, and the severe consequences of failing to do so.

Another aspect of speech which Kohelet touches on is *lashon hara,*[55] or evil talk. It is crucial to be mindful not only of the words that we speak but also of those that we hear. The danger of hearing evil talk is exemplified in the story of King Saul.[56] Rashi tells us that because Saul was receptive to malicious words, he ordered the murder of the priests who lived in the city of Nov (R 7: 21).

Even to think evil words is dangerous, as Kohelet states:

> Don't revile a king even in your thoughts. Don't revile a rich man even in your bedchamber. For a bird of the air may carry the utterance, And a winged creature may report the word (10:20).

Rashi explains:

> *Do not revile a king* (R 10:20) – Do not provoke the King of the Universe.... *For a bird of the air* – The soul placed within you that will eventually fly up to the heaven. *And a winged creature* – The angel who escorts you, as it states, "For He will order His angels to guard you" (Ps. 91:11).[57]

54. See *Kohelet Zuta* 5:5; Ecclesiastes Rabba 5:5.
55. Regarding the seriousness of this sin in Rashi's eyes, see Avigail Rock, *Great Biblical Commentators: Biographies, Methodologies, and Contributions* (Maggid Books, 2023), 54–58.
56. See 1 Samuel 22.
57. See Ecclesiastes Rabba 10:23. Whereas Ecclesiastes Rabba describes the journey of the evil thought to heaven when the offender sleeps (a nightly accounting of one's

Thus, caution is advised even in one's innermost thoughts, as the soul will ultimately be held accountable for them.

Finally, Rashi recognizes the virtue of silence. In the face of the devastating loss of his two eldest sons, Nadab and Abihu, Aaron chose not to protest against God but remained silent. His acceptance of the divine decree without complaint earned him a unique priestly commandment addressed exclusively to him (R 3:7), illustrating that in certain circumstances, silence is golden.

Heart

Rashi's commentary also delves into the commandments of the heart.

On the verse "Wisdom strengthens the wise more than ten rulers that a city may contain" (7:19), Rashi explains that the wisdom referred to is the wisdom that guides a wise man toward repentance.[58] However, what is the significance of the "ten rulers" mentioned at the verse's conclusion? Rashi elaborates:

> *Than ten rulers* (R 7:19) – We find regarding Josiah, that Scripture testified about him, "There was no king like him before [or after him who returned to God]" (II Kings 23:25). His wisdom remained with him, and he examined his actions, and it was better for him than "ten rulers" who acted wickedly and did not repent. *That a city may contain* – In Jerusalem: Rehoboam, Abijah, Ahaziah, Joash after the death of Jehoiada, Amaziah, Ahaz, Manasseh, Amon, Jehoiakim, and Zedekiah.

Rashi identifies the ten rulers with the ten wicked kings of Jerusalem during the First Commonwealth, contrasting their refusal to repent with king Josiah's transformative repentance. Josiah's actions, inspired by his wisdom, led to significant religious reforms, including the eradication of

sins), Rashi describes the ascension of the soul itself after death. Rashi offers another interpretation, according to the contextual meaning, warning against speaking ill of an earthly king because bystanders might overhear the slanderous speech.

58. See Nedarim 32b. It is interesting that the Talmud notes that wisdom leads both to repentance and good deeds, whereas Rashi notes repentance only.

idol worship in Judah, thereby restoring the sole worship of God (see II Kings, 23). Regarding his actions, the Bible states: "There was no king like him before who turned back to God with all his heart and soul and might, in full accord with the teaching of Moses; nor did any like him arise after him" (II Kings 23:25).

The identification of the "ten rulers" with the ten Judaean kings is original to Rashi. While Rashi takes the number ten literally, other exegetes understand it as a general number signifying many.[59]

Later in his commentary, Rashi returns to the theme of repentance, which he finds in the verse "For to him who is joined with all the living there is hope; even a live dog is better than a dead lion" (9:4). During the biblical period the dog was seen as a lowly and despised creature (I Sam. 17:43), while the lion symbolized royalty and strength (Gen. 49:9); yet to Kohelet the living dog is superior to the dead lion, because for the living dog "there is hope." As to the nature of this hope, Rashi elucidates:

> *For to him who is joined with all the living, there is hope* (R 9:4) – For as long as he lives, even if he is wicked and associates with the wicked, as it is written, "To all the living" – even for the wicked – there is hope that he will repent before his death.

There is hope for "all" the living to repent, even if the individual is wicked and associates with others who are evil. Rashi gives a historical example:

> *Even a live dog is better than a dead lion* (R 9:4) – And they are both wicked. It was better for Nebuzaradan, who was a wicked slave and became a proselyte, that death did not overtake him sooner than Nebuchadnezzar, his master, who is called a "lion," as it states, "The lion has come up from his thicket" (Jer. 4:7),

59. Such as the commentary that some attribute to Rashbam: "More than ten rulers; these ten are not meant to be taken literally, meaning neither more nor less. It is rather like 'than many rulers,' as in 'ten women shall bake your bread' (Lev. 26:26), which is not to be taken literally." Regarding authorship of this commentary, see S. Japhet and R.B. Salters, *The Commentary of R. Samuel Ben Meir (Rashbam) on Qoheleth* (Magnes, 1985), 19–33.

> and who died in his wickedness. He is in Gehinnom, while his slave [Nebuzaradan] is in the Garden of Eden.[60]

Nebuzaradan, the servant of King Nebuchadnezzar, repented; his master, likened to the lion, remained wicked. Hence the servant merited eternal bliss while the king was condemned to eternal suffering.

Action

Other verses connect to the world of action.

Kohelet recommends the continuous wearing of white clothing (9:8), with Rashi providing a metaphorical explanation:

> *At all times, let your garments be white* (R 9:8) – Prepare yourself at all times with a good deed, so that if you die today, you will enter [the hereafter] in peace. Solomon the wise compared this to a man whom the king invited for a day of feast, without setting a date for him. If he is wise or clever, he will immediately launder his garments, bathe, and anoint himself. And similarly, he will do the same thing the next day [and every day], until the time that he will be summoned to the feast. All this time his garments are white [i.e., laundered] and he is bathed and anointed. So did our Rabbis expound this verse in Tractate Shabbat (153a).

White clothing symbolizes the good deed that one should do daily in preparation for the day of death.[61] It is noteworthy that one opinion in Tractate Shabbat connects white garments with the specific commandment of repentance, and another opinion links it to the commandment of tzitzit (because the ritual fringes are attached to a white garment), yet Rashi does not mention these specifications but speaks generally of "a good deed."[62]

---

60. See Sanhedrin 96b and Gittin 57b.
61. In the Bible the color white is associated with purity and forgiveness from sin; see Isaiah 1:18.
62. See *Kohelet Zuta* 9:8.

Kohelet advises throwing bread upon the waters (11:1), a piece of advice that cannot be taken literally, since the bread would become soggy and unusable. Rabbi Josef Kara interprets this advice as a recommendation to sow seeds in a moist area, so that even during a drought year the seeds will have the necessary moisture to grow. Rashi, by contrast, explains the verse metaphorically:

> *Cast your bread upon the waters* (R 11:1) – Do goodness and kindness to a person about whom your heart tells you that you will never see him again, like a person who casts his food upon the surface of the water.

Thus Rashi recommends doing a good deed for someone who will likely never repay the act of kindness. Rashi continues:

> *For in the abundance of days, you will find it* – Days will yet come, and you will receive your recompense. Look what is stated about Jethro: "Ask him in to break bread" (Ex. 2:20), and he thought that he [Moses] was an Egyptian and that he would never see him again. What was the end? He became his son-in-law and reigned over Israel, and [Moses] brought him under the wings of the Divine Presence, and his grandsons merited sitting in the Chamber of Hewn Stone.[63]

The Jethro incident and our verse in Ecclesiastes are connected by the word "bread."[64] Jethro extended kindness to Moses, the Egyptian fugitive, welcoming him into his house and sharing bread, without expecting to see him again or to be repaid for his gesture. Eventually, Jethro was rewarded by becoming Moses's father-in-law, and his descendants became part of the legislative body in Israel. This biblical example illustrates that recompense can come unexpectedly.

---

63. See Sanhedrin 106a.
64. It is noteworthy that Exodus Rabba (27:6) notes an additional link: the motif of water. Kohelet recommends throwing bread upon the "water," and Moses was drawn from the "water." It is unclear whether Rashi was familiar with this source.

Kohelet follows this with another piece of advice: "Give a portion to seven and also to eight, for you do not know what evil will befall the earth" (11:2). Rashi continues his allegorical line of explanation:[65]

> *Give a portion to seven and also to eight* (R 11:2) – If you shared your food and possessions with seven people who need kindness, share further with eight more who come after them, and do not say, "Enough." *For you do not know what evil* – Perhaps days will yet come and you will need [help from] them all. Then you will be saved from the misfortune because of this charity, and if not now, when?

One should give charity to as many as possible, so as to be able to call on them in one's own hour of need.[66]

Kohelet here employs the literary device of enumerating consecutive numbers ("seven and… eight")[67] to signify many. This pattern recurs elsewhere in the Bible with different consecutive numbers. In Amos we find: "Thus said God: For three transgressions of Damascus, for four, I will not revoke the decree" (Amos 1:3);[68] in Proverbs, "Six things the Lord hates; seven are an abomination to Him" (Prov. 6:16).[69] This structure implies not only X, but also one more: Y. However, Rashi's commentary on our verse in Ecclesiastes contains a slight deviation:

> *Give a portion to seven and also to eight* (R 11:2) – If you shared your food and your possessions with seven people who need kindness, share further with eight more who come after them.

Rather than advising one to give to the eighth person in addition to the previous seven, Rashi suggests giving to eight more, for a total of fifteen

65. Rabbi Josef Kara recommends dividing belongings among numerous associates.
66. Similarly, Rashi explains "'Sow in the morning' (11:6): If you performed charitable acts in your youth, perform charitable acts in your old age."
67. Similarly, see Micah 5:4.
68. So, too, Amos 1:6, 9, 11, 13, 2:4.
69. So, too, Prov. 30: 18, 21, 29. See Robert Gordis, *Koheleth: The Man and His World, a Study of Ecclesiastes* (Schocken Books, 1973), 330.

people! This alteration shows the importance Rashi attaches to giving charity generously and without limits. However, Rashi's explanation of 11:1–2 also emphasizes a "profit" motive – the eventual benefit to oneself of giving charity.

Rashi continues with two additional explanations, drawn from the realm of Jewish ritual, that fit the numerical pattern of seven and eight:

> Our Rabbis (Eiruvin 40b), however, said: "Give a portion to seven"; these are the seven days of Creation. Give one of them as a portion to your Creator, by resting on the Sabbath. "And also to eight"; these are the eight days preceding circumcision.
>
> Another explanation: "Give a portion to seven": the communal sacrifices of the seven days of Passover. "And also to eight": the eight days of the festival [Sukkot].[70] "For you do not know what evil will befall": If the Temple will be destroyed, and you will no longer bring sacrifices, the sacrifices that you offered before will avail. Another explanation: "For you do not know, etc.": You do not know what was decreed on the festival regarding the rains, and the sacrifices will avail to annul an evil decree.[71]

Performance of the ritual commandments preserves the community against disaster. This is the only instance in his commentary on Ecclesiastes where Rashi mentions these specific ritual acts.

On the other hand, neglect of religious obligations endangers the community. Kohelet observes, "Through slothfulness the ceiling leaks; through lazy hands the house caves in" (10:18), and Rashi clarifies:

> *Leaks* (R 10:18) – The dripping rain leaks, meaning: When Israel is lazy with Torah, they melt away, and the House [i.e., the

70. See Ecclesiastes Rabba 11:5.

71. It is noteworthy that these latter explanations of Rashi – the Sabbath and circumcision (second explanation) and festival offerings (third explanation) – both relate to the realm of sacred time, thereby reinforcing Shapira's previously noted thesis about multiple explanations in Rashi's commentary.

> Temple], the pride of their strength (see Ezek. 24:21), becomes destroyed and lowly.[72]

Neglect of obligations has detrimental effects not only on the community, but also on the individual. Reflecting on the "crookedness" pervasive in the world, Kohelet observes: "A twisted thing that cannot be made straight, a lack that cannot be made good" (1:15), a sentiment further elucidated by Rashi:

> *A twisted thing* (R 1:15) – Our Sages explained this as referring to... a student[73] who separates from the Torah, who was originally straight, and became crooked. *And that which is wanting cannot be counted* – The one who excluded himself from the number of the righteous cannot be counted among them to share their reward.

A look at Rashi's source sheds light on his intention. The Talmud[74] applies the initial segment of our verse to an individual who intentionally skips a morning or evening prayer ("a twisted thing"). Since this omission was deliberate, it cannot be rectified afterward ("cannot be made straight"). Because this individual removed himself from the righteous quorum, he cannot share in the reward the others will receive.

If neglect of obligations yields adverse effects, then certainly the transgression of even a single commandment carries far graver consequences. Kohelet asserts, "Just as dying flies turn the perfumer's ointment fetid and putrid, so a little folly outweighs massive wisdom" (10:1), and Rashi expounds:

> *Dying flies* (R 10:1) – If one falls into a perfumer's oil and becomes mixed with the perfumes – it causes it to become putrid.... We see that an insignificant thing spoiled a precious thing.... Suppose that a man was equally divided between transgressions and merits, and

72. Taanit 7b connects our verse to laziness with Torah but makes no mention of the Temple.
73. Rashi's source, Ḥagiga 9a, reads "a scholar/*talmid ḥakham*" and not a student.
74. Ḥagiga 9a–b; Berakhot 26a.

> he came and committed one transgression, which tipped the scale [causing him] to be guilty. The result is that this one small folly is worth more and weighs [more] and is heavier than all the wisdom and honor that he possessed, for behold, it outweighed them all.[75]

Thus, the transgression of even a single commandment can cause the individual to be found guilty, especially when the scales are evenly balanced.

Benefits

Throughout our analysis, a recurring theme has been the benefits of study and performance. At this juncture, let us briefly explore who reaps the rewards from the study of Torah and the fulfillment of commandments by the individual. Undoubtedly, the individual performing these acts benefits personally; and in the case of good deeds, the recipient of the kindness also gains. However, surprisingly, Rashi expands the category of beneficiaries.

When Kohelet says that the rich man's abundance does not let him sleep (5:11), Rashi explains metaphorically:

> *But the rich man's abundance* (R 5:11) – The many oral traditions [that a man has transmitted]. *Does not allow him to sleep* – In the grave, as it states, "Causing the lips of the sleeping to murmur" (Song. 7:10). Every Torah scholar in whose name a law is recited, his lips murmur in the grave.[76]

When a student recites the teachings in the name of the departed Torah scholar, it symbolically grants the scholar a form of eternal life. Thus the student brings benefit to those who preceded him.

The benefits can also extend to future generations. Kohelet states: "Because the wise man, just like the fool, is not remembered forever; for, as the succeeding days roll by, both are forgotten. And how can the death of the wise man be [like the death] of the fool!" (2:16). And Rashi explains:

---

75. See Ecclesiastes Rabba 10:1.

76. See Yevamot 97a.

> *And how can the death of the wise man be [like the death] of the fool* (R 2:16) – I observe the righteous succeeding in their deaths and availing their children, for example, "And I will remember My covenant with Jacob, etc." (Lev. 26:42) [and] "I remember for you the kindness of your youth" (Jer. 2:2).

While humans may forget both the righteous and the wicked after their deaths, thus blurring the distinction between them, God does not. Divine remembrance is demonstrated by the ability of the righteous to pass on merit to their children. In our next chapter, dedicated to the theme of reward and punishment, we will go further into the concept of *zekhut avot,* the passing on of merit.

The final beneficiary, however, is perhaps the most unexpected. Kohelet says that as wealth accumulates, so does the number of those desiring to consume it, leaving the owner with little beyond "feasting his eyes" (5:10). Rashi interprets "wealth" as "good deeds," which give God the benefit of satisfaction:

> *As good increases* (R 5:10) – When Israel increase their good deeds. So there is an increase of the number of those who benefit from the reward given for observing the commandments. *What benefit does its owner* – The Holy One, blessed be He, get from the improvement of their deeds. *Only feasting his eyes* – That He sees that they are subservient to Him, and He has satisfaction *(naḥat ruaḥ),* that He said and His will was done.[77]

Rashi identifies the "owner" as God and interprets "the increase in good" as the improvement of Israel's deeds. When this occurs, not only are the people of Israel rewarded for their enhanced observance, but God Himself finds satisfaction in witnessing their obedience to His will.

In sum, Kohelet's unorthodox discourse on life's transience and the apparent futility of human endeavor undergoes a radical shift in Rashi's commentary. Whereas toil "under the sun" is devoid of value, replacing it with spiritual pursuits yields profound results. Numerous skeptical

77. No known source.

thoughts are reinterpreted to urge the importance of Torah study and adherence to commandments, all while holding the promise of eventual divine reward. Seemingly mundane elements like dying flies, soggy bread, white laundry, and snake charmers are imbued with religious significance, so that the text becomes a cohesive spiritual guide based on traditional beliefs and values.

HISTORICAL IDENTIFICATIONS

The process of spiritualization is also evident in Rashi's application of verses to historical personalities and events. While we are familiar with this exegetical technique from Rashi's commentary on Proverbs, its use is particularly extensive in his Ecclesiastes commentary, as demonstrated in the following comparison.

	Approximate number of verses which contain historical identifications	**Number of total verses**	**Percentage**
Rashi on Proverbs	80	915	9 percent
Rashi on Ecclesiastes	70	222	32 percent

We see that in Rashi's commentary on Ecclesiastes, he connects approximately every third verse to historical figures or events, thereby enhancing the spiritual depth of the text. Moreover, the actual frequency is even higher, as we shall see.

Generally the historical figures are from the biblical period,[78] with certain personalities being invoked in multiple verses, including Moses,[79]

78. A small number are identified from the talmudic period: Elisha b. Abuya: R 7:8; Joseph son of Phukhsas the priest: R 7:15; R. Akiva: R 11:6.

79. Fourteen times: 1:1, 3:7, 4:2, 7:1, 7, 21, 8:1, 8:17, 9:2, 11, 17, 12:10, 11.

David,[80] Saul,[81] and Aaron,[82] These figures are praised for their virtuous behavior and critiqued for their shortcomings. For example, Moses is commended for enduring forty days and nights without sustenance (R 7:21), but he is criticized (R 7:7)[83] for letting Dathan and Abiram provoke him into an accusation against God (following a midrashic understanding of Exodus 5). For this, God will not let Moses witness the defeat of the thirty-one kings of Canaan.

Rashi applies verses in Ecclesiastes not only to Israelites, but also to foreigners.[84] Rashi identifies gentiles – ranging from commoners to kings – as seen in the following example. In 10:12–14, a contrast is drawn between the speech of the wise and that of the foolish, with the latter attributed to Balaam:

> *But a fool's lips are his undoing* (R 10:12) – This refers to... Balaam, who broke the restrictions that the nations had imposed upon themselves regarding immorality since the time of the generation of the flood and onward, and he advised them to offer their daughters for prostitution.[85]

Although the wickedness of Balaam is a widespread theme in rabbinic literature,[86] its invocation here is original to Rashi. The identification of Balaam with the fool continues in Rashi's interpretation of the next two verses.

---

80. Five times: 4:2, 6:12, 7:10, 8:8, 9:2, and twice the Kingdom of David: 3:7, 12:6 (in Rashi's long explanation drawn from the Midrash).
81. Five times: 1:3, 7:16, 17, 18, 21.
82. Four times: 3:7, 7:1, 9:2, 12:6 (in Rashi's long explanation drawn from the Midrash).
83. Rashi's comment on 7:7 ("oppression makes a wise man mad") is a combination of sources: Ecclesiastes Rabba 7:17 and Sanhedrin 111a. See Rashi's commentary on Exodus 6:1, where he expresses the same idea.
84. Belshazzar: R 2:1; Nergal-sarezer: R 3:16; Titus: R 5:9; Pharaoh: R 8:9; Nebuzaradan: R 9:4; Nebuchadnezzar: R 8:2, 9, 9:4, 10:8, 12:6 (in Rashi's long explanation drawn from the Midrash); Balaam: R 10:12–14; Jethro: R 11:1; Sennacherib: R 8:9.
85. See Sanhedrin 106a; Genesis Rabba 70:12.
86. Regarding the rabbinic appraisal of Balaam, see J. Milgrom, "Balaam: Saint or Sinner," *The JPS Torah Commentary: Numbers* (Jewish Publication Society, 1990), 469–71.

In a similar vein, Rashi connects verses in Ecclesiastes that depict the fleeting nature of riches (5:12–13) to the wealth of Korah, a prominent midrashic motif.[87] This connection of Korah to the book of Kohelet is also Rashi's innovation.

Only a handful of verses are applied to biblical women,[88] the most extensive being the following:

> *Wisdom is more valuable than weapons of war* (R 9:18) – The wisdom of Serah, of whom it is stated, "The woman came to all the people with her clever plan" (II Sam. 20:22), availed them more than the weapons that were in their hands, to wage war against Joab. *But a single error destroys much of value* – Had she not slain Sheba the son of Bichri, they would all have been destroyed by him.[89]

The "wise woman" depicted in the book of Samuel saves the inhabitants of the rebellious city of Abel from the "weapons of war," i.e., the siege placed upon the city by Yoav, David's commander in chief (see II Sam. 20). The midrashic tradition identifies this anonymous woman with Serah the daughter of Asher and the granddaughter of Jacob, who enjoyed exceptional longevity (see Gen. 46:17).[90]

---

87. See Pesahim 119a; Numbers Rabba 18:15.
88. Esther: R 2:26; Deborah: R 3:7; Miriam: R 7:1; Eve: R 7:29.
89. See *Kohelet Zuta* 9:18; Ecclesiastes Rabba 9:18.
90. According to one later tradition, Serah's long life is attributed to her manner of delivering the news of Joseph's survival to Jacob, her grandfather. By gently revealing the truth through music, she did not shock him but rather revived his spirit, thus prolonging his life. For this Jacob blessed her with immortality. (See *Sefer HaYashar, Vayigash*, ch. 14.) It is apparent from the genealogical list at the end of Genesis (46:17) that she journeyed to Egypt and was alive during the census in the desert before entering the land of Canaan (Num. 26:46). Therefore, if she was still living during the period of David, she would have been several hundred years old at that time. For an analysis of the rabbinical treatment of Serah, see Leila Leah Bronner, "Serah and the Exodus: A Midrashic Miracle," in *A Feminist Companion to Exodus to Deuteronomy*, ed. A. Brenner-Idan (Sheffield Academic, 2000), 179–99.

Rashi applies verses not only to individuals but to various groups, such as Israel's archenemies Amalek, Egypt, Babylonia, and Edom,[91] as well as subsets within the nation: priests, Levites and Israelites.[92] Also invoked are "generations" – the generations of the dispersion, Enoch, the desert, Joshua, David and Rehoboam,[93] along with the 974 generations that were never brought into existence.[94] Rashi focuses especially on the generation of the flood, whom he mentions six times.[95]

In certain instances, Rashi's commentary includes multiple identifications due to the structure of the biblical verse. Kohelet bemoans the shared destiny of both the righteous and the wicked, presenting a series of examples:

> For the same fate is in store for all: [1] for the righteous, and for the wicked; [2] for the good and pure, and for the impure; [3] for him who sacrifices, and for him who does not; [4] for him who is pleasing, and for him who is displeasing; [5] and for him who swears, and for him who shuns oaths. (9:2)

Rashi, who does not adhere to the principle that "the Torah speaks in the human vernacular,"[96] interprets verbosity and repetition in the bib-

---

91. R 1:11, 3:15, 8:9.
92. R 12:6 (in Rashi's long explanation drawn from the Midrash).
93. R 2:17, 3:14, 4:15–16, 7:10.
94. R 4:3. See *Kohelet Zuta* 1:11; Ecclesiastes Rabba 4:3. According to the Midrash, God's original plan was for the Torah to be given to the thousandth generation after Creation, but it was actually given twenty-six generations after the creation of the world. Hence there were 974 generations that did not come into existence; see Genesis Rabba 28:4.
95. R 2:1, 21, 3:14, 4:15, 7:3, 10:12.
96. Traditional scholarship aligned Rashi's perspective with that of R. Akiva, who maintained that any superfluous phrase, word, or letter in the Bible carries added meaning. This view contrasts with that of R. Yishmael, who argued that since the language of the Bible mirrors human speech, repetition does not inherently convey additional ideas (Sanhedrin 64b; Rock, *Great Biblical Commentators*, 45–49). However, this traditional division between R. Akiva and R. Yishmael is now being questioned by contemporary scholars, as evidenced by Richard Kalmin's article "Rabbinic Midrash of Late Antiquity," *HBOT* 1/1 (1996), 295–99. Thanks to Professor M. Lockshin for bringing this article to my attention.

lical text as conveying nuanced ideas rather than mere emphasis. Consequently, based on midrashic sources, he links each contrasting pair with historical personalities who shared similar fates:

> [1] *The righteous* (R 9:2) – Noah. *And the wicked* – Pharaoh Necho.[97] This one became crippled, and that one became crippled.
>
> [2] *The good* – Moshe. *And the pure* – Aaron. *And the impure* – The spies; one group of them spoke in praise of the Land of Israel, and the other group spoke derogatorily about it. [Nevertheless,] neither group entered [the land]; hence, they have the same fate.
>
> [3] *To him who brings offerings* – Josiah, [as it states,] "And Josiah offered a sacrifice" (II Chr. 35:7). *And to him who does not bring offerings* – … Ahab, who abolished Israel's festival pilgrimage. [Nevertheless,] one of them was killed by arrows and the other one was [also] killed by arrows. (I Kings 22:34; II Chr. 35:23)
>
> [4] *As is with the good man* – This is David. *So is it with the sinner* – This is Nebuchadnezzar. One of them built the Temple, and the other destroyed it; [nevertheless,] one of them reigned for forty years, and the other one [also] reigned for forty years. (II Sam. 5:4; Megilla 11b)
>
> [5] *As is with one who swears* – Zedekiah, who swore falsely, as it states, "And he also rebelled against King Nebuchadnezzar, who had made him swear, etc." (II Chr. 36:13). *So is it with the one who fears an oath* – Samson, as it states, "And Samson said to them, 'Swear to me, that you, yourselves, will not strike me'" (Judges 15:12). We learn that he believed in the strict observance of an oath. [Nevertheless,] one of them died after his eyes were gouged out, and the other one [also] died after his eyes were gouged out (Judges 16:21; II Kings 25:7).[98]

97. Pharaoh Necho is mentioned in II Kings 23:29 and II Chronicles 35:20.
98. See *Kohelet Zuta* 9:1; Ecclesiastes Rabba 9:1.

These contrasting pairs share a common destiny in this world. However, as Rashi explicitly states, "There is distinction between them in the World to Come" (R 9:2). Thus, Rashi's explication of one verse yields eleven identifications![99]

Rashi's commentary also connects the verses of Ecclesiastes with historical events, spanning both those described in the Bible and episodes exclusively found in rabbinic writings. For instance, when Kohelet asserts that everything that God created remains constant and this constancy is in order that man should fear God (3:14), Rashi inverts the meaning of the verse:

> [1] Seven days, the course of the sun was changed in the generation of the flood, to rise in the west and set in the east, in order that they fear Him.[100]
>
> [2] The ocean broke through its boundary in the generation of Enoch and inundated a third of the world, and God did this so that they would fear Him.[101]
>
> [3] The sun went back ten degrees in the days of Hezekiah (see Is. 38:8).
>
> [4] And in the days of Ahaz his father, the day was shortened and the night was lengthened on the day of his death, so that he should not be eulogized.[102]

According to Rashi, it is actually the *breach* of the laws of nature (and not the unchanging nature of the created order itself) that instills fear.[103] Of the four occurrences where the natural order was altered, only one – the reversal of the sun's movement in the reign of King Hezekiah – is

99. Rashi's commentary on 9:11 contains five identifications.
100. See Sanhedrin 108b.
101. See *Mekhilta Yitro, BaḤodesh* 6.
102. See Sanhedrin 96a.
103. As noted by M.V. Fox, *JPS Bible Commentary: Ecclesiastes* (Jewish Publication Society, 2004), 24.

explicitly mentioned in the biblical text; the remaining three instances are documented solely in midrashic writings.

In sum, Rashi consistently associates verses from Ecclesiastes with historical events and personalities. Although many of these connections are drawn from midrashic literature specific to Ecclesiastes, others build upon themes found across rabbinic writings, and some are entirely original to Rashi. Approximately seventy verses are linked to historical figures or events, yet the number of individual applications almost doubles this count. This plethora of applications – whether chastising the wicked or praising the righteous – significantly deepens the spiritual dimension of this commentary and strengthens its connection with the other scriptural books.

Chapter Seven

Internal Contradictions

Kohelet contradicts himself frequently. Time after time, he finds himself at odds with his own assertions. This inconsistency is so glaring that the Talmud even considered removing the book of Ecclesiastes from general circulation, citing its contradictory statements.[1] How does Rashi reconcile the divergent elements within this text? What exegetical strategies does he employ to unify the composition?[2]

WOMEN

Kohelet initially voices his distrust of women (7:26–29), only to later counsel enjoying life with the woman one loves (9:9). Let us examine both the biblical verses expressing these opposing viewpoints, along with Rashi's explanations.

Kohelet negatively states:

1. Shabbat 30b.
2. Kohelet's contradictory statements about wisdom will be examined in the next chapter, which explores the topic of Solomonic authorship.

> Now, I find woman more bitter than death; she is all traps, her hands are fetters and her heart is snares. He who is pleasing to God escapes her, and he who is displeasing is caught by her. (7:26)

Rashi explains:

> *Now I find more bitter and severe than it [i.e., death] the woman* (R 7:26) – This is heresy (*minut*).[3] ... *Her hands are fetters* – When she seizes a man, he is as though tied with thick ropes.

Rashi interprets the woman as a metaphor for heresy, specifically Christianity, aligning with his understanding of the "strange woman" in Proverbs.[4] The description of her hands and heart as "fetters" and "snares" implies that once Christianity ensnares an individual, it becomes nearly impossible to escape its grasp.[5]

Continuing with the theme of women, Kohelet observes that in his search he found only one human being among a thousand:

> What my soul sought and did not find, one man in a thousand, and a woman among all these I did not find. But, see, this I did find: God made man straight, but they sought many stratagems. (7:28–29)

Regarding these verses, Rashi explains in a nonmetaphorical sense:

> *My soul sought* (R 7:28) – A proper one among women, *but did not find* – Because they are all lightheaded ... therefore, you must be cautious with her.

3. Standard printed editions read *haapikorsut* due to censorship. See *Sifrei, Shelaḥ* 115; Ecclesiastes Rabba 7:26.
4. See our extensive analysis in the previous chapter on Proverbs.
5. Similarly, see Rashi's commentary on Proverbs 2:19. Nevertheless, if one manages to return to the Jewish fold, Rashi asserts in his responsa that the individual should be treated with compassion and must not be humiliated or disgraced. See Israel Elfenbein, "Rashi in His Responsa," in *Rashi: His Teachings and Personality,* ed. S. Federbush (World Jewish Congress, 1958), 90–92.

This characterization of women as lightheaded is a common rabbinic motif,[6] based on Eve's susceptibility to the words of the serpent in the Garden of Eden.[7] And indeed Rashi mentions Eve in his gloss to the following verse:

> *But, see, this I did find* (R 7:29) – For a stumbling block was brought to the world through her. *That* – The Holy One, blessed be He, *made* the first man straight.[8] *But they* – When Eve was paired up with him, and they became two and were called "they" – *sought many stratagems* – Plans and designs of sin. So is it expounded in the Midrash.[9]

This homily, as cited by Rashi, relies on a grammatical shift within the verse from singular to plural: "God made *man* straight, but *they* sought out many stratagems" (7:29). The singular term "man" refers to Adam in his initial state of innocence, while the plural pronoun "they" denotes the sinful schemes of Adam and Eve after she was joined with him.[10] Thus, Eve, the first woman, serves as the archetype for all women; her surrender to temptation and subsequent act of leading Adam to sin establishes a pattern of female behavior.[11]

Although this gloss denigrates women, Grossman notes that it does not reflect Rashi's overall perspective on females. On the contrary,

6. It carried with it halakhic ramifications, such as the prohibition against teaching women Torah. See Avraham Grossman, *Pious and Rebellious: Jewish Women in Medieval Europe,* trans. J. Chipman (Brandeis University Press, 2004), 155–57.
7. See Rashi on Genesis 3:15.
8. According to a midrash, Adam's righteousness is implied by God's comparison of man to the angels: "Now that man (*haadam*) has become like one of us" (Gen. 3:22). Just as an angel is straight, so is Adam. See *Midrash Rabbah: Koheles,* ArtScroll Series (Mesorah, 2015), 23.
9. See *Kohelet Zuta* 7:29; Ecclesiastes Rabba 7:29.
10. Other exegetes interpret the term "man" as encompassing humanity as a whole, explaining the verse as follows: Mankind (singular) is initially fashioned in an upright state, but it is from some of its members (plural) that perversion arises.
11. For an analysis of this stereotypical perception of women, see Leila Leah Bronner, *From Eve to Esther: Rabbinic Reconstructions of Biblical Women* (Westminster John Knox, 1994), 22–41.

Rashi held them in high esteem and endeavored to protect their honor and rights. For example, in Rashi's commentary on the Creation story in Genesis, he avoids incorporating midrashic material that disparages females, as Grossman states:

> Medieval Jewish commentators used the biblical account of Creation and the midrashim disparaging women to bear out their predisposition to prove women's inferiority. Man was created first, his body from the earth and his spirit from God.... Not only was woman created later than man, but she was created from his rib, demonstrating that she was secondary and man primary.... But these ideas do not appear in Rashi's interpretation of the Creation narrative. He cites not one of the midrashim that disparage women, and it is hard to see that as a mere coincidence.[12]

In sum, from an exegetical standpoint, Rashi's commentary on Kohelet's negative portrayal of women can be divided into two. Explicating the initial verse as a metaphor for Christianity, he then views the subsequent verses as referring to women of flesh and blood.

Returning to the problem of contradictions within Ecclesiastes, how does Rashi reconcile the aforementioned negative characterization with the author's positive endorsement to "enjoy happiness with the woman you love" (9:9)? Rashi explains:

> *With the woman* (R 9:9) – With the Torah study that you possess."[13]

Thus, Rashi harmonizes the conflicting verses largely by means of metaphor: While the "woman more bitter than death" symbolizes Christianity, her positive counterpart represents Torah study.

---

12. Grossman, *Rashi*, 269.
13. See *Kohelet Zuta* 9:9; Ecclesiastes Rabba 9:9. Similarly, Rashi identifies the "capable wife" (Prov. 31:10–31) with Torah; see our comprehensive discussion of this topic in the previous chapter.

LAUGHTER AND JOY

Laughter and joy is another subject concerning which Kohelet contradicts himself. The Talmud points out:

> It is written: "Vexation is better than laughter (*miseḥok*)" (Eccl. 7:3), and it is written: "I said of laughter (*liseḥok*), it is *meholal* (praiseworthy)" (Eccl. 2:2).... [Likewise,] it is written: "So I commended mirth (*hasimḥa*) (Eccl. 8:15), and it is written: "And of mirth (*ulesimḥa*): What does it accomplish?" (Eccl. 2:2).[14]

Rashi resolves these conflicting views through a scrutiny of the context in which each phrase or term is found. Let us begin with an analysis of the first contradiction noted in the Talmud regarding the term *seḥok* (laughter/merriment).

S-Ḥ-K (שח״ק)

Kohelet states that anger (*kaas*) is preferable to laughter (*seḥok*) (7:3). According to the standard explanation, the verse refers to the emotions of an individual: It is better for a person to feel anger (*kaas*) than to indulge in laughter (*seḥok*). Rashi, however, significantly alters the meaning of this verse:

> *Anger is better than laughter* (R 7:3) – It would have been better for the generation of the flood if the Holy One, blessed be He, had showed them an angry countenance because of their sins, rather than the laughter that He laughed with them.... It would have been better for Adonijah had his father caused him grief for every sin that he committed, rather than the laughter that he showed him, and for which he was ultimately killed.[15]

According to Rashi, the verse deals with the way a person is treated by a superior: It is better to be treated with displeasure (*kaas*) than with laughter (*seḥok*). If God had expressed displeasure with the generation

14. Shabbat 30b.
15. See *Kohelet Zuta* 7:3; Ecclesiastes Rabba 7:3.

of the flood for their misconduct, and if King David had expressed displeasure with his son's sinful behavior,[16] both stories would have had a different outcome. Because displeasure was not expressed in either case, they continued with their *seḥok*, which led to their downfall.[17] Thus, in this verse (Ecclesiastes 7:3), the connotation of *seḥok* is negative.

How can this negative perception of merriment be reconciled with the explicit praise it receives: "Of merriment I said, 'It is to be praised (*meholal*)'" (2:2)?

The key lies in the interpretation of the root H-L-L in our Ecclesiastes verse. While the Talmud reads it as "to praise," most exegetes give it the meaning "to be senseless."[18] Rashi also understands it as negative. He homiletically links it to the verb *mahul*, which means "to mix" or "to dilute," as illustrated in the verse "Your silver has become dross, your wine mixed (*mahul*) with water" (Is. 1:22). When we are speaking about the realm of ideas, "mixing" suggests a blending of thoughts that produces madness or foolishness, as in the following gloss by Rashi:

> *Madness (holelut)* (R 1:17) – Dullness and confusion of thoughts, an expression of mixing, as in "diluted (*mahul*) with water" (Is. 1:22).

Thus, Rashi interprets the aforementioned verse (2:2) not as commending *seḥok*, but actually denigrating it:

> Of laughter I said it is mingled (*meholal*) (R 2:2) – Mixed with cries and sighs.[19]

---

16. Adonijah considered himself heir to the throne and proclaimed himself king unbeknownst to his father; see I Kings 1.
17. Similarly, in Rashi's commentary on Proverbs 14:13, he explains that God enables the wicked to laugh in this world, but their hearts will ache in the future.
18. Koehler and Baumgartner, *HALOT*, vol. 1, 249, s.v. III: הלל "Foolish; senseless." In I Samuel 21:14 it has the meaning of crazy.
19. See *Kohelet Zuta* 2:2; Ecclesiastes Rabba 2:2. Similarly, Rashi writes in his commentary on Isaiah 1:22: "But the Midrash Aggada explains (Eccl. 2:2): 'Of laughter I said, it makes one mad (מְהוֹלָל)' to mean that it is confused, or mixed up."

Yet in Kohelet's "catalog of seasons" (3:1–8), there is "a time for *weeping* and a time for *laughing* (*liseḥok*)" (v. 4). Given the poetic structure of the text – juxtaposed antonyms – *seḥok* is explicated by Rashi in a positive sense, as the laughter that will be heard at the time of redemption.[20]

S-M-Ḥ (שמ"ח)

What about the meaning of the root S-M-Ḥ? Its meaning is similarly determined by the context in which it is situated.

In the course of Kohelet's quest, he delves into joy (*simḥa*) and experiences pleasure (*tov*), only to ultimately deem them *hevel,* futile (2:1). The failed outcome of this experiment – *hevel* – undoubtedly shapes an exegete's interpretation of the word *simḥa* mentioned earlier in the verse, and, indeed, Rashi writes:

> *I said to myself* (R 2:1) – Since that is so… I will constantly indulge in drinking (*mishteh*). *I will mix (anaskha)* [joyfully (*besimḥa*)] – wine.

According to Rashi, the *simḥa* referenced in the verse is not wholesome joy but rather drunken revelry. He reinforces this interpretation by explicating the verb *anaskha* (root N-S-K), which is followed by the adverb *besimḥa,* as the mixing of wine.[21] Thus the *simḥa* (joy) referred to in the verse is superficial and futile.

However, when the term *simḥa* stands alone, it represents a central theme of this composition: finding happiness and contentment with one's lot in life. True happiness results from appreciating what one has, rather than constantly seeking more. Rashi reiterates this theme throughout his commentary. Here are some examples:

---

20. Similarly, the laughter of the "capable wife" (Prov. 31:25) is heard as positive because the context is a song of praise for her diligence.
21. Similar to: "Mixed (*maskha*) her wine" (Prov. 9:2). Other exegetes explicate the verb from the root N-S-H (נסה), "to test or experiment" – see the second interpretation of Ibn Ezra and that of Gersonides.

> *And I praised joy (simḥa)* (R 8:15) – That he should be *happy with his lot* and engage in the upright commands which cause the heart to rejoice (see Ps. 19:9), and he should not be immersed in increasing his wealth by means of usury, interest, and robbery.
>
> *There is nothing better* (R 3:12) – For man than to *rejoice with his portion,* "and to do that which is good" in his Creator's eyes, while he is yet alive.
>
> *That man should rejoice in his work* (R 3:22) – In the toil of his hands, he should *rejoice* and eat, but not [to aspire] to widen his desire like the grave, to covet riches, to accumulate that which is not rightfully his (Hab. 2:5–6). *For that is his lot* – The toil of his hands, *that is the portion given him from Heaven,* and with it he should *rejoice.*
>
> *[It is good and proper] for one to eat and drink and to enjoy the good* (R 5:17) – To engage in Torah, which is "good instruction" (Prov. 4:2), but he should not accumulate much wealth; rather, he should *rejoice with the portion given him,* for that is his portion.

Genuine happiness (*simḥa*) is achieved not through excessive indulgence or hedonistic pursuits. Instead, it is found by adhering to God's commandments and deriving joy in one's labor and possessions, recognizing them as blessings bestowed from above.

Thus, context is the decisive factor in Rashi's explication of the terms "laughter" and "joy." Sometimes this context is the natural setting in which the term appears in the biblical text; at other times it is the context that Rashi himself constructs.

REWARD AND PUNISHMENT

The most agonizing dilemma that consumes Kohelet's thoughts is the issue of reward and punishment. If God is just, why do the wicked prosper while the righteous suffer? This troubling disparity deeply disturbs Kohelet, prompting him to repeatedly revisit this injustice:

> In my own brief span of life, I have seen both these things: Sometimes a good man perishes in spite of his goodness, and sometimes a wicked one endures in spite of his wickedness. (7:15)

> Here is a frustration (*hevel*) that occurs in the world: Sometimes an upright man is requited according to the conduct of the scoundrel, and sometimes the scoundrel is requited according to the conduct of the upright. I say all that is frustration (*hevel*). (8:14)

> For the same fate is in store for all: for the righteous, and for the wicked; for the good and pure, and for the impure. (9:2)

Yet in other passages, Kohelet contradicts himself and perceives fairness in the realm of reward:

> One who keeps the commandments will not suffer harm. (8:5)

> The fact that a sinner may do evil a hundred times and his [punishment] still be delayed, yet surely I am aware that "it will be well with those who revere God since they revere Him." (8:12)

EXEGETICAL TECHNIQUES

In an attempt to harmonize these conflicting views, Rashi employs a variety of exegetical techniques.

Shifts of Emphasis

Sometimes the solution hinges on subtle shifts of emphasis, such as in the following instances.

The Preposition Bet

Kohelet states:

> In my own brief span of life, I have seen both these things: Sometimes a righteous man perishes *betzidko,* and sometimes a wicked one endures in his wickedness. (7:15)

Explicating the letter *bet* prefixed to the word *tzidko* (his righteousness), Rashi writes:

> *Sometimes a righteous man perishes in his righteousness* (R 7:15) – Although he is perishing, he is nonetheless steadfast in his righteousness.

It would seem natural to take the letter *bet*, "in," in the sense of "in spite of." Although he is righteous, he perishes. Rashi, however, gives it a sense of "maintaining": Although he is on the verge of death, he steadfastly maintains his righteousness. This interpretation shifts the focus from the seemingly unjust death of the righteous to their unwaveringly virtuous behavior until their final breath.

Rashi provides a historical example of such a righteous person – Joseph son of Phukhsas the priest. When Joseph developed a festering sore on his leg, a physician was called to amputate it. Joseph instructed the physician to inform him when the procedure was nearly finished. As instructed, the physician did so, and Joseph then called his son, saying, "My son, until now, you were tasked with caring for me, but now your duty ends, as a priest cannot risk ritual impurity from a limb severed from his living father."[22] Thus Joseph maintained his righteousness even during a perilous procedure.

Designation of Subject

Sometimes the solution hinges upon a novel designation of the subject of the verse. Kohelet heretically declares:

> Consider God's doing! Who can straighten what He has twisted? (7:13)

Rashi explains:

22. See Y. Nazir 7: 1 [55d], *Kohelet Zuta* 7:15. Interestingly, in *Kohelet Zuta*, Joseph is called the son of Boethus.

> *Consider God's doing* (R 7:13) – How everything is prepared according to man's actions, the Garden of Eden for the righteous and Gehinnom for the wicked. Consider to which you should cling. *Who can straighten* – After death that which he made crooked during his life?

Who is the subject of the phrase "what He has twisted?" Presumably, it refers to God, mentioned in the first part of the verse, suggesting that Kohelet holds God accountable for distorting justice. However, Rashi interprets the phrase differently, identifying the subject as the human sinner: "*he* has twisted."[23] Thus Rashi reverses this seemingly blasphemous assertion, attributing the distortion of justice to the wicked rather than to God.

Transforming a Question

When Kohelet asks, "Who knows if a man's spirit does rise upward and if a beast's spirit does sink down into the earth?" (3:21), he is brazenly questioning whether there exists a distinction between humans and animals after death.

The verse contains two linguistic markers signaling that we are dealing with a question. The first is the presence of the word "who" at the beginning of the verse; the second is the interrogative Hebrew letter *heh* prefixed to both verbs: "Does rise upward (*haola*)... does sink down (*hayoredet*)."[24] Rashi reinterprets the verse in the following way:

---

23. More specifically, midrashic literature on Ecclesiastes applies this verse to Adam; see *Kohelet Zuta* 7:13; Ecclesiastes Rabba 7:13; but Rashi omits this specification.

24. Generally, the interrogative *heh* is vocalized differently. Shadal suggests that the punctuation was intentionally altered, transforming the interrogative *heh* into a definite article to soften the sacrilegious nature of Kohelet's words. By contrast, Gordis attributes the unusual vocalization to the positioning of the letter *heh*. When it precedes the letters *alef* and *yod*, there is a tendency to vocalize the *heh* with full vowels and with a *dagesh*. See Shmuel Vargon, "The Identity and Period of the Author of Ecclesiastes According to S.D. Luzzatto (Shadal)," in *Studies in Bible and Exegesis: Presented to Uriel Simon*, vol. 5 (Bar-Ilan University Press, 2000) [in Hebrew], 370, 376–77, and Gordis, *Koheleth*, 238. See also M. Lockshin, "Is Kohelet's Wisdom Vanity of Vanities," www.thetorah.com/article/is-kohelets-wisdom-vanity-of-vanities.

> *Who knows* (R 3:21) – As in, "Whoever knows, let him repent" (Joel 2:14), [i.e., he] who understands, knows that "the spirit of man" ascends on high and stands in judgment, "and the spirit of the beast" descends to the earth, and does not have to give a justification and reckoning.

Rashi transforms this heretical question into a definitive statement: "He who understands, knows."[25] This rephrasing defuses the theological uncertainty, so that Kohelet, once the skeptic, now affirms the mainstream traditional belief in the differing destinies of humans and beasts after death: While human souls rise to be judged, beasts descend to the earth.[26]

Attributing to Others

In the following example, Rashi employs the stratagem of attributing a problematic phrase to a speaker other than Kohelet. The verse states:

> That is the sad thing about all that goes on under the sun: that the same fate is in store for all. Not only that, but men's hearts are full of evil, and their minds of madness, while they live; and then – to the dead! (9:3)

Regarding which, Rashi writes:

> Therefore, *men's hearts are full of evil* (R 9:3) – For they say that there is no judgment of retribution for the wicked. Everything is according to fate, [benefiting] sometimes the righteous, and sometimes the wicked.

25. Similarly, in Rashi's commentary on 6:12, he transforms a question into a statement.
26. It is noteworthy that some *Geonim* did believe in divine compensation for animals; see Daniel J. Lasker, "The Theory of Compensation ('Iwad) in Rabbanite and Karaite Thought: Animal Sacrifices, Ritual Slaughter, and Circumcision," *Jewish Studies Quarterly*, vol. 11, nos. 1–2 (2004): 59–72. I am grateful to Professor Marty Lockshin for pointing out this enlightening source.

According to Rashi, Kohelet is not the speaker of the blasphemous phrase "the same fate is in store for all"; rather, he is quoting the words of men whose "hearts are full of evil," mentioned in the latter part of the verse. Other exegetes, both medieval and modern, employ this stratagem of attributing problematic statements to others.[27]

Addition of Interpretive Words

However, in the majority of cases Rashi smooths out challenging and self-contradictory verses through the addition of interpretive words absent in the biblical text.

For instance, Kohelet challenges the value of wisdom over foolishness by noting that ultimately both the wise and the foolish face the same fate: death and oblivion. This reflection leads him to conclude that wisdom, like foolishness, is *hevel* (2:15–16). Rashi elucidates his words in the following way:

> *And I said to myself, etc.* (R 2:15) – Meaning, since they both die, perhaps I will think in my heart from now on: As it happens to the wicked man, so will it happen to me, so why should I be more righteous? *Then I said to myself* – That if I will think so, that is *hevel* (vanity).

Rashi's interpretation suggests that it is not the shared destiny of the righteous and wicked that renders righteousness *hevel*. On the contrary, what is *hevel* is this erroneous notion of a shared fate! Thus, once again, Rashi's interpretation aligns Kohelet's words with traditional Jewish thought.

Often Rashi's additional interpretive words focus upon the world of sinners, thus preserving the integrity of the righteous, as in the following examples.

> Kohelet states: For I have set my mind to learn wisdom and to observe the business that goes on in the world – his eyes went without sleep both day and night. (8:16)

27. Such as Ibn Ezra, Menahem HaMeiri, and Robert Gordis; see G. Cohn, *Textual Tapestries*, 318–20.

Kohelet notes that "the business that goes on in the world," seemingly alluding to questions about divine providence, results in sleeplessness. But who suffers from this sleepless state? According to Rashi it is not the righteous individual engrossed in understanding God's governance, but rather the wicked.[28] Consumed by their relentless pursuit of wealth and illicit desires, they are unable to find rest.

Likewise, the following comment of Rashi directs us to the world of sin. Kohelet asserts:

> So in a time of good fortune enjoy the good fortune; and in a time of misfortune, reflect: The one no less than the other was God's doing; consequently, man may find no fault with Him (*aḥarav meuma*). (7:14)

This enigmatic verse implies that both fortune and misfortune experienced by an individual are divinely ordained, so that one has no grounds for criticizing God's actions.[29] Rashi explains the verse as follows:

> *So in a time of good fortune enjoy the good fortune* (R 7:14) – On a day in which you have the ability to do good, be among those who do good. *And in a time of misfortune, see* – When evil comes upon the wicked, be among the observers.[30]

---

28. This explanation can find support in the grammatical shift in the verse from first person ("I have set," i.e., Kohelet, the righteous individual) to the third person ("his eyes," i.e., the evildoer).

29. M.V. Fox offers a different interpretation of the verse. He explains that what unsettles Kohelet is not the lack of rationale for both good and misfortune, but rather the proximity of the two, one following the other. This proximity prevents individuals from knowing what the future holds. Therefore, he reads the verse as follows: "In a time of good fortune, enjoy the good fortune; and in a time of misfortune, ponder. God has orchestrated these experiences one after the other; consequently, an individual cannot discover [or anticipate] anything [about what will happen] next." Whereas the explanation written above interprets the phrase *aḥarav meuma* as "fault or blemish with Him" (referring to God), Fox understands the phrase as modifying the individual: "anything [that will happen] after him" (meaning subsequently); see Fox, *JPS Bible Commentary: Ecclesiastes*, 48.

30. See Ecclesiastes Rabba 7:14.

Rashi's interpretation shifts the focus. According to Rashi, the verse does not describe the same individual experiencing both fortune and misfortune. Instead, it distinguishes between the two: Good is associated with the virtuous, while misfortune befalls the evildoer. This dichotomy, absent in the biblical text, "solves" the issue of the suffering of the righteous by transferring misfortune to those who engage in wrongdoing.

Similarly, when Kohelet laments the dire plight of the persecuted, stating: "I further observed all the oppression that goes on under the sun: the tears of the oppressed, with none to comfort them" (4:1), Rashi elucidates as follows:

> *I further observed* (R 4:1) – Through divine inspiration. *All the oppression* – In Gehinnom – who were made oppressed in Gehinnom because of the deeds [that were done] *under the sun* [i.e., while the person was still alive].... *The tears of the oppressed* – Weeping for their souls... these are the ones who descended to Gehinnom.[31]

In Rashi's interpretation, the oppression is not happening in this world but in Gehinnom, where punishment is meted out to evildoers. It is not the innocent who are being oppressed, but rather the wicked, who deserve such a fate. Thus, by fleshing out the biblical text through the addition of interpretive words, Rashi neutralizes the verse's theological sting.

In summary, Rashi employs a range of techniques to reconcile Kohelet's seemingly blasphemous and contradictory statements about divine governance. While some of these techniques are rooted directly in the language of the biblical text, others stem from Rashi's interpretive additions.

COHESIVE THEOLOGY

Using these exegetical methods, Rashi's commentary reveals a cohesive theology of divine providence. This theology, which places greater

31. Rashi gives his source: *Sifrei* (*Re'eh* 53).

emphasis on the fate of the wicked than on that of the righteous, spans both the present world and the World to Come. Let us explore the elements of this philosophy.

The Present World: The Wicked

The prosperity of the wicked is fleeting; evildoers will eventually face retribution at an *appointed time,* as illustrated by the following examples.

> *A season is set for everything* (R 3:1) – Let not the one who gathers wealth out of vanity rejoice (see Prov. 13:11), for even though he possesses it now, the righteous will ultimately inherit it; only the time has not yet arrived, for everything has *a set time* when it will be.

> *A wise man, however, will bear in mind that there is a time of justice* (R 8:5) – The wise person knows that there is *a set time for the punishment* of the wicked, and there is judgment before the Holy One, blessed be He, with which He will ultimately punish them.[32]

The setting of a set time explains the apparent *delay* in the arrival of punishment:

> *I mused, etc.* (R 3:17) – Therefore, I say: the Holy One, blessed be He, judges everything after a time, and even though the matter is delayed, it will eventually reach its time, for there is a time for every experience; even for retribution and for the visitation of judgment there is a time that will come.

The timing of punishment is determined by the extent of the evildoer's *measure of evil.* Punishment is meted out when the sinner's iniquity reaches a certain threshold.

---

32. See Numbers Rabba 14:17.

> *When the evil of man is great upon him* (R 8:6) – When man's evil is great and his measure is piled up (*use'ato gedusha*),[33] then his punishment arrives.[34]

The concept of an evildoer's "full measure" is rooted in the Genesis narrative. In the vision of "the Covenant Between the Pieces" (Gen. 15), God informs Abraham that his descendants will be exiled from the land of Canaan for four generations because "the iniquity of the Amorite will not yet be full until then" (Gen. 15:16). Rashi explains that God delays punishment of this Canaanite nation until their sins have accumulated sufficiently to warrant their expulsion from the land.[35] This connection between the two narratives, expressed through Rashi's use of similar phraseology,[36] underscores the principle that God administers punishment – whether on an individual or national scale – only when transgressions have reached a certain threshold, rather than gradually meting out punishment.

The lag in punishment *emboldens the wicked to continue sinning* because they do not believe that retribution will come.

> *The fact that the sentence (pitgam) imposed for evil deeds* (R 8:11) – Punishment for evil deeds [is not executed] swiftly – For the Holy One, blessed be He, does not rush to mete out retribution upon the evildoers, and therefore, they think there is no judgment, and they are emboldened to do evil.

Not only do evildoers doubt divine retribution, but this misconception is pervasive among humanity at large:

---

33. A similar phrase is used earlier in his commentary: "That their measure should be full" (R 5:7).
34. See Numbers Rabba 14:17.
35. See Rashi's commentary on Genesis 15:16; his source is Sota 9a.
36. Rashi on Genesis 15:16: *Shetitmalei se'atah* (measure is full); Rashi on Ecclesiastes: *use'ato gedusha* (measure is piled up). Both glosses use the noun סאה, which is a type of measure. Drawing from the verse in Isaiah: "In full measure (בְּסַאסְּאָה), when you send her away, you contend with her" (27:8), the Talmud in Sota (9a) interprets this to mean that punishment is exacted only when the measure is full.

And here is another (R 8:10) – One of the vanities that were given to the world to weary mankind, for the Holy One, blessed be He, does not rush to mete out retribution [upon evildoers], and mankind thinks that there is neither judgment nor Judge.

The fact that a sinner, etc. (R 8:12) – Because they see that the sinner does evil a hundred,[37] a thousand, or myriads [of times], and the Holy One, blessed be He, grants him an extension, without meting out retribution.

The lag, however, does afford the wicked an opportunity to repent:

For him who is joined to all the living, there is hope (R 9:4) – For as long as he lives, even if he is wicked and is connected with the wicked, as it says, "To all the living"– even [for] the wicked, there is hope; perhaps he will repent before his death.

When retribution finally arrives, it strikes suddenly and unexpectedly:

When it is on the point of happening (R 8:7) – The punishment. *Who can tell him* – To discuss with him and to ask permission, for suddenly it will befall him.

Kohelet again stresses the abrupt nature of misfortune: "Even so are the sons of men snared in an evil time, when it falls *suddenly* on them" (9:12).[38]

The Present World: The Righteous

Turning his attention to the righteous, Rashi addresses their plight in the following gloss:

37. According to Rashi, the word מְאַת (*me'at,* a hundred) does not mean exactly one hundred but signifies a large, indefinite number: "a hundred, a thousand, or myriads." Due to the elliptic nature of the verse, one should add the words "of times." Thus, the meaning of the phrase becomes: does evil a hundred, a thousand or myriads [of times].

38. Similarly, see Hab. 2:7

> *If the wrath of the ruler* (R 10:4) – The Ruler of the Universe, flares up against you – to scrutinize you with the divine attribute of judgment.... *Don't give up your post* – Don't give up your virtuous attitude, saying, "Of what avail is my righteousness?" *For a cure* – The stringencies of the judgment through the afflictions that come upon you are a cure for your sins, and will ease for you grave offenses.

Taking the term "ruler" to mean the Ruler of the Universe, Rashi explains that the suffering of the righteous, resulting from the meticulous application of divine judgment, serves to purify their sins. This commentary encapsulates two well-known rabbinic axioms: first, that God's providential accounting is more rigorous (verb: D-K-D-K) with the righteous,[39] and second, that suffering brings atonement.[40]

Both principles are illustrated in a story from the Talmud. R. Neḥunya, known for his exceptional righteousness, dedicated himself to digging cisterns for the community's benefit. Despite his piety, calamity struck: His son perished from thirst. How can this tragic event be understood? The Talmud explains that "the Holy One, blessed be He, is exacting (*medakdek*) with those who surround Him (i.e., the righteous that follow His ways) to [the extent of a] hairsbreadth."[41] This implies that R. Neḥunya's son met his fate due to his father's sin,[42] exemplifying the meticulous justice applied to the righteous by God. The application of these principles to our verse in Ecclesiastes is original to Rashi.[43]

---

39. See also Rashi's commentary on Psalms 99:9. Regarding God's rigorous punishment of the righteous, see M. Lockshin, "Does God Punish People Who Are Close to Him More Harshly?" thetorah.com: www.thetorah.com/article/does-god-punish-people-who-are-close-to-him-more-harshly.
40. See Leviticus Rabba 27:1.
41. Yevamot 121b.
42. As is written in the Ten Commandments, "For I, your God, am an impassioned God, visiting the guilt of the parents upon the children" (Ex. 20:4).
43. Rashi's commentary concludes with a quote from the verse in Ecclesiastes: "Will ease [for you] great offenses." If the verse is indeed describing a righteous person, as Rashi suggests, how can there be great offenses? Despite this apparent contradiction, Rashi maintains his interpretation of the verse.

The World to Come

The true distinction between the righteous and the wicked will occur in the World to Come (R 9:2). The Garden of Eden is prepared for the righteous, while Gehinnom awaits the wicked (R 7:13).

Before the final verdict, there will be a day of judgment when the wicked will witness the glory given to the righteous:

> *The fool* (R 4:5) – The wicked... eats his own flesh, on the day of judgment, when he sees the righteous being honored, while he is being judged; so it is explained in the *Sifrei*.[44]

The righteous are encouraged to enjoy goodness in this world, knowing that they have merited the World to Come:

> *Go eat your bread in gladness, etc.* (R 9:7) – But you, the righteous man, whose good deeds the Holy One, blessed be He, has already accepted: "Go, eat your bread in gladness" – in this world, because the Holy One, blessed be He, has already accepted your good deeds, and you will merit the World to Come.

In sum, Rashi constructs a cohesive theology of divine governance, based on the actions of the individual. However, this systematic philosophy encounters complexity with the introduction of the notion of vicarious merit.

Transfer of Merit to Others

Kohelet bemoans the equalizing effect of death, noting that both the wise and the fool die and are forgotten thereafter (2:16). Rashi, however, reinterprets Kohelet's words to convey the opposite message:[45]

> *And how can the wise die with the fool* (R 2:16) – I see the righteous succeeding after their deaths and being of use still to their children,

44. *Sifrei, Re'eh* 53.

45. The strategy employed by Rashi is the addition of interpretive words.

> such as, "And I will remember My covenant with Jacob" (Lev. 26:42); "I remember to you the kindness of your youth" (Jer. 2:2).[46]

Death distinguishes between the two because the righteous [wise], unlike the wicked [fool], can bestow merit upon their children. To support this notion of the transference of merit, Rashi presents two textual proofs. The first, from Leviticus, speaks of the benefits derived from the merit of the Patriarchs. The idea that the merit of the forefathers *(zekhut avot)* benefits future generations features prominently in rabbinic literature.[47]

Marmorstein elaborates on this doctrine:

> The Patriarchs, as well as other personages of the Bible, accomplished or came near to perfection by their faith and love, unselfishness and charity, observances and performances, studies and works – of those ideals for which alone the world was worthy to be called into existence, and for which it deserves to exist. Thus they gathered treasures in heaven not for themselves but for others. By their works and charity their descendants experienced miracles and wonders in the course of historical life. By their merits Israel escaped thousands of perils and dangers. For their sake Israel's immortality and eternity are assured.[48]

The second proof, from Jeremiah, is less commonly cited. It refers to the loving-kindness shown by the Israelite nation toward God after the Exodus. But what specific kindness is intended? Rashi's gloss on this verse in Jeremiah provides clarity:

> *I remember to you* (R Jer. 2:2) – Were you to return to Me, I would desire to have mercy on you, for I remember the loving-kindness

46. See *Kohelet Zuta* 2:144. This source evokes a similar proof text regarding the Patriarchs (Ex. 32:13) but makes no mention of the merit of the nation.
47. See Solomon Schechter, *Some Aspects of Rabbinic Theology* (Macmillan, 1910), 171–76; E.E. Urbach, *The Sages*, 496–511.
48. A. Marmorstein, *The Doctrine of Merits in Old Rabbinical Literature* (Ktav, 1968), 155–56.

> of your youth.... Now what was the loving-kindness of your youth? Your following My messengers, Moses and Aaron, from an inhabited land to the desert without provisions for the way since you believed in Me.[49]

The loving-kindness referred to is the nation's willingness to follow their leaders into the barren desert, trusting in God despite having no provisions.[50]

Notice the recurring words "I" and "remember" present in both proof texts cited by Rashi:

> And *I will remember* My covenant with Jacob. (Lev. 26:42)

> *I remember* for you the kindness of your youth. (Jer. 2: 2)

This repetition emphasizes that God actively recalls the deeds of the righteous by transferring their merit across generations.

It is noteworthy that Rashi's gloss blurs the boundaries between the various categories of intergenerational merit: the merit (covenant) of the Patriarchs (Leviticus), the merit of the Israelites leaving Egypt (Jeremiah), and the merit of a righteous parent (Ecclesiastes). In doing so, he demonstrates the fluidity between these concepts.

Rashi revisits the theme of merit in his gloss to the following verse: "Wisdom is good with an inheritance (*naḥala*), and even better, for those who behold the sun" (7:11), explicating it in the following fashion:

> *Wisdom is good [with an inheritance (naḥala)]* (R 7:11) – Their wisdom lasted for them, together with the inherited merit of their fathers (*naḥalat zekhut avotam*).

49. See *Mekhilta, Bo* 14; *Tanḥuma, Bo* 9.
50. In Rashi's commentary on Jeremiah, the transfer of the merit of the exiting Israelites is conditional upon the generation's repentance: "*Were you to return to Me,* I would desire to have mercy on you, for I remember the loving-kindness of your youth." However, this stipulation of repentance is absent in Rashi's commentary on Ecclesiastes when discussing the transfer of the same merit.

While the word *naḥala* generally refers to inherited property,[51] Rashi spiritualizes this term to refer to ancestral merit.[52] Thus "their wisdom," i.e., the wisdom of the righteous mentioned in his gloss to the previous verse, is enriched when combined with ancestral merit (*naḥala*), "benefiting all of mankind" ("those who behold the sun").

The Limits of Ancestral Merit

Inherited merit does not remove all problems. In the book's closing chapter, Kohelet poetically portrays the harsh effects of aging on the human body, including, according to Rashi, a waning sexual drive: "*And the desire (haaviyona) will fail* (R 12:5) – The desire for women."[53]

Rashi also offers a homiletical interpretation that extends this verse to the nation of Israel:

> *And the desire will fail* – This refers to ancestral merit; the support of your Patriarchs will fail; *haaviyona* is derived from *av* (father).[54]

Thus, *zekhut avot* does not endure forever.[55] Similarly, on an individual scale, parental merit has its limitations. Descendants may forfeit the inherited benefits due to their own sinful behavior, as in Rashi's interpretation of the verses:

> Here is a grave evil I have observed under the sun: riches hoarded by their owner to his misfortune; when those riches are lost in some unlucky venture, if he begets a son, nothing is left for him. (5:12–13)

---

51. Koehler and Baumgartner, *HALOT*, vol. 2, 687–88: "Inalienable, hereditary property."
52. See Ecclesiastes Rabba 7:11.
53. *Haaviyona*, derived from the root A-V-H (אבה), denotes wanting something. Modern exegetes explicate this term in a similar fashion; see Gordis, *Koheleth*, 345–46.
54. This comment is found in Rashi's commentary on 12:6 in his long explanation drawn from Lamentations Rabba, *Petiḥta* 23.
55. However, rabbinic literature is divided on this point. See Marmorstein, *The Doctrine of Merits in Old Rabbinical Literature*, 154.

According to the contextual explanation, the passage depicts a wealthy man, who, having lost his fortune, has nothing material to bequeath to his offspring. Rashi presents an alternative reading:

> *Riches hoarded by their owner to his misfortune* (R 5:12) – Like the wealth of Korah, because of which he became haughty and descended into the grave. *Nothing is left for him* (R 5:13) – Not even the merit of his fathers.

Korah, who hailed from the same esteemed lineage as Moses,[56] was exceedingly affluent according to midrashic tradition.[57] However, when he instigated a failed uprising against the leadership of Moses and Aaron, he not only lost his riches but also "had nothing left," signifying the forfeiture of his ancestral merit. While midrashic sources associate Korah's wealth with the verse in question, its connection to the curtailment of merit seems original to Rashi.

Merit of the Children

Merit is not only passed forward to future offspring, but it can also be extended back to previous generations, as alluded to in the following gloss:

> *In all that goes on, etc.* (R 9:6) – The merit of a son or a daughter did not avail those wicked men who worshipped idols.[58]

It can be inferred that if the parent had not worshipped idols, the merit of the child could have benefited them.[59] Here, too, notice the notion of

---

56. According to Exodus 6:21, Korah is the great-grandson of the patriarch Levi and a first cousin to Moses and Aaron.
57. See Ecclesiastes Rabba 5:12; Pesaḥim 119a; Sanhedrin 110a.
58. Although there is no known source linking engagement in idolatry with the forfeiture of merit, rabbinic sources do associate the term "zealous" with idolatry, and this word is present in our Ecclesiastes verse: "Their jealousies (*kinatan*) have long since perished"; see Ecclesiastes Rabba 9:6.
59. Surprisingly, according to some, the belief that a child can bring merit to a parent is the rationale for the recitation by mourners of *Kaddish*. As M. Lamm explains, the

limitation; violation of a cardinal precept annuls the intergenerational transfer of merit.

These constraints on the transfer of merit carry a significant theological implication, as Solomon Schechter observes: "There can be no doubt that the *zechut* of the fathers in no way served to silence the conscience of the individual, relieving him from responsibility for his actions."[60] Thus each person remains accountable for his own deeds; individual conduct is of importance in determining one's destiny.

Merit of the Generation

Until now we have examined the notion of merit along a diachronic axis, transferring both forward and backward across generations. However, merit also possesses a synchronic dimension – the capacity of a virtuous generation to distribute merit among all its members. Rashi expresses this concept:

> *Don't say, "How has it happened that former times," etc.* (R 7:10) – Do not wonder about the goodness that was given to the righteous men of the past, in the generation of the wilderness, the generation of Joshua, and the generation of David. *For it is not wise of you to ask* – For everything depends upon the merit of the generation.[61]

This explanation suggests that the collective merit of a generation can influence the fortunes of all its individuals, illustrating the power of communal righteousness.

In summary, Rashi's commentary harmonizes seemingly conflicting verses to present a cohesive theology of divine governance, where each individual receives his due rewards or punishments in this world and/or the World to Come. However, this straightforward framework

---

sages believed that a son's recitation of *Kaddish* confirms a parent's life of goodness and can even effect repentance for a parent's life of sin. (Maurice Lamm, *The Jewish Way in Death and Mourning* [Jonathan David Publishers, 1969], 161).

60. Schechter, *Some Aspects of Rabbinic Theology*, 183.

61. See Rosh HaShana 25b.

can be modified by the diachronic or synchronic transfer of merit. The accumulated merit from previous and future generations (diachronic) and the collective righteousness of the current generation (synchronic) can influence the distribution of reward and punishment, adding layers of complexity to this theological system.

Limitations of Human Understanding

Ultimately, when all is said and done, Rashi writes:

> *That man cannot discover, etc.* (R 8:17) – Mankind is unable to fathom the ways of the Holy One, blessed be He, what the reward is for all the work that is done under the sun, for they see wicked men prospering and righteous men deteriorating.... *And even though a wise man declares* – That he understands it, he will not be able to, for [even] Moses our teacher could not comprehend this matter, as when he said, "Please make Your way known to me" (Ex. 33:13).[62]

Thus, according to Rashi, both Kohelet (Solomon), the wisest of all men, and Moses, the greatest of all prophets, acknowledge that ultimately the ways of God are beyond human comprehension.

In conclusion, Rashi uses a variety of techniques to harmonize the divergent voices within Kohelet. At times he harmonizes the text through nuanced readings, reinterpreting prefixes or altering the punctuation of verses. In other instances, he employs metaphor to resolve apparent contradictions, offering symbolic interpretations that reconcile disparate elements. More frequently, Rashi embellishes the biblical text by adding interpretive words that serve to clarify and unify its message. Through these methods of explanation and expansion, Rashi transforms Ecclesiastes into an internally coherent and unified composition.

---

62. While Berakhot 7a explains Moses's request to God as a desire to understand why the righteous suffer (see Rashi's commentary on Ex. 33:13), Rashi's application of this concept to our Ecclesiastes verse is uniquely his own.

Chapter Eight

Additional Manifestations of Wholeness

AUTHORSHIP

The unity of the narrative is closely tied to the question of authorship. Ecclesiastes is unique in its use of first-person narrative to recount personal experiences, thoughts, and observations. But who is the "I" sharing his insights with us? Who is the Kohelet mentioned in the book's superscription: "The words of Kohelet son of David, king in Jerusalem" (1:1)? Given that the Bible records only one son of David who was crowned as king, Kohelet is naturally identified with Solomon. This identification is widely supported in rabbinic literature: "He was called by three names: Yedidya, Kohelet, Solomon."[1]

Rashi explains the epithet "Kohelet" in the following way:

> *Kohelet* (R 1:1) – Because he gathered much wisdom... and the *darshanim* (homiletic interpreters) say that he would say all his words in *hakhel* (public assembly).[2]

1. Ecclesiastes Rabba 1:1.
2. See *Kohelet Zuta* 1:1; Ecclesiastes Rabba 1:1. *Hak'hel* is a biblical commandment

Rashi offers two interpretations for the root K-H-L, which means to gather. The first interpretation pertains to the wisdom that Kohelet accumulated internally, while the second connects to the assembly of people, the occasions when Kohelet shared his wisdom with the public. This dual explanation highlights both the internal and external dimensions of Solomon's wisdom.

Although Rashi does not explicitly state at the outset of his Kohelet commentary that Solomon penned this composition, Solomonic authorship is indicated repeatedly throughout his gloss.[3] For example, while discussing the gender of the word *kohelet*, Rashi writes:

> *Kohelet* (R 7:27) – Is a feminine noun, and when it is used in the masculine form (see Eccl. 1:2), it refers to the one who gathers it, i.e., Solomon.

In this specific verse, the feminine noun "Kohelet" is accompanied by a feminine verb, indicating that it refers to something else, not a person. However, elsewhere, near the beginning and end of the book (1:2, 12:8), its association with a masculine verb indicates that it refers to Solomon.

Additionally, Rashi states that when Solomon inaugurated the Temple, his initial pleas failed to summon fire to the altar. However, the moment he invoked the merit of David, his father, the fire immediately descended (R 4:2).[4] When Rashi says that Kohelet used the phrase "my father David," he unmistakably identifies him as Solomon. Similarly, when Kohelet acknowledges the superiority of earlier generations (7:10),

(Deut. 31:10–13) that mandated that every seven years, during the Sukkot holiday following the Sabbatical year, the entire nation should assemble at the Temple in Jerusalem. At this gathering, the king would read verses from the book of Deuteronomy.

3. In his commentary on the book of Kings, Rashi explicitly acknowledges Solomonic authorship of Ecclesiastes. Upon identifying Solomon's songs, Rashi writes: "And his songs numbered [... and] five (1 Kings 5:12) – the above three, and Song of Songs and Ecclesiastes."
4. See Shabbat 30a; *Kohelet Zuta* 4:3; Ecclesiastes Rabba 4:6.

Rashi lists previous generations, all of which predate Solomon,[5] further hinting at Solomon as the author.

PORTRAIT OF KING SOLOMON

Another unifying factor in Rashi's commentary is from aligning the book's content with Solomon's life. Many of Kohelet's experiences and observations resonate deeply with the accounts of Solomon's experiences and wisdom as detailed in other parts of the Bible.

Wealth

King Solomon's wealth was legendary and unmatched. He accumulated immense riches through extensive trade, prosperous economic policies, and hefty tributes from other nations. His daily provisions were immense and reflected the grandeur of his court. According to the Bible, his household consumed vast quantities of food each day:

> Solomon's daily provisions consisted of 30 *kor* of semolina, and 60 *kor* of [ordinary] flour, 10 fattened oxen, 20 pasture-fed oxen, and 100 sheep and goats, besides deer and gazelles, roebucks and fatted geese. (1 Kings 5: 2–3)

These provisions were necessary to sustain the large number of people in Solomon's royal household, evidencing the prosperity of his reign.

Kohelet also speaks of his extensive acquisitions, including houses, vineyards, gardens, and parks, and the amassing of silver, gold, and treasures (Eccl. 2:4–8). Regarding Kohelet's daily food needs, Rashi explains:

> *Nor is bread won by the wise* (R 9:11) – For example, I, [Kohelet,] whose daily bread was "thirty *kor* of semolina, etc." (1 Kings 5:2).[6]

"Thirty *kor* of semolina" is the amount of Solomon's daily bread provision as listed in 1 Kings.

5. They include the generations of the desert, of Joshua, and of David.
6. See Ecclesiastes Rabba 9:11.

The most significant overlap, however, lies in the realm of wisdom. Kohelet articulates a complex relationship with wisdom, expressing both its profound value and its inherent limitations. This dual perspective is a theme that Rashi connects to the personality and life of Solomon.

Wisdom

According to the book of Kings, Solomon was endowed with exceptional wisdom:[7]

> I grant you a wise and discerning mind; there has never been anyone like you before, nor will anyone like you arise again. (1 Kings 3:12)

This incomparable wisdom included a profound understanding of the natural world, encompassing both fauna and flora, which Rashi links to Kohelet's expertise in horticulture. Concerning the fruit trees Kohelet planted in his estate, Rashi writes:

> *Every kind of fruit tree* (R 2:5) – For Solomon with his wisdom recognized the veins of the earth, which vein goes to Ethiopia, and there he planted peppers; which one goes to a land of carobs, and there he planted carob trees. For all the veins of the lands come to Zion, from where the world was founded, as it states, "Out of Zion, the perfect beauty" (Ps. 50:2). Therefore, it states, "Every kind of fruit tree" in *Midrash Tanḥuma*.[8]

In Rashi's gloss, Kohelet is explicitly identified as Solomon. His remarkable ability to discern the optimal tracts of land for each species of tree, understanding the subterranean channels connecting Israel to the rest of the world, enabled him to plant and cultivate non-native plants successfully in the Land of Israel. This extraordinary insight demonstrates the depth of Solomon's wisdom and his profound connection to the natural world.

7. See 1 Kings 3:5–28, 5:9–14.
8. *Tanḥuma*, Buber, *Kedoshim* 10.

Kohelet also acknowledges the frustrations and perils of the quest for knowledge:

> All this I tested with wisdom. I thought I could fathom it, but it eludes me. [The secret of] what happens is far off and deep, deep down; who can discover it? I put my mind to studying, exploring, and seeking wisdom and the reason of things, and to studying wickedness, stupidity, madness, and folly. (7:23–25)

Rashi correlates these verses with religiously dangerous topics that may provoke doubt in a believer:

> *What happens is far off* (R 7:24) – The distant things that were in the Creation. *And deep, deep down; who can discover it* – For I am not permitted to delve into them, what is above and what is below, what is before and what is after.[9]

It is forbidden to study what is indiscernible, such as the mysteries of the universe at the time of Creation, because these matters are beyond human comprehension. Engaging in such speculative study can lead to theological confusion and doubt.

In his commentary on the next verse, Rashi discourages study of an additional three realms of wisdom:

> Furthermore, *I put my mind... to studying, exploring, and seeking* (R 7:25) – The wisdom of the section of the Red Heifer, and the computation (*ḥeshbon*) of the end [of exile] for redemption.[10] *And to know* the *wickedness of folly* – To fathom the depths of the reasoning of *minut* (heresy),[11] and the confusion of foolish-

9. See Ḥagiga 11b.
10. See *Pesikta Rabbati* 14:7.
11. English translations erroneously translate the phrase "*laamod al sof datta*" as "To foresee the ultimate end of." The correct translation is "To fathom the depths of reasoning," as stated in the text above. That is the meaning of the phrase in the Talmud (Eiruvin 13b), as well as in Rashi's commentary ad loc.

> ness (*vesikhlut holelot*): the mixture of foolishness and the idiocy therein.

Let us examine each of these three enigmas: the Red Heifer, the calculation of the end of exile, and the reasoning involved in heresy.

The Torah describes the Red Heifer as a *ḥukka* (Num. 19:2), a type of law that the Sages consider beyond human comprehension. The paradox of the Red Heifer is that its ashes purify those who are spiritually unclean, yet those involved in its preparation become unclean themselves. This ritual is traditionally regarded as the ultimate example of a commandment that defies logic. Following in the footsteps of the Sages,[12] Rashi links Solomon, the wisest of all men, with the quest to unravel this mystery, which ultimately leads him to admit, "I thought I could fathom it, but it eludes me" (Eccl. 7:23).

The calculation of the end of exile involves attempting to pinpoint from biblical verses an exact date for the arrival of the Messiah. The Talmud, recognizing the complexities and uncertainties inherent in such calculations, adamantly discourages this pursuit.[13]

> R. Shmuel bar Naḥmani says [that] R. Yonatan says: May those who calculate the end of days be cursed [*tippa... meḥashvei kisin*], as they would say, once the end [of days that they calculated] arrived and [the Messiah] did not come, [that] he will no longer come [at all]. Rather, [the proper behavior is to continue to] wait for his [coming], as it states, "Though it tarry, wait for it" (Hab. 2:3).[14]

The strong stance against calculating the date of the final redemption stems from the concern that an incorrect prediction could shake people's faith. Individuals engaging in this discouraged pursuit are

12. See *Kohelet Zuta* 7:23.
13. Despite the warning, Rashi does indulge in this practice; see Rashi's commentary on the book of Daniel: 7:25, 8:14, 12:11–12.
14. Sanhedrin 97b. *Koren Talmud Bavli, Tractate Sanhedrin, Part Two, Commentary by Rabbi Adin Even-Israel Steinsaltz* (Koren Publishers, 2017), 317.

termed *meḥashvei kisin* (calculators of the end) by the aforementioned Gemara – note the linguistic similarity between the word *meḥashvei* and the term *ḥeshbon* in our verse in Ecclesiastes, both sharing the same root. However, it is Rashi's original contribution to establish this connection and to explicate our verse within the context of eschatological predictions.[15]

Finally, according to Rashi, Kohelet attempted to fathom the reasoning behind *minut* (which, as we have seen, is a code word for Christianity in Rashi's commentary),[16] only to find that it contains "*the confusion of foolishness (vesikhlut holeilot)* (R 7:25) – the mixture of foolishness and idiocy."[17]

In his Ecclesiastes commentary, Rashi consistently takes the root H-L-L to mean a blend or confusion.[18] He may be hinting at illogical beliefs present in Christian doctrines. Although his precise intention is not entirely clear, the polemical nature of his words was not overlooked by medieval censors. A twelfth-century manuscript of Rashi's Bible commentary replaces the term *minut* (מינות) with the word "mitzvot" (מצוות),[19] two words that visually resemble one another.[20] This substi-

15. Ecclesiastes Rabba connects Solomon's desire to understand the timing of the end of days to Ecclesiastes 12:10.
16. Note the anachronism: Solomon lived a thousand years before Christianity.
17. Jastrow, *A Dictionary of the Targumim*, 1161, "*She'amum* – dullness, idiocy."
18. In Rashi's commentary on 1:17, he clearly states: "*holeilot* – dullness and confusion of thoughts, an expression of mixing." Similarly, see his commentary on 10:13.
19. Manuscript Oxford-Bodleian Corpus Christi Coll. 165 (Neubauer 2440), as noted by Gila Prebor, "The Use of Midrash in Rashi's Commentary on Ecclesiastes" [in Hebrew], in *Shnaton, An Annual for Biblical and Ancient Near Studies*, ed. S. Japhet, XIX, p. 226, n. 29. The same manuscript also features the subsequent polemical interpolation not present in other manuscripts and printed editions checked by Prebor. It contains a sharp expression of Rashi's attitude toward Christianity (folio 396v): "All the mitzvot [should read: heresy] of the hanged one, which says 'I have spread my couch with coverings' (Prov. 7:16), 'I have perfumed my bed' (Prov. 7:17) – they weary themselves to seduce and continue to פרדייר in Old French, twisting the Scriptures to their divinity, which is not so with any other nation." In personal communication, Professor Cyril Aslanov believes that the Old French word should be corrected to *plaidier* meaning "to plead."
20. The standard Rabbinic Bible edition (reprinted from the Venice edition, 1524–25) similarly reads *mitzvota* (מצותה). So too, in Rashi's commentary on Prov. 2:12, the

tution may be a scribal error.[21] In any case, it seems clear that Solomon advises against delving too deeply into Christian theology.

Thus Rashi's commentary on verse 25 strongly discourages intellectual inquiry in three areas. Whereas the first two are divine mysteries beyond human comprehension, the third is a matter of muddled human thought.

Kohelet also acknowledges the danger of excessive wisdom: "For in much wisdom is much grief; and he who increases knowledge increases sorrow" (1:18). Rashi explains:

> *For in much wisdom* (R 1:18) – A person relies on his great wisdom and does not distance himself from the prohibition, and much grief comes to the Holy One, blessed be He. I said, "I will get many horses, but I will not return the people to Egypt" (Deut. 17:16), but ultimately, I returned them (see 1 Kings 10:28–29). "I will take many wives, but they will not turn my heart away" (Deut. 17:17), but it is written about me, "His wives swayed his heart" (1 Kings 11:4). And, similarly, he states that he relied on his great wisdom and did [many things], as it states, "the words of this man to Itiel, because God is with me, I will be able" (Prov. 30:1).[22]

Rashi elucidates the thought process that led Solomon to violate the specific prohibitions given to a king – prohibitions for which the Torah explicitly states the rationale. Solomon reasoned that since the Torah provided the rationale, he was exempt from the prohibition, since his immense wisdom would protect him. This belief is reflected in the cited verse from Proverbs, where the epithet "Itiel (God is with me)" gives assurance that "I will be able (*ve'ukhal*)."[23]

---

aforementioned edition reads: *hamitzva* in place of *haminut.*

21. *Apikorsut*: Judaica Press edition (p. 94); *mitzvot*: standard Rabbinic Bible edition (reprinted from the Venice edition, 1524–25). Similarly, in Rashi's commentary on Proverbs 2:12 the standard Rabbinic Bible edition reads *hamitzva* in place of *haminut.*
22. See *Tanḥuma, Va'era* 5.
23. Similarly, see Rashi's commentary on Proverbs 30:1 and our discussion earlier, p. 115.

Punishment for Sin

Was Solomon punished for transgressing the prohibitions enumerated above? While the book of Kings indicates that his primary punishment – the division of his kingdom – was deferred until the reign of his son Rehoboam (1 Kings 11:11–12), Rashi's Ecclesiastes commentary reveals that Solomon faced serious repercussions during his own lifetime.

Kohelet states, "I, Kohelet, was king in Jerusalem over Israel" (1:12), and Rashi explains:

> *I, Kohelet, was king* (R 1:12) – Over the whole world, and later, over Israel, and then, over Jerusalem only, and finally, over my staff, for it says: I was king in Jerusalem – but now I am no longer king.

Drawing from rabbinic sources, Rashi interprets the use of the past tense "was" and the specific mention of "Jerusalem" – unlike other more general biblical references to kingship – as evidence that Solomon was gradually dethroned.[24] Initially, Solomon ruled over the entire world. Then his domain was restricted to Israel only, subsequently to Jerusalem alone, and finally he was left ruling only over his staff.

Tuller Keiter notes that Solomon's punishment was "measure for measure."

> If Solomon's great sin was pride in his wisdom, his assuredness that he could violate the letter of the law without violating its spirit, then the proper punishment for such a sin, in the rabbinic mind, would be humiliation.[25]

According to Rashi, Kohelet continues to reflect on his pitiable condition:

24. See Sanhedrin 20b; Song of Songs Rabba 1:10.
25. Sheila Tuller Keiter, *Perils of Wisdom: The Scriptural Solomon in Jewish Tradition* (Gorgias, 2021), 236.

> *I said to myself* (R 1:16) – Now that I have sunk from my greatness, I speak to myself, saying, "Who would have said about me that I would come to such a state?" *Behold, "I have grown," etc.*

> *And this was my portion* (R 2:10) – And after doing all these, I have nothing more than this. Rav and Samuel, one says, his walking stick, *maklo,* and one says, his cup, *makkeida,* [which is] an earthenware cup from which people drink.[26]

Both the walking stick and the earthenware cup are utensils used by those on a journey, far from home,[27] signifying Solomon's loss of stature and material wealth.[28]

Repentance

Does Solomon repent of his misdeeds? The book of Kings and Rashi's commentary there remain silent on this issue. However, in Rashi's commentary here, Solomon does acknowledges his sins:

> *For in much wisdom* (R 1:18) – I said, "I will get many horses, but I will not return the people to Egypt" (Deut. 17:16), but ultimately, I returned them (see 1 Kings 10: 28–29). "I will take many wives, but they will not turn my heart away" (Deut.17:17), but it is written about me, "His wives swayed his heart" (1 Kings 11:4).

Acknowledgment of sin is the beginning of repentance.

Further on in the book, Rashi gives a different meaning to that phrase "Because God is with me, I will be able." Rashi's reframing of the principle "Because God is with me," evident in the following gloss, hints at penitence:[29]

---

26. See Sanhedrin 20b and Rashi's commentary there.
27. Regarding the cup, see Rashi on Ezekiel 12:3.
28. The Talmud in Gittin (68b) describes the crucial role played by the demon Ashmedai in Solomon's loss of the throne. While Ashmedai is not mentioned in Rashi's Ecclesiastes commentary, he is briefly mentioned in connection to Solomon in Rashi's commentaries on II Samuel 7:14 and Psalms 89:33.
29. This reinterpretation is original to Rashi. Exodus Rabba 6:1 links a later verse in

> *And my heart conducted itself with wisdom* (R 2:3) – Even if my body is soaked with wine, my heart conducted itself with wisdom – Torah. *And to grasp folly* – With things that appear foolish to me, concerning them I said, "Because God is with me, I will be able" (Prov. 30:1). For example, wearing *shaatnez*[30] and mingled species in a vineyard,[31] which Satan challenges and the nations of the world challenge.[32]

It is difficult to see a reason for the laws of *shaatnez* and mingled species, and according to rabbinic texts, these laws were often mocked by Satan and the nations of the world. Solomon asserts that despite the seemingly "foolish" nature of these commandments, he could uphold them because *Itiel ve'ukhal* (meaning "God is with me; I will be able"). Rashi has cleverly reinterpreted this principle, which Solomon originally used to rationalize his *violation* of prohibitions for which the Torah gave an *explicit reason. Now it becomes an assertion of his resolution* to *uphold* laws that *defy human reason*. Thus what once symbolized the breaking of God's law now signifies its fulfillment, hinting at Solomon's repentance.[33]

Forgiveness

Is Solomon forgiven? This question partially hinges on whether he regained his throne. While the Talmud debates this issue, Rashi holds that at the time Solomon wrote the book of Ecclesiastes, late in his life,[34] he had not been restored to kingship; where Kohelet says, "I was king

---

the chapter (Eccl. 2:12) to "*Itiel ve'ukhal*," but it is unclear if Rashi was aware of this source.

30. Clothing that contains a mixture of wool and linen; Leviticus 19:19.
31. See Deuteronomy 22:9.
32. Yoma 67b identifies *shaatnez* as a type of law, or *ḥok*, that Satan and other nations challenge, listing it alongside laws such as eating pork and purifying a *metzora*. However, this source does not connect to our verse in Ecclesiastes or to the concept of *Itiel ve'ukhal*.
33. Regarding a similar discussion of Solomon's repentance in rabbinic literature, see Tuller Keiter, *Perils of Wisdom*, 252–55.
34. This late timing is evident not only from the reflective tone of the book but also from Solomon's admission of his sins concerning his many wives. Rashi notes: "But

over Israel in Jerusalem," Rashi supplies: "But now he is no longer king" (R 1:12). Thus, Solomon's return to the throne is uncertain at best.

While Solomon may not have been forgiven in the public realm, Rashi evidently believes that he did attain forgiveness in his personal, religious life. We may infer this from the fact that Rashi attributes prophecy or divine inspiration (*ruaḥ hakodesh*) to Solomon no less than six times:

> *That, too, I found was futile* (R 2:1) – For I saw *prophetically* that much evil is caused by lighthearted frivolity.
>
> *And so I loathed life* (R 2:17) – He was *prophesying* about the members of the generation of Rehoboam, who were wicked.
>
> *In the place of justice, etc.* (R 3:16) – I saw with *divine inspiration* the place of the Chamber of Hewn Stone in Jerusalem, which had been "full of justice" (Is. 1:21).[35]
>
> *I further observed* (R 4:1) – With *divine inspiration.* "All the oppressed [people]" in Gehinnom – who were oppressed in Gehinnom for the deeds that were committed.[36]
>
> *And then* (R 8:10) – *In this prophecy,* "I saw how the wicked were buried" – who were worthy of being buried in the dust, for they were held in contempt by the nations.[37]
>
> *Folly was placed on lofty heights* (R 10:6) – For I see with *divine inspiration* that they are destined to extend their hand against His Temple.

---

it is written about me, 'His wives swayed his heart'" (R 1:18). This swaying of the heart happened only during Solomon's old age, as noted in the book of Kings: "In his old age, his wives turned away Solomon's heart after other gods" (1 Kings 11:4).

35. See Sanhedrin 103a.
36. Rashi clearly states that his source is *Sifrei* (*Re'eh* 53).
37. See Gittin 56b. According to this interpretation, the "wicked" are the Romans.

Note Rashi's use of the terms "divine inspiration" and "prophecy" to describe communication with the Divine. These terms are related but not identical. Some rabbinic sources intimate that divine inspiration serves as the intermediary through which prophecy is received;[38] later sages, such as Maimonides, held that the terms refer to different levels of divine communication, prophecy being the higher.[39] In any event, divine inspiration or prophecy implies that the person receiving it is reconciled with God. Greenspahn notes:

> Isaac, Jacob, Moses, the elders, Jeroboam and Hananiah all are said to have "lost" the Holy Spirit[40] at various times. Its presence is thus a sign of Divine favor and its departure reflects lower status.[41]

Thus Rashi, by attributing divine inspiration to Solomon, seems to imply that Solomon had achieved personal reconciliation with God.

In sum, Rashi views Solomon as the author of Ecclesiastes and presents a comprehensive portrait of him. Despite being blessed with incomparable wisdom, Solomon violated Torah prohibitions and faced punishment as a result. Acknowledging his wrongdoings, he pursued repentance and received divine forgiveness, as evidenced by the gift of prophecy, which signified his reconnection with God. By applying the biblical verses to Solomon, Rashi's commentary on Ecclesiastes constructs a detailed narrative of Solomon's life.

---

38. For example, *Seder Olam Rabba* 30 states that until the time of Alexander the Great, "prophets prophesied with divine intervention: hereafter, incline your ears and obey the sages' words." For further discussion, see Chaim Milikowsky, "The End of Prophecy and the Closure of the Bible in Judaism of Late Antiquity" [in Hebrew], *Sidra: A Journal for the Study of Rabbinic Literature* 10 (1994): 83–94.
39. *Guide for the Perplexed,* II:45.
40. I.e., *ruaḥ hakodesh,* or divine inspiration.
41. Frederick Greenspahn, "Why Prophecy Ceased," *JBL* 108/1 (1989): 47.

FINAL SUMMARY

Unorthodox, heretical, and riddled with contradictions – what is Ecclesiastes doing in the biblical canon? Rashi's commentary skillfully unravels this perplexing narrative, creating harmony on three distinct levels.

To begin with, skeptical thoughts are reinterpreted to emphasize the importance of Torah study and adherence to commandments, with the promise of eventual divine reward. Whereas "toil under the sun" is *hevel* (devoid of value), replacing it with spiritual pursuits yields profound results. In this reinterpretation, dozens of seemingly mundane elements such as dying flies, soggy bread, white laundry, and snake charmers are imbued with religious significance, contributing to the narrative's evolution into a cohesive spiritual guide that espouses traditional beliefs and values. Genuine happiness is not achieved through excessive indulgence or hedonistic pursuits. Rather, it is found by adhering to God's commandments and deriving joy in one's lot in life (*same'aḥ beḥelko*), recognizing them as blessings bestowed from above.

The spiritualization of the narrative is further enriched by application of the verses to historical figures and events. Characters like Moses, Serah, Elkanah, and Balaam are invoked over seventy times, modeling both pious and ungodly behavior. These lessons deepen Ecclesiastes's spiritual dimension and strengthen its connection with other scriptural books. Thus, the first level of harmonization operates on the broadest scale, aligning Ecclesiastes with traditional theology and integrating its content within the wider canon.

Narrowing the lens, the second level of harmonization addresses the internal cohesiveness of the narrative itself. Employing a range of techniques, Rashi reconciles Kohelet's divergent voices. Sometimes, these methods are rooted directly in the language of the text, such as differentiating between synonyms, explicating prefixes, or altering the punctuation of verses. At other times he takes heretical words in a metaphorical sense, or attributes them to other speakers. In the majority of instances, the harmonization is achieved through the addition of interpretive words. Rashi particularly focuses on reconciling Kohelet's unorthodox views on reward and punishment. His exegetical efforts result in a comprehensive theology concerning divine governance. By using the aforementioned methods of explanation and expansion, Rashi transforms Ecclesiastes into an internally unified composition.

Finally, zooming in on the notion of authorship reveals an additional dimension of unity. Who is the "I" sharing his story with us? Kohelet is traditionally identified with Solomon. This identification, initially suggested by the book's superscription, is further reinforced through a meticulous analysis of the book's content. Rashi aligns the themes, reflections, and experiences described in Ecclesiastes with the events and wisdom of Solomon's life.

Endowed with unprecedented wisdom, Solomon misused his gifts by overstepping the boundaries set by the Torah. As a consequence of his transgressions, he faced significant punishment but also recognized his wrongdoings and embarked on a path of sincere repentance. Despite the uncertainty about his return to the throne, Solomon received divine favor in his personal and spiritual life, as evidenced by the bestowal of prophetic powers upon him – a divine gift noted no less than six times. This implies his spiritual reconciliation and enduring relationship with God.

By aligning the biblical verses with Solomon's biography, Rashi's Ecclesiastes commentary paints a comprehensive portrait of Solomon's life. It presents Solomon not as a saint, untouched by sin, nor as the unrepentant sinner of the book of Kings, but as a complex figure who experiences success, failure, and ultimately, repentance. This holistic portrayal constitutes the third level of unity within this narrative, enriching our understanding of his character and journey.

Thus Rashi's commentary redeems not only the book of Ecclesiastes, but also the legacy of Solomon himself.

Conclusion

In our examination of Rashi's commentaries on the books attributed to King Solomon, we have focused on a tendency to create unity across the whole of the text. In conclusion, we may now reflect on the overarching strategies by which this is achieved, and also ask about the timing of this holistic quest and about its ultimate source.

TWO SCHEMATA

In Rashi's commentaries on the books traditionally attributed to Solomon, we uncover two exegetical schemata employed to convey unity. The first, resembling a *horizontal line*, is evident in his allegorical interpretation of the Song of Songs. Here Rashi presents the narrative as a love story between the Congregation of Israel (female beloved) and God (male beloved), tracking their tumultuous relationship throughout history. This relationship unfolds through significant historical events such as the Exodus, the entry into the Promised Land, and the subsequent exiles and returns, each event marking a milestone on the national timeline. A consistent motif throughout history is the "indwelling of God" (*hashraat haShekhina*), which Rashi repeatedly describes in spatial terms:

Mount Sinai, the Tabernacle, the Temple, houses of prayer and study, and the future Temple. These sacred spaces, each representing a distinct point on the historical continuum, symbolize the enduring connection between God and His beloved nation. This divine-human connection is indissolubly linked to the Congregation of Israel's fidelity to Torah study and adherence to God's precepts, with the congregation representative of all strata of Israelite society – legislators and laymen, men and women, scholars and disciples, the devout and the impious – thus embracing the entire collective.

Rashi introduces new terminology to articulate an allegorical timeline. Rather than using the more general term *midrasho,* he coins the term *dugma* to more precisely capture the notion of exact comparison between the biblical text and its corresponding message. While the word *dugma* appears in midrashic literature, it is Rashi who infuses it with exegetical import. Drawing generously from rabbinic literature to construct his sequential allegory, Rashi meticulously selects and edits those sources that align with his exegetical agenda. When no suitable source material is available, he formulates original explications to fill the exegetical void, seamlessly interweaving all elements into a cohesive and organic whole.

The second schema can be likened to a wheel, where the central hub and outer rim are connected by radiating spokes. In Rashi's commentaries on Proverbs and Ecclesiastes, central themes extend outward from a core concept, uniting all parts of each composition. At the heart of these commentaries is the fundamental identification of "wisdom" with the Torah, with the spokes representing the practical application of this wisdom in both thought and action. Hundreds of sayings in Proverbs and philosophical musings in Ecclesiastes are "reread" to emphasize the study of Torah and the observance of its commandments. While this reinterpretation is rooted in rabbinic literature, Rashi refines and expands it, adding additional spokes to better align and strengthen the compositional frame. Through his reinterpretation, Rashi transforms these seemingly secular and randomly arranged compositions into cohesive, holistic narratives, unified within a singular thematic framework that promotes traditional Jewish values and actions.

It is highly significant that, with respect to both the linear and circular schemas, the unification of the narrative is primarily achieved within the midrashic tier. This more flexible exegetical level is crucial in providing Rashi with the interpretive latitude necessary to weave a cohesive narrative. By operating within this pliable framework, Rashi is able to highlight key motifs and ensure a consistent overarching message, thereby creating thematic coherence within the text.

BETWEEN PROVERBS AND ECCLESIASTES

Despite their similarities, fundamental differences exist between the commentaries on Proverbs and Ecclesiastes. In his commentary on Proverbs, Rashi begins with an explicit declaration of intent to interpret the text on two distinct exegetical levels. This is an unusual move and is further distinguished by the introduction of original terms: *mashal* and *melitza*. The term *mashal* refers to the allegorical or homiletical interpretation, while *melitza* pertains to the literal, contextual understanding of the text. These terms, although present in the Proverbs text (1:6), are transformed by Rashi into exegetical categories.

By contrast, Rashi's commentary on Ecclesiastes lacks both this explicit declaration and the introduction of any new terminology. Instead, his approach is more implicit, relying on the reader's understanding of his method without the formal framework provided in Proverbs. Readers will recognize the dual interpretations by the presence of terminology familiar from his other biblical commentaries, such as *peshuto, mashmao,* "our Rabbis *darshu/peirshu,*" and *davar aḥer* (another interpretation).

The two commentaries are also distinguishable by content. Nearly 150 verses in Proverbs are applied to the world of Torah study, thereby transforming the narrative into an educational Torah manual for student and teacher. This comprehensive manual explores vital components for successful Jewish education, such as curriculum planning, motivational factors, and essential pedagogical tools and methods, homing in on both the intellectual and emotional needs of student and teacher. These components divide into two overarching categories, the mind and the soul, emphasizing that successful education necessitates the fusion of both. Hence, Rashi's educational philosophy reveals its inherent holistic nature.

By contrast, in Rashi's Ecclesiastes commentary we are thrown into the world of thoughts and ideas. Dozens of unorthodox, skeptical thoughts on the meaning of life and the apparent futility of human endeavor are reinterpreted to underscore the importance of Torah study and adherence to commandments, with promise of eventual reward. Reward is one of the central themes of this narrative, with Rashi addressing the issue of theodicy head-on. A coherent theology of divine governance emerges from his commentary, in which each individual receives his due rewards or punishments in this world and/or the World to Come. At the same time, Rashi takes into consideration the notion of inherited merit, which challenges the overall reward system.

Thus, if Rashi's Proverbs commentary can be considered a practical educational manual, his Ecclesiastes commentary is more akin to a treatise on Jewish religious thought. If one were to enroll in Rashi's Online University, his commentary on Proverbs would be the required reading for "Jewish Education 101," whereas his commentary on Ecclesiastes would serve as the core text for "Introduction to Jewish Religious Thought." These nuanced differences arise naturally from the distinct natures of the original biblical texts being explicated. Despite these differences, both commentaries emphasize the paramount importance of Torah study and performance of commandments.

THE DRIVE TOWARD UNITY: TIMING AND MOTIVE

The question of when Rashi embarked on the search for unity in King Solomon's writings is bound up with the question of why. If this quest were prompted by developments in the historical environment or on his personal trajectory, then it would have been timed to these events.

The Question of Timing

There is a hypothesis that the commentaries on the Solomonic books were written late in Rashi's life, that Rashi developed a heightened interest in the concept of unity over time. However, this hypothesis is built upon two assumptions that are difficult to substantiate.

The Dating of Rashi's Commentaries

The first assumption is that the order in which Rashi wrote his commentaries can be established. Poznanski believed that Rashi began with his commentary on the Pentateuch, continued with his glosses on the Prophets, and concluded with the Hagiographa, the final section of the Bible, of which the Solomonic books are a part.[1] Gelles supports this view and asserts that Rashi completed his Talmud commentary by the mid-1080s and then began writing his Bible commentary.[2] According to their views, Rashi's commentaries on the later Prophets and the Hagiographa were written at a more advanced stage in his life. However, Grossman does not believe there is sufficient data to suggest a specific timeline.[3]

There is linguistic evidence suggesting that Rashi authored his commentary on Proverbs late in his life, based on its connection to his commentary on Job, the book that follows Proverbs in the sequence of Hagiographa. Rashi uses the term *melitza* in his Proverbs commentary to denote the contextual meaning. This term also appears at the beginning of his commentary on Job (chs. 1–15) but is subsequently dropped.[4] Evidence from both printed editions and manuscripts indicates that Rashi was unable to complete his Job commentary before his death.[5] This suggests that the commentary on Proverbs, written immediately before his work on Job, was composed near the end of his life.

However, there are no clear indications regarding the timing of his Ecclesiastes commentary; and while it is possible that his commentary on the Song of Songs, with its strong anti-Christian thrust, reflects the deteriorating conditions for the Jews of northern France around the time of the First Crusade (1096), this premise lacks strong substantiation.

---

1. Samuel Poznanski, *Mavo al Ḥakhmei Tzarfat Mefarshei HaMikra* [in Hebrew] (Mekize Nirdamim, 1913), xiv.
2. Benjamin Gelles, *Peshat and Derash in the Exegesis of Rashi*, 137–43.
3. See Grossman, *The Early Sages of France* [in Hebrew], 182, n. 204.
4. First noted by Isaac Maarsen, chief rabbi of the Hague, murdered in Auschwitz; see Gelles, *Peshat and Derash in the Exegesis of Rashi*, 80.
5. The commentary from chapter 40, verse 25, through chapter 42, as it appears in printed editions, was not penned by Rashi. See J.S. Penkower, "The End of Rashi's Commentary on Job. The Manuscripts and the Printed Editions," *JSQ* 10 (2003): 18–48.

Thus the dating of these two works to Rashi's old age remains tentative at best.

Increased Interest in Unity?

The second assumption is that Rashi developed an increasing interest in the concept of unity as he aged. However, the tendency to perceive a thematic whole is already evident in his commentary on the Torah, which may well have been an earlier work (see above). Notably, in his commentary on Numbers, Rashi draws from the midrashic treatise *Yesodo shel Rabbi Moshe HaDarshan* numerous times, employing this material to elucidate groups of verses within a unified thematic framework.[6] For instance, in Rashi's commentary on the laws of the Red Heifer (Num. 19:1–22), he begins by explicating the verses individually and concludes with the following statement:

> *Shall be unclean until the evening* (R 19:22) – This is its explanation according to what it literally implies (*mashmaa*) and according to the halakhot connected with it. And the [following] Midrash Aggada I copied from *Yesodo shel Rabbi Moshe HaDarshan.*

Drawing from this homiletic work, Rashi elucidates nearly the entire section (vv. 1–17) as an atonement for the sin of the Golden Calf. In a similar vein, based on the same treatise, Rashi interprets the details of the princely offerings at the inauguration of the Tabernacle (Num. 7:18–23) as symbolizing essential components of the world, such as Adam, Noah, the seventy nations, the Torah, and the Ten Commandments.[7]

A similar interest in unity can be discerned in his commentary on the Prophets. For instance, in Isaiah's vineyard parable (5:1–7), the prophet compares God to a vintner who diligently cultivates his vineyard, anticipating a bountiful harvest. Yet, the vineyard yields only inferior grapes,

6. Rashi explicitly references this source more than twenty times in his Bible commentary. However, he often uses it to elucidate a single word or verse rather than a unit of verses; see Mack, *The Mystery of Rabbi Moshe Hadarshan* [in Hebrew], 133–41.
7. Similarly regarding his commentary on tzitzit (Num. 15:38) and on the second census in Numbers (26:24).

symbolizing the nation's failure and betrayal. Rashi first explicates this section according to its contextual meaning, then gives a meticulous application of the metaphor, first to Adam and then to the nation of Israel. Adam's treachery in the Garden of Eden prefigures the nation's betrayal later in history.[8] Interestingly, Rashi introduces this interpretive approach with the term *dugma,* which we noted in his commentary on the Song of Songs. Likewise, his explication of Ezekiel's vision of dry bones (ch. 37) as a reference to the nation's restoration is prefaced by the same exegetical term.

Evidence of Rashi's inclination toward thematic coherence can also be found in his commentary on Psalms. For instance, Rashi relates the verses of psalm 2 to David's life and those of psalm 22 to the exiled Jewish people of his own time.[9]

Thus, that interest in the thematic whole which we have noted in these three commentaries is also evident in his other works. True, the unity is on a much smaller scale, differing not only not only quantitatively but also substantively. In his commentaries to the other biblical books, unity emerges from verses already linked by the biblical text, either through shared themes (like the Red Heifer or the inaugural ceremony), the use of allegory (Parable of the Vineyard; Is. 5:1–7), or the confines of a single chapter. Contrastingly, in his commentary on Solomon's works, Rashi creates coherence across seemingly unrelated verses, sections, and chapters.

Thus, although Rashi embeds many ideas into his commentaries, and overarching themes can be pieced together through a close reading of his comments on the Pentateuch and Prophets, this is all implicit and up to the skillful reader to discover.[10] By contrast, the cohesion within

8. For an in-depth analysis of Rashi's treatment of this Song, see Kamin, *Rashi,* 80–82.
9. For a more in depth analysis, see M.Z. Cohen, "Psalms for Our Times: Rashi Counters Christological Readings," TheTorah.com: www.thetorah.com/article/psalms-for-our-times-rashi-counters-christological-readings.
10. For example, Devorah Schoenfeld's analysis of Rashi's commentary on the near-sacrifice of Isaac reveals a coherent narrative which can be constructed by the reader. See Devorah Schoenfeld, *Isaac on Jewish and Christian Altars: Polemic and Exegesis in Rashi and the Glossa Ordinaria* (Fordham, 2013), 10–11.

his commentaries to Solomon's writings is explicit and demands no detective work.

Notwithstanding these distinctions, the recognition of textual unity appears to be ongoing in Rashi's work. Therefore, we must question the initial hypothesis that posits the passage of time as the primary factor contributing to the unity in Solomon's writings.

The Narratives and Their Author

Instead, we propose that the inherent nature of the narratives and the role of their author are the crucial factors. The inclusion of all three works – Song of Songs, Proverbs, and Ecclesiastes – within the biblical canon is highly problematic due to their content and form. The erotic imagery of Song of Songs, the pragmatic wisdom of Proverbs, and the existential questioning of Ecclesiastes stand in stark contrast to the content of other biblical books.

Regarding their literary structure, the episodic nature of Song of Songs, the pithy format of Proverbs, and the reflective, often contradictory discourse of Ecclesiastes challenge traditional notions of biblical coherence. What justifies the sanctification of these works?

These problems are further exacerbated by the attribution of authorship to Solomon. How is it conceivable that Solomon, builder of the holy Temple and renowned for his unparalleled wisdom, would produce literature that appears so secular?

Rashi's holistic interpretive framework offers a compelling solution to the challenges posed by these texts. Beneath their seemingly secular exteriors, he uncovers profound, overarching spiritual messages. By meticulously constructing and applying either a linear or circular interpretive template, Rashi reveals the underlying thematic unity and spiritual depth embedded within Solomon's writings. These compositions, once considered for exclusion from the biblical canon, are thus transformed into integral components of Scripture, firmly rooted in biblical theology and essential for the reader's religious growth.

Rashi's capacity to synthesize seemingly disparate elements into a unified thematic tapestry necessitates a reassessment of his exegetical acumen. Traditionally perceived as a meticulous verse-by-verse commentator who segmented the biblical text into discrete units for detailed analysis, our study uncovers an unrecognized dimension of his interpretive artistry. This localized style, we find, is remarkably adept at constructing a panoramic, thematically coherent reading of the text. Thus, with regard to the Solomonic corpus, Rashi emerges not merely as a master of exegetical minutiae, but as a visionary interpreter capable of perceiving the biblical text as a unified whole.

Appendix

Rashi's Commentary on the Song of Songs and the Aramaic *Targum*

There is a striking similarity between Rashi's *dugma* and the historical allegory created by the Aramaic *Targum* (eighth century).[1] Both view the young lovers as an allegory for the relationship between God and the Congregation of Israel, systematically tracking that relationship in sequence from the Exodus until future redemption.

In certain instances the demarcation of the beginning of a new era is identical, such as both interpreting the phrase "I have come to my garden" (Song of Songs 5:1) as marking the start of the First Temple period, with the *Shekhina* resting upon this holy edifice. Similarly, both Rashi and the *Targum* view the beginning of chapter 6 as signaling the

1. Based on linguistic considerations, a recent study proposes a later eleventh-century composition date for the *Targum* on the Song of Songs. See Hsin-chih Perng, "The Date and Provenance of the Aramaic Targum to Canticles," *JJS* vol. 74, n. 2 (2023): 345–58.

construction of the Second Temple through the permission granted by Cyrus, with Rashi identifying this transition in verse 1, while the *Targum* places it in verse 2.

Additionally, the cyclical nature of the divine-human bond is highlighted in both compositions. This pattern, exemplified by the wilderness period – the Exodus/Sinai experience, followed by the sin of the Golden Calf, and then the construction of the Tabernacle – is replicated (redemption, sin, reconciliation) in subsequent periods of Jewish history.

Furthermore, the descriptions of the protagonists' bodies in the *Targum* and Rashi's *dugma* are also allegorized in a similar fashion,[2] with their body parts identifiable with subsets within the nation, such as scholars and commoners, consistently reinforcing the importance of Torah study, mitzva performance, and legislation.

For example, the female beloved is praised for her lovely "feet in sandals" (7:2), which the *Targum* and Rashi explicate in identical fashion:

> *Targum*: "How beautiful are the feet of Israel when they go up to appear before the Lord three times a year in sandals of badger skin.[3]
>
> Rashi: How fair were your feet – In the festive pilgrimages, O daughter of nobles!

Both compositions share similar leitmotifs, such as the resting and withdrawal of God's presence (*Shekhina*), the serious sin of idolatry, the merit of the righteous, and the importance of houses of study, to name just a few.

Despite the strong similarities between Rashi's commentary and the *Targum*, earlier scholars did not believe that Rashi drew directly from the *Targum*,[4] primarily due to Rashi's explicit statement in his commentary

2. Female beloved: 4:1–7, 6: 4–7, 7:2–8; male beloved: 5:10–16.
3. *The Aramaic Bible: The Targum of Canticles*, trans. Philip S. Alexander, v. 17A (Michael Glazier Books, 2003), 176.
4. Abraham Berliner, "The History of Rashi's Commentaries" [in Hebrew], in *Sefer*

on the Talmud: "For there is no Aramaic *Targum* [established] for the Hagiographa."[5]

This statement is further supported by an examination of Rashi's commentaries on the Hagiographa. When Rashi draws from the *Targum* in these commentaries,[6] he culls material from other Aramaic sources, such as *Targum Onkelos* on the Torah and *Targum Yonatan* on the Prophets, rather than directly from the Aramaic *Targum* on the book of the Hagiographa being explicated.

For instance, regarding the phrase in Psalms "There is Benjamin, the youngest, ruling them" (68:28), Rashi writes:

> *There is Benjamin* – The youngest became the ruler over them. *Ruling them* – From there, he merited to become king because he descended first into the sea, and so did Samuel say to Saul: "Even if you are small in your own eyes, are you not the head of the tribes of Israel?" (I Sam. 15:17), *which [Targum] Yonatan paraphrases:* The tribe of Benjamin crossed the sea at the head of all the other tribes.

Rashi is quoting from *Targum Yonatan* on the book of Samuel, even though the *Targum* on Psalms expresses the same idea. This suggests that Rashi did not have access to this latter source.[7]

Similarly, in his commentary on the Song of Songs, Rashi quotes from the *Targum* five times: Four times he is referring to *Targum Onkelos*[8]

Rashi, ed. Y.L. HaCohen Maimon (Mossad HaRav Kook, 1955), 151–52. Poznanski, *Mavo al Ḥakhmei Tzarfat Mefarshei HaMikra*, xviii. So, too, more recently, Sarah Kamin, *Rashi*, 259, n. 112.

5. Rashi on Tractate Megilla 21b, s.v. *vaasara metargemin*. It is unclear how to reconcile this statement with his explicit acknowledgment of the *Targum* on Esther, a book of the Hagiographa, in his commentary on Deuteronomy 3:4. Thank you to Dr. Hsin-chih Perng for bringing this Rashi comment to my attention.
6. Often prefacing these comments with the term T-R-G-m (to translate), but not always.
7. This example (as well as others) is noted by E.Z. Melammed, "Rashi's Commentary on the Bible" [in Hebrew], *Bible Commentators*, vol. 1 (Magnes, 1978), 379.
8. R 2:11, 4:1, 5:1, 2.

and once to *Targum Yonatan*.[9] Likewise, in his commentary on Proverbs, Rashi draws from the *Targum* six times – three times from *Targum Onkelos* and three times from *Targum Yonatan*.

Additional support can be drawn from Japhet's analysis of Rashi's explanation of the term "Lebanon" in his commentary on the Song, where she explains:

> Unlike his customary approach in commentaries on the Torah and the Prophets, in his commentary on the Song of Songs, there is no connection between Rashi's interpretation of the word "Lebanon" and the Aramaic translation of the book.[10]

Japhet notes that Rashi's interpretation of the word "Lebanon" in the Song doesn't align with how the Aramaic translation understands the same word, which is a departure from Rashi's typical approach in other biblical books, where the translation of this term often matches the Aramaic translation.

Thus, there is textual evidence, besides Rashi's statement in his talmudic commentary that there is no *Targum* on the Hagiographa, that he did not have access to the *Targum* on the Song and was not influenced by it.

Nevertheless, many modern scholars believe that Rashi's commentary is directly dependent on the *Targum* because of the close affinity between the two. For example, Alexander, who translated the Aramaic *Targum* to the Song into English, writes:

> The influence of the Targum on Rashi is more clear-cut. Rashi as usual, is his own man and attempts to "improve" on the Targum, but at times he seems to be doing a little more than summarizing or paraphrasing it, which surely indicates that he actually possessed a copy of the Targum and was not simply relying on a third-party report.[11]

9. R 1:6.
10. Sara Japhet, *Collected Studies in Biblical Exegesis* [in Hebrew] (Bialik Institute, 2008), 91.
11. *The Aramaic Bible: The Targum of Canticles*, trans. Philip S. Alexander, 45.

Marcus believes that the dual thrust in Rashi's commentary was drawn from the *Targum*:

> Like the Targum, Rashi focuses on the Song of Songs as being a chronological collective allegory. Like the Targum, Rashi's commentary on Songs is at the same time an implicitly anti-Christian Judeo-centric reading of God's romance with Israel, understood as Jews not Christians.[12]

This question of dependency demands an in-depth, systematic, verse-by-verse comparison between the two compositions that is beyond the scope of this work, but nevertheless I would like to briefly address the two points raised by Marcus.

HISTORICAL ALLEGORY

The idea of historicizing the Song predates the *Targum*. Midrashic literature is replete with the application of some of the Song's verses to different biblical events, albeit in a haphazard manner. However, as Alexander cogently notes, the *Targum* is the oldest extant source that *systematically* creates a *linear* historical storyline.[13]

While the storyline of the *Targum* shares many similarities with Rashi's commentary, there are fundamental differences that warrant attention. For the Targumist, the idyllic period depicted in the Song is the Solomonic era, representing the "pinnacle of national perfection for Israel."[14] The descriptions of Solomon's "bed" and "palanquin" made from "the wood of Lebanon" (3:7–11) are understood as symbolizing the

---

12. Ivan G. Marcus, "The 'Song of Songs' in German Hasidism and the School of Rashi: A Preliminary Comparison," in *Rashi, 1040–1090: Homage to Ephraim E. Urbach,* ed. G. Sed-Rajna (Editions du Cerf, 1993), 267.
13. Philip Alexander, "Tradition and Originality in the Targum of the Song of Songs," in *The Aramaic Bible: Targums in Their Historical Context,* ed. D. Beattie and M. McNamara (Sheffield Academic, 1994), 336–37.
14. Alexander, "Introduction: The Argument and Structure of Targum Canticles," *The Aramaic Bible: The Targum of Canticles,* 18.

building and dedication of Solomon's Temple. As noted by Alexander, for the Targumist, "Israel as a polity reached perfection in Solomon's reign."[15]

Furthermore, in the Targumist's historical schema, the later Hasmonean period is portrayed in a very positive light, as if "to assert the reestablishment of the Solomonic polity in the post-exilic era."[16]

In stark contrast, Rashi downplays the historical significance of Solomon. As we saw earlier regarding Rashi's exegesis of the Song, there is no mention of the historical Solomon whatsoever! Even when Solomon's name is explicitly stated in the text, it is consistently allegorized to represent either God or other spiritual entities.[17] Thus, in Rashi's commentary, Solomon has essentially been erased from the Song that he himself composed!

Similarly, the Hasmonean period is downplayed. Rashi notes their ascent to power (R 6:10), but then just two verses later describes their forfeiture of this power due to causeless hatred and internecine rivalry, resulting in political servitude to Rome and subsequent subjugation by foreign powers.

Rashi's *dugma* and the *Targum* also differ significantly in their treatment of the subject of redemption. The Targumist delves into great detail, outlining this future period. He envisions the ingathering of the exiles (8:1–5), who will partake in the messianic feast of Leviathan (8:2), and the defeat of Gog and Magog (8:4, 7). While in earlier chapters he describes two Messiahs, the Messiah son of Ephraim and the Messiah son of David (4:5; 7:3), in the closing chapter he focuses solely on the Messiah son of David, presumably because the Messiah son of Ephraim will have already fallen in battle during the messianic war. Mention of the Messiah is present throughout the narrative, and Alexander aptly describes it as an "immensely Messianic document."[18]

Contrastingly, Rashi is tight-lipped regarding the future days. No mention of Messiahs, messianic feasts, or Gog and Magog. The

15. Ibid., 16.
16. Ibid., 17.
17. Solomon=God: R 1:1, 8:11; Solomon=Tabernacle: R 3:7, 9.
18. Alexander, "Introduction," 23.

commentary ends not with redemption but with a fervent plea for deliverance (R 8:14).

Consequently, key differences exist between the *Targum* and Rashi's reading regarding core elements of the narrative.

ANTI-CHRISTIAN, JUDEO-CENTRIC READING

Moving on to Marcus's second point: If both compositions share an anti-Christian orientation, do we really need to assume dependence to explain Rashi's anti-Christian reading of the Song? Polemical material is already present in rabbinic literature, from which Rashi gleaned his commentary. Moreover, Rashi's commentaries on the Hagiographa are replete with anti-Christian readings, and as we demonstrated regarding his Proverbs commentary, anti-Christian polemic permeates this composition from start to finish. In Professor Avraham Grossman's recent book *Rashi and the Jewish-Christian Polemic,* eighty-seven pages are dedicated to Rashi's anti-Christian polemic in his commentaries to the Later Prophets and the Hagiographa.[19]

Furthermore, even within the realm of polemics, one detects a fundamental difference between Rashi and the *Targum*. The adjuration to the "daughters of Jerusalem" serves as a primary motif within the Song:

> I adjure you, O daughters of Jerusalem, by gazelles, or by hinds of the field: Do not wake or rouse love until it please.

This adjuration appears three times in almost identical form (2:7, 3:5, 8:4), and the *Targum* consistently identifies this female chorus as the Congregation of Israel. In all three passages they are asked to pledge not to hasten their return to the land, first by Moses (2:7, 3:5) and then by the Messiah (8:4).

By contrast, Rashi consistently identifies the "daughters of Jerusalem" with the nations of the world primarily those contemporary to him. The

19. Grossman, *Rashi and the Jewish-Christian Polemic (*Bar-Ilan University Press, 2021) [in Hebrew], 69–155.

Congregation of Israel beseeches the nations not to try to entice them away from their beloved God.

This difference in the identification of the "daughters of Jerusalem" profoundly influences the narrative's storyline. According to the *Targum*, the Song remains a passionate description of the relationship between the two lovers – God and the Congregation of Israel – through all its vicissitudes. However, according to Rashi, the narrative is recast as a triadic relationship involving two females (Israel and the nations) competing for the same love, that of the Beloved (i.e., God).[20] Thus, the dialogue within the narrative is no longer between two but among three main actors – God, the Congregation of Israel, and the nations of the world – the latter primarily synonymous, in Rashi's eyes, with Christians. This transformation effectively turns the frame story itself into a polemical one.

CONCLUSION

Fundamental differences exist between the two compositions. In an effort to explain these differences, scholars may claim that Rashi is "improving" upon the *Targum*.[21] However, based on this preliminary study, we dispute this assertion, holding that these differences are not merely surface level or a "cosmetic" reworking of the text but rather demonstrate divergent perspectives on the core narrative.

Given these fundamental differences, coupled with Rashi's statement that there is no *Targum* on the Hagiographa, and the supporting evidence of his lack of direct quotations from the *Targum* on the Hagiographa,[22] we question the claim of direct dependency on the *Targum*.

Instead, we posit that Rashi's comprehensive, chronological, allegorical reading of the Song is his own creation.[23] However, regarding his explication of certain verses, it is possible that he drew from

20. Stern, "Ancient Jewish Interpretation of the Song of Songs," 106–7.
21. As does Alexander; see his "Introduction," 46.
22. The exception being Rashi's acknowledgment of the *Targum* on Esther in his commentary on Deuteronomy 3:4.
23. Of course, it is molded from rabbinic sources.

midrashic source material similar in content to that of the *Targum* which is no longer extant.[24] This would explain the similarities between their commentaries while maintaining the overall independence of Rashi's *dugma.*

24. This is the position articulated by J. Rosenthal regarding interpretations of Rashi in his Song of Songs commentary that are similar to the Aramaic *Targum,* with no antecedents found in any other rabbinic literature; see Rosenthal, "Rashi's Commentary on the Song of Songs," 134.

Index of Rashi's Commentary

RASHI'S BIBLE COMMENTARIES

Job

Song of Songs

RASHI'S COMMENTARIES ON THE TALMUD

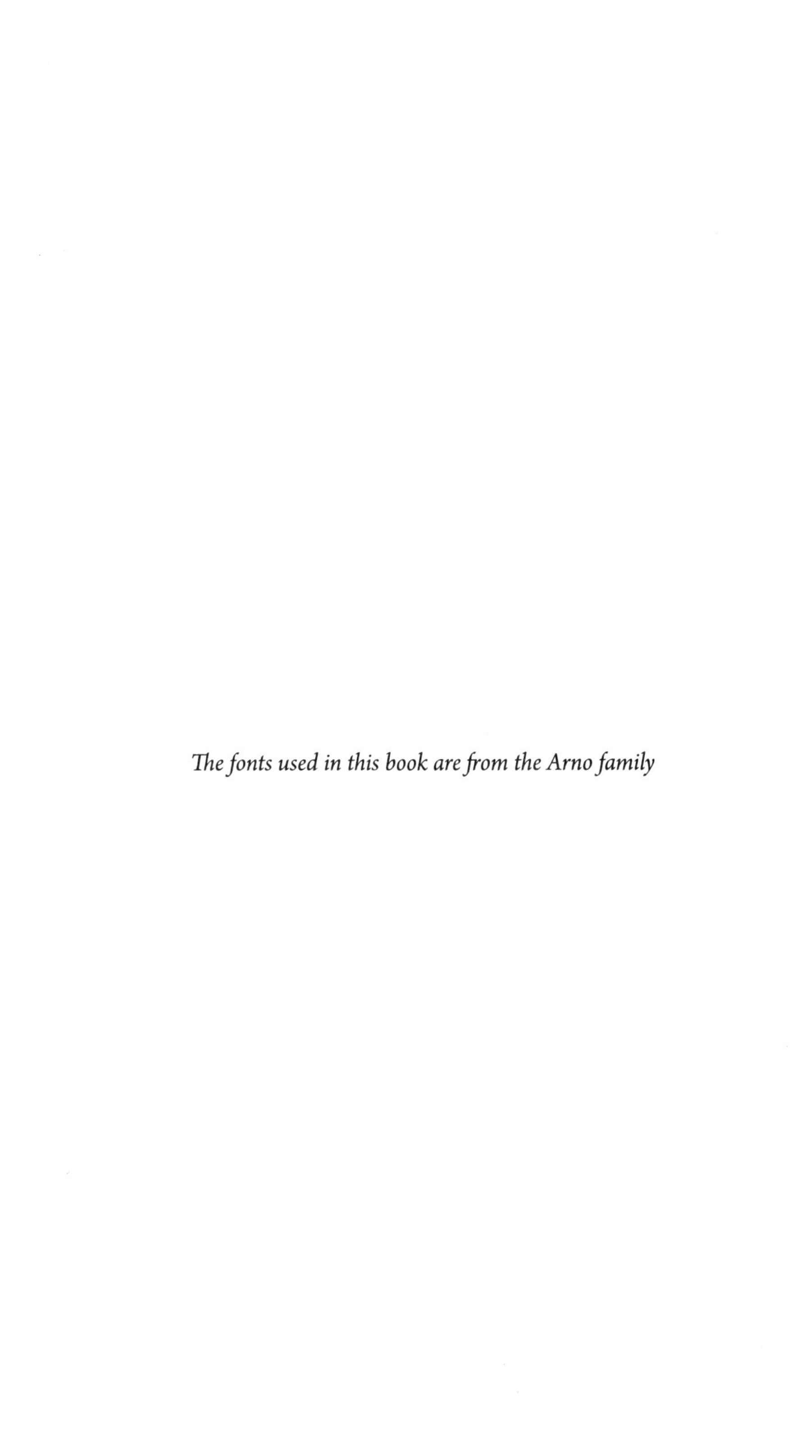

The fonts used in this book are from the Arno family

Maggid Books
The best of contemporary Jewish thought from
Koren Publishers Jerusalem Ltd.